MIDWAY SUBMERGED

American and Japanese Submarine Operations at
the Battle of Midway, May–June 1942

MARK W. ALLEN

CASEMATE
Philadelphia & Oxford

This is a fully revised edition of Mark W. Allen, *Midway Submerged: An Analysis of American and Japanese Submarine Operations at the Battle of Midway, June 1942* (iUniverse, 2012)

Published in the United States of America and Great Britain in 2023 by
CASEMATE PUBLISHERS
1950 Lawrence Road, Havertown, PA 19083, USA
and
The Old Music Hall, 106–108 Cowley Road, Oxford OX4 1JE, UK

Copyright © 2023 Mark W. Allen

Hardcover Edition: ISBN 978-1-63624-281-1
Digital Edition: ISBN 978-1-63624-282-8

A CIP record for this book is available from the British Library

All rights reserved. No part of this book may be reproduced or transmitted in any form or by any means, electronic or mechanical including photocopying, recording or by any information storage and retrieval system, without permission from the publisher in writing.

Printed and bound in the United Kingdom by CPI Group (UK) Ltd, Croydon, CR0 4YY
Typeset in India by DiTech Publishing Services

For a complete list of Casemate titles, please contact:

CASEMATE PUBLISHERS (US)
Telephone (610) 853-9131
Fax (610) 853-9146
Email: casemate@casematepublishers.com
www.casematepublishers.com

CASEMATE PUBLISHERS (UK)
Telephone (0)1226 734350
Email: casemate-uk@casematepublishers.co.uk
www.casematepublishers.co.uk

Front cover image: Diorama by Norman Bel Geddes, depicting the attack by USS *Nautilus* (SS-168) on a burning Japanese aircraft carrier during the early afternoon of 4 June 1942 as seen through the submarine's periscope. *Nautilus* thought she had attacked *Soryu*, and that her torpedoes had exploded when they hit the target. However, the ship attacked was *Kaga*, and the torpedoes failed to detonate. The ship shown in this wartime diorama does not closely resemble either of those carriers. (Official U.S. Navy Photograph #: 80-G-701871 Naval History and Heritage Command)

To the officers and crews of Task Groups 7.1, 7.2, and 7.3

It was to the Submarine Force that I looked to carry the load until our great industrial activity could produce the weapons we so sorely needed to carry the war to the enemy. It is to the everlasting honor and glory of our submarine personnel that they never failed us in our days of great peril.

Chester W. Nimitz
Fleet Admiral, U.S. Navy
Foreword, in *United States Submarine Operations in World War II*
by Theodore Roscoe, p. v, 1949

Contents

Foreword by Thomas J. Goetz   vii
Preface   xi

1	Introduction	1
2.	Japanese Naval Doctrine	9
3.	Japanese Submarine Strategy and Tactics	17
4.	United States Naval Doctrine	27
5.	United States Submarine Strategy and Tactics	33
6.	Japanese Submarine Actions at Midway	41
7.	United States Submarine Actions at Midway	57
8.	Analysis: Undersea Warfare at Midway	75
9.	Midway Submerged: Conclusions	91

Appendices

    Appendix 1. Patrol Reports of U.S. Task Group 7.1 Submarines   103
    Appendix 2. Patrol Reports of U.S. Task Group 7.2 Submarines   163
    Appendix 3. Patrol Reports of U.S. Task Group 7.3 Submarines   165
    Appendix 4. Patrol Reports of U.S. Submarines on Patrol   169
    Appendix 5. Extracts From the United States Strategic Bombing Survey: Interrogations of Japanese Officials   183

Appendix 6. Interrogation of Vice Admiral Paul H. Weneker   185
*Appendix 7. Navy Cross Citation for Lieutenant Commander
William Herman Brockman, Jr.*   187
Endnotes   189
Bibliography   213
Index   223

Foreword

The Battle of Midway, in June 1942, is rightly considered one of the most important naval battles in history, and perhaps the pivotal naval battle of World War II in the Pacific. It is certainly one of the best-known battles of the Pacific War, and the most written-about naval battle of the war.

The broad outlines of the battle are familiar to anyone with even a passing acquaintance with the history of World War II—how the armed forces of Imperial Japan, beginning with the crushingly successful surprise attack on the Hawaiian Islands, swept all before them in a stunning campaign of conquest in the western Pacific. So successful was this naval blitzkrieg that the Japanese achieved all their pre-war territorial goals faster than their most optimistic estimates had forecast. By the spring of 1942 they had, while sustaining only minimal casualties, essentially completed their conquest of the "Greater East Asian Co-Prosperity Sphere." This produced significant debate within the Japanese high command as to the nature and target of their next major offensive. That there would be another major offensive was accepted by the high command without question. What the Japanese would later term "Victory Disease"—a belief the Japanese military could accomplish any goal it set for itself, with minimal losses—had already become the standard mindset in the Japanese military.

Various options were considered for the next Japanese victory such as operations against British India, either overland through Burma or by sea against Ceylon or eastern India; efforts to isolate and perhaps invade Australia; or a drive to the east to engage and destroy the remnants of the U.S. Pacific Fleet that had escaped destruction at Pearl Harbor, most notably the American aircraft carriers, coupled with the possible occupation of the Hawaiian Islands. This last option had the powerful support of Admiral Yamamoto Isoroku, the architect of the Pearl Harbor attack, and his support ultimately carried the debate, although a limited move against Australia, in the form of an amphibious assault against Port Moresby in New Guinea, was also approved, as was an operation to occupy several of the Aleutian Islands in the far northern Pacific.

The operation to destroy the U.S. Fleet would take the form of a massive naval attack to occupy the tiny base on Midway Island, to the northwest of the Hawaiian Islands. This attack on, and occupation of, Midway would, so the plan went, force the U.S. Navy to respond and, in so doing, the Japanese forces of *Kido Butai* (Mobile Force), the innovative Japanese naval task force comprised of their fleet aircraft carriers, would then locate and destroy the American carriers as they sailed to engage the Japanese fleet, leaving the Japanese with complete dominance throughout the Pacific.

The major events of the campaign are well known—how U.S. Naval Intelligence had been able to break Imperial Japanese naval radio codes and was able to provide enough advance intelligence to allow Admiral Nimitz, the U.S. naval commander in the Pacific, to know the target of the Japanese operation in advance. This information enabled the Americans to plan to ambush the Japanese naval forces, by pre-positioning all of their available carriers to the north and east of Midway and operating with the support of land-based airpower on Midway itself. The advantage of surprise would, in theory, help to offset the Japanese advantage of numbers and concentration of force.

The initial stages of the battle appeared to signal yet another impressive Japanese victory, as Japanese airpower swept the American planes from the skies, and they appeared to be on the verge of occupying Midway and fending off American air strikes, and eventually finishing off the American carriers, just as Yamamoto had hoped to do. Yet in one of the most stunning reversals of fortune of the entire war, in a matter of moments American Dauntless dive bombers from USS *Enterprise* and USS *Yorktown* arrived, essentially simultaneously over the Japanese fleet, and, unmolested by Japanese fighters or antiaircraft fire, proceeded to obtain direct hits on three of the four Japanese fleet carriers. These ships, due to hectic combat operations, were strewn with poorly stored bombs and torpedoes, as well as quantities of aviation gasoline as refueling operations were underway. The American bomb hits ignited raging infernos, which Japanese damage control and firefighting measures were inadequate to control.

In a matter of minutes, three Japanese aircraft carriers were reduced to flaming wrecks, and although the fourth carrier, *Hiryu*, survived long enough to launch a crippling strike on *Yorktown*, it too succumbed to American airpower a short time later. The Japanese lost all four of their fleet carriers that had engaged in this battle, as well as a heavy cruiser. American losses were limited to *Yorktown* and a destroyer that had been assisting in the efforts to recover the carrier. The results of this battle indeed altered the nature of the war in the Pacific, although not in the fashion envisioned by Admiral Yamamoto. Almost exactly six months after the attack on Pearl Harbor, the Japanese Navy was deprived of its primary striking power and would never again engage in a major offensive operation.

All of this is well known, and rightfully so. But this information is not the entire story of the battle. There is another aspect of the battle that also deserves to be known. While airpower bore the brunt of the combat, there was another element of naval power on both sides that was one of the few elements of either fleet to actually see combat during the battle. This "hidden" element of the Battle of Midway is, appropriately, the submarine forces of both the Japanese and American navies.

Mark Allen has produced a comprehensive examination of this little-known aspect of this pivotal naval battle. This project originated as a master's thesis which I had the privilege of supervising. Delving deeply into the archives, Mark has studied not just the battle itself, but submarine design and construction, as well as tactical and operational doctrine for both the United States and Japan. He has also examined the intended role of the submarine in the plans and doctrine of both navies, and what the submarines were supposed to accomplish for both fleets during the battle.

From this foundation, he has examined the actual accomplishments, successes, and failures of the submarine service of both the Japanese and

American navies. Of particular importance, he has also analyzed how well these vessels fulfilled the expectations placed on them by their respective naval planners. Submarines turned out to be far more important to the outcome of the battle than has been previously understood.

I believe this work enhances the understanding of one of the most pivotal battles of the 20th century. A complete account of the Battle of Midway requires a study of the role of the "Silent Service" in its outcome, and Mark's book provides that.

Thomas J. Goetz
Professor of Military History
American Military University
Charles Town, West Virginia
May 25, 2011

Preface

Most literature examining the Battle of Midway usually focuses on American and Japanese carrier operations. Intertwined are discussions of naval aviation, the sinking of four Japanese carriers and one American carrier, the chess match between Admirals Chester W. Nimitz and Yamamoto Isoroku, and what some have called the turning point of the war in the Pacific. These discussions do not normally examine detailed submarine operations during the battle. Any reference to submarines usually criticizes their lack of involvement and operational mismanagement. This re-evaluation of the Battle of Midway presents an in-depth look at Japanese and American submarine operations before, during, and after the battle.

Initially, my argument was to focus on the deployment of submarines by both Japan and the United States. I would show how both sides misused their submarines which, for Japan, contributed to defeat. Two Japanese submarine cordons were late getting on station, allowing American forces to position themselves northeast of Midway unseen. Therefore, Japanese naval leaders were unaware there were American carriers in the area. I would next point out how Admiral Nimitz incorrectly placed his submarines in an arc west of Midway when he knew, based on information from his code breakers, where the Japanese Striking Force would appear. I figured both statements would be easy concepts to prove.

The only thing I proved was that going into a project with preconceived ideas was a dangerous thing to do. It is easy to play "Monday Morning Quarterback" years after an event and with significantly more information then was available at the time. This was the course I started down, reading secondary sources that made statements I accepted as fact, assuming previous authors based their research on primary sources. It was only when I dug deeper into primary sources myself that I realized my initial preconceived ideas were not quite correct. I therefore started from scratch, researching both Japanese and American naval doctrine and how that related to submarine strategy and tactics. I next reviewed operational orders for both sides, evaluating Yamamoto's attack/invasion plan and how Nimitz planned to counter it. Then it was a matter of tracking submarine activity throughout the battle, relying heavily on the patrol reports and after-action reports by both Admirals Nimitz and Robert H. English.

It was at this point that I realized Nimitz did not plan to use the submarines of Task Group 7 offensively; he and English deployed them in defensive sectors against the anticipated Japanese occupation force. In most instances, information on the Battle of Midway is so focused on carrier actions and naval aviation that the fact the Japanese were sailing a force to occupy Midway gets lost. However, Nimitz was keenly aware of this fact. He employed the assets he had and used them in their proper role at the time—to stop the invasion. This was not the popular move. Just ask English, Commander Submarines Pacific, who wanted to vector the submarines towards the Japanese Striking Force and attack the carriers. Moreover, it is not the popular move according to many historians and authors years after the event.

Additionally, research into the Japanese side of the battle indicates there was more to the fiasco with the late arrival of their submarines then I initially thought. The problem was not so much the late arrival on station as it was a faulty strategic and tactical plan by Admiral Yamamoto and the strict adherence to this plan by his admirals.

Nimitz has taken a lot of criticism over the years due to what some think was an improper use of his submarines at the Battle of Midway. Most authors and historians suggest he should have sent the submarines to attack the Japanese Striking Force. But then the question is, "How would you propose to defend against the Japanese invasion?" In terms of submarine deployment at Midway, Nimitz got it right. And this book tells this story. In hindsight, I greatly admire Admiral Nimitz; his tactical genius has humbled me.

I grew up not far from the World War II fleet submarine USS *Batfish* (SS-310). This "cool" place to visit turned into fascination and then admiration. Since then, I have grown increasingly interested in the Silent Service during World War II. The concept for this book originated from my master's thesis at American Military University. Before I started graduate school, I knew I wanted to write my thesis on some type of submarine warfare in the Pacific Theater, something significant that had not been written about in detail. I settled on submarine actions at the Battle of Midway because, as previously mentioned, most texts focus on the carrier aspect of the battle.

Along the way, several people, in one way or another, have helped me formulate this concept. I thank Dr. Thomas Goetz and Dr. Don Sine, both of American Military University, for guidance during the completion of my thesis while finishing my master's degree in Military History, World War II emphasis. I am also indebted to Dr. Goetz for writing the Foreword to this book. I appreciate the effort of Mike Constandy of Westmoreland Research Group (WestmorlandResearch.org) who obtained all the period photographs from the National Archives and Records Administration and the Washington Naval Yard. I am grateful for Bobby Sammons of MilSpecManuals.com for making many hard-to-get primary sources available at a very reasonable price. A special thanks to my late parents, Joe and Kathleen Allen, for their life-long example and educational encouragement. Finally, a very special thank you to my wife, Leilani, who assisted with typing and initial editing, but mostly for the sacrifice of time as I worked on my degree and then the publication of this work. Even with all this help, I alone am responsible for the opinions and conclusions herein, and for any errors or omissions.

Finally, I must point out that this is a fully revised edition of the book. The 2012 edition, self-published with iUniverse, was my thesis, as mentioned above, essentially unchanged from when I submitted it to the graduate school for completion of my degree. Over the next few years, I wanted to re-write some sections, clean up inconsistencies, and reduce some repetition. I also felt a few more figures were needed. My agent, Theodore Savas of Savas Beatie, put me in touch with

Casemate Publishers, and their editorial staff has worked wonders in finalizing the text, figures, and cover. I cannot be more pleased with the final product and feel this edition is a far superior book than the first edition.

Mark W. Allen
Owasso, OK
July 29, 2022

CHAPTER I

Introduction

Midway was *the* decisive battle.[1]

The Battle of Midway is one of the most analyzed battles of World War II's Pacific Theater. Most studies focus on Japanese vs. American carrier operations as naval air power ultimately decided the battle's outcome. Japan's operational objectives at Midway were clear. The first objective focused on the invasion and capture of the island itself. The second objective was to draw out the American Pacific Fleet to engage and destroy it in a decisive battle. Once the 3,500-strong Occupation Force secured Midway, Japanese naval forces would reposition themselves around the island to intercept and destroy the U.S. fleet Admiral Yamamoto Isoroku anticipated would sail in defense of Midway.[2] In total, Japanese forces included 11 battleships and four carriers, as well as assorted cruisers and destroyer squadrons, troopships, and supply ships.[3]

Figure 1.1: Admiral Yamamoto Isoroku. Imperial Japanese Navy portrait photograph, taken during the early 1940s, when he was Commander-in-Chief, Combined Fleet. (Naval History and Heritage Command)

Three American carriers and aircraft stationed on Midway opposed Japan's carrier armada. Many authors have described the battle both from the Japanese and American perspectives and how, in a matter of minutes, American dive bombers destroyed three Japanese carriers and sank a fourth later that same day. In comparison, the American Pacific Fleet lost only one carrier. Some claim Midway was an intelligence victory; the United States capitalized on it while the Japanese ignored it. Others state luck played a big part. However, they all agree that naval air power won the battle.

What authors have not focused on in any detail are Japanese and American submarine operations before, during and after the battle. Most authors criticize Admiral Chester Nimitz, claiming he should have placed his submarines farther away from Midway to strike at Japan's carriers before they could launch air strikes against the island. However, Nimitz assigned American submarines to defensive roles, acting as a strike force against an anticipated Japanese amphibious assault on Midway, leaving only American carrier aircraft to strike at Japan's carriers. It was a matter of mobility and defense, and Nimitz correctly assigned his available assets to their proper role.

Literature that addresses submarine operations at Midway mostly focus on their failure and operational mismanagement. Most authors and some Japanese military leaders claim the late arrival of one of the Japanese submarine scouting

Figure 1.2: Admiral Chester W. Nimitz, December 1942. As Commander-in-Chief, Pacific Fleet, Nimitz had operational control over all Allied units in the Pacific, including air, land, and sea forces. (National Archives)

lines significantly contributed to Japan's defeat. For example, "Among the several factors that contributed to the Japanese disaster at Midway, the failure of SubRon 5 took high place"[4] or "This delay in stationing submarines is considered to be a major flaw in the Japanese plan."[5]

From the American perspective, authors almost exclusively claim Nimitz and Admiral Robert English deployed American submarines too close to Midway, which prevented their offensive deployment against Japan's Carrier Striking Force. Some examples include:

> Whoever created the submarine plan, it was bad. Most of the submarines were disposed for a concentrated defense close in to Midway, instead of being offensively placed farther out where they may have had an opportunity to torpedo a Japanese carrier before the decisive battle.[6]

> U.S. submarines had been poorly deployed to intercept the Japanese fleet attacking Midway. They were too close to the island. They needed to be much farther away to spot, report and attack the Japanese carriers heading for Midway.[7]

> The placement of submarines at Midway and poor command and control by the CINC and ComSubPac precluded their massing to attack in concert with Midway based and carrier-based aircraft. Better placement of the arcs further out would have reduced submarine transit time as well as allowed the submarines to attack and disrupt the force before the arrival of U.S. aircraft.[8]

Normally, discussions concerning American and Japanese submarines center around these topics and only in generalities, claiming both sides failed to use their submarines correctly and successfully.

To understand failure or success of Japanese and American submarines at Midway, we must understand the following relationship:

Doctrine → Strategy → Tactics → Deployment

In essence, this states that tactics define submarine deployment. Tactics are a by-product of strategy and strategy develops from naval doctrine. Leaders of the interwar maritime countries not only believed in battleship supremacy but also shared a philosophy about the role of sea power in national defense. They all subscribed to the tenets of Mahanian doctrine.[9] In his 1941 book *Armed Forces of the Pacific*, W. D. Puleston, a captain in the U.S. Navy and head of the Office of Naval Intelligence, compared the military power of the United States and Japan and arrived at certain conclusions based on doctrine and tactics of that time. Puleston concluded operations of the two fleets would determine the outcome of a war between the two countries, operations that included submarines, naval aviation, and all available Army aviation. Both fleets would endeavor to gain and exercise control of the western Pacific to ensure its use to friendly ships and deny it to hostile ones. Puleston suggested the quickest way to gain this control was to defeat the opposing fleet. Based on treaty limitations, the Commander-in-Chief of the U.S. Fleet, which would be stronger, would attempt to bring the Japanese to action in the open sea. The Commander-in-Chief of the Japanese Fleet would try to reduce American superiority by submarines, aviation, and minefields before accepting a daylight action in which he would risk defeat and possible annihilation. Japan would attempt a war of attrition as soon as hostilities commenced and would take full advantage of its geographical position to wage it.[10]

Although Japan created its navy on a Western model, its operational methods remained essentially Oriental. Japanese leaders were aware of the Western doctrines of singularity of aim and concentration of force. They had failed to rid themselves, nonetheless, of ancient Asian notions of the value of complexity and diffusion. Yamamoto argued strongly to abandon the old naval strategy, of interception operations and systematic reduction of the enemy fleet as it reached out to the western Pacific. He advocated for more offensive operations, such as the invasion and occupation of the Hawaiian Islands.[11]

Admiral Yamamoto designed his Midway plan to confuse the enemy. He divided his fleet into five separate bodies, each committed to a different geographical objective or operational aim.[12] Japanese plans required their submarines to patrol along scouting lines, or cordons, to hunt for and intercept American task forces. Japan's use of submarines in support of fleet operations was typical of their use at Midway.[13] Yamamoto was confident the U.S. fleet would not be in the area prior to the initial attack on Midway and he therefore did not emphasize reconnaissance in the early stages of the operation.[14] He anticipated any major naval engagement with American forces would occur after Japanese occupation forces occupied Midway.[15]

Yamamoto's plan counted on the Americans sailing from Pearl Harbor in response to Japan's "surprise" attack on Midway and, on arrival of the U.S. fleet, Japanese submarines and carriers would deliver the first attack.[16] There was no contingency plan if American forces acted in a way Yamamoto did not expect.

As previously stated, historians place significant blame for Japan's defeat at Midway on the late arrival of submarine scouting line SubRon 5. The blame is rooted in SubRon 5's failure to spot the American carriers, preventing Admiral Chuichi Nagumo's Striking Force from knowing enemy carriers were in the area.[17] This would have put the American carriers as top priority instead of continuing the attack on Midway Island. American carriers were already northeast of Midway by June 1 and would have escaped detection even if SubRon 5 had been on station at the designated time. Furthermore, the Japanese fleet was operating under the assumption American forces would not be in the vicinity of Midway until at least June 7, sailing after the island's occupation. Based on Yamamoto's *anticipated* timeline, Japanese submarines, even though two days late, were still on station in plenty of time to intercept and attack any American ships racing to Midway in response to the Japanese invasion.[18]

Figure 1.3: Japanese Admiral Chuichi Nagumo. Nagumo led Japan's main carrier battle group at the Battle of Midway. (National Archives)

The American and Japanese pre-war models of naval warfare were similar with submarines being auxiliaries to the battle fleet. However, the Japanese attack at Pearl Harbor changed this role for the United States. With the battle fleet destroyed or damaged, submarines and aircraft carriers became the offensive striking force of the American Pacific Fleet. Submarines adopted the role of commerce raiders and targeted the supply line of Japan, mimicking the role German U-boats successfully used against Great Britain. However, when American naval intelligence discovered the Japanese plan to invade Midway, Nimitz needed all his fleet assets to defend the island. He therefore temporarily removed American submarines from their role as commerce raiders and placed them back into the fleet support role, not in defense of the fleet itself, but in defense of Midway against an anticipated Japanese amphibious assault.

Many historians make statements like "Twenty-six submarines were deployed by Nimitz although in the course of the battle of Midway, they proved largely ineffective,"[19] or "The American submarines as a whole had performed poorly."[20] Broad statements like these diminish the role American submarines played during the conflict and downgrade their accomplishments. Researchers should look at the previously mentioned statements and ask, "Why did submarines fail at Midway?" or "Why did submarines perform poorly at Midway?" "Is it true that American and Japanese submarines had little effect in the battle?" The researcher will find answers to questions surrounding submarine failure, performance, and deployment in the answer to one additional question: "What role did American and Japanese submarines perform at Midway?"

When analyzing submarine actions at the Battle of Midway, historians should consider three things. First, carrier operations and naval aviation overshadow the role submarines had at Midway. Second, there does not appear to be enough research into Admiral Ernest King's operational orders to Admiral Nimitz. Third, there is a timing misconception regarding when Japanese submarines were to be on station versus when American carriers were to sail in defense of Midway.

The first statement is not a criticism of carrier naval aviation. It is a known fact that naval aviation won the battle. The problem regarding the submarine is that with the voluminous amount of research written about the battle, submarine actions for the most part are just footnotes in the overall history. Most texts briefly mention submarine actions and, in doing so, continue with the line of reasoning that submarines failed at Midway.

As for the second statement, it appears most historians direct criticism of submarine deployment squarely at Nimitz and indirectly at English. In hindsight, these historians feel Nimitz should have used his submarines offensively, as Admiral English preferred. Nimitz overruled English and placed the submarines in defensive arcs west of Midway. Why did he do that? Researching *that* question should reduce much of the criticism. A complication from a literature standpoint is it seems that some authors quote past authors (instead of reading the primary sources themselves) and accept previous research as accurate. This type of reasoning contributes to the continued criticism directed at Nimitz and to the confusion surrounding submarine actions at Midway.

As stated, most historians and Japanese naval leaders suggest the late arrival of SubRon 5 was a significant reason for the defeat at Midway. The scouting line arrived on June 3, two days late. However, whether SubRon 5 submarines were on time or two days late did not make a difference in the battle's outcome, as it was Yamamoto's plan that failed, not the tardiness of the submarines arriving to their station. This study examines the roles of Japanese and American submarines and concludes that neither failed in their missions at the Battle of Midway.

CHAPTER 2

Japanese Naval Doctrine

> Having for many years been preoccupied with fleet drills centering on the battleship, I could not make a mental switch, and even after the great success of the task force in the Pearl Harbor attack, I believed that the task force should be assigned auxiliary operations and that the main prop of the decisive fleet encounter was the "big battleships and big guns."[1]

Japan's sea power doctrine in World War II was overwhelmingly a product of its naval leaders closely studying Alfred Thayer Mahan.[2] The Japanese had translated Mahan's works well before the turn of the century and, as far as Mahan knew, more of his works, which were required reading at Japan's military schools and colleges, were translated into Japanese than any other language.[3] On no point was Mahan more emphatic: the primary mission of a battle fleet is to engage the enemy's fleet. "The one particular result which is the object of all naval action is the destruction of the enemy's organized force, and the establishment of one's own control of the water." Both strategically and tactically, navies should be employed offensively.[4] This doctrinal focus explains all of Japan's naval energies, and much of their innovation.[5]

In *The Influence of Sea Power on History*, Mahan argued that great national wealth and power had, in the past, always been synonymous with control of the seas. Sea power, in turn, rested on an oceangoing fleet prepared and strong enough to reengage and destroy any enemy fleet that challenged it in a decisive sea battle.[6] Mahan ridiculed *guerre de course*, or commerce raiding, as the strategy of the weaker power, hopeless in the face of a navy able to exercise overbearing sea power.

Instead, his followers sought titanic clashes between concentrated fleets of battleships.[7] Mahan's writings, while appropriate to maritime nations with far-flung aspirations like Great Britain or the United States, held only limited relevance for a fledgling power such as Japan, with aspirations confined to regional waters and coastal areas.[8]

The exact nature of Mahan's influence on Japan's naval establishment is a matter of some dispute. One view draws a straight line between Mahanian precepts and prewar Japanese ideas about sea power.[9] It is impossible to overstate Mahan's influence on the Japanese Navy. Besides the adoption of his texts in Japanese military colleges, the decisive-battle idea is evident in their armament programs, their maneuvers, their staff work, and their strategy. Japan desired superior quality in the decisive battle and this prompted the Navy to train small numbers of pilots. Since victory was anticipated from one quick confrontation, quality rather than quantity of aviators would make the difference.[10]

A different view suggests Mahan was far from the only influence on Japan's doctrine. The Japanese Naval War College provided basic study of strategy and tactics. Of all the instructors of the college, two figures stood out: Akiyama Saneyuki, commonly known as the "father of Japanese naval strategy," and Satō Tetsutarō, "Japan's Mahan."[11] These two drew intellectual inspiration from many sources, ranging from studying abroad in the United States and Great Britain to the writings of Sun Tzu.[12] Akiyama studied tactics and strategy in the United States from 1897 to 1900 and had private tutorship from Mahan. During almost the same period, Satō visited Britain to study how important the influence of sea power was in relation to the rise and fall of nations. After returning to Japan, the college appointed both men as instructors; Akiyama taught tactics and Satō taught strategy and naval history. The training provided by these two men was the basis of Japanese naval strategy and tactics.[13]

In the first decade of the 20th century, Japanese naval strategists mapped out the basic contours of their naval strategy. A blend of Mahan's doctrines and traditional Chinese and Japanese military concepts, their thinking emphasized the subjugation of the enemy through maneuver, strategy, and attrition, rather than by strict quantitative superiority.[14] For the Japanese, surprise was essential, and they sought to fold into their operational plans the best and most significant elements of the Sun Tzu style of war fighting: surprise, secrecy, and deception.[15]

Mahanian strategy continued to dominate Japan's naval thinking in the interwar period.[16] However, the Japanese Navy's adoption of Mahan's ideas was highly selective and arbitrary as naval strategists used them to ratify preconceived ideas about how to configure and use their force.[17] As it took shape, Japanese naval strategy bore only a partial resemblance to the sea power-minded strategy Mahan championed.[18]

Treaty Limitations

What was Japan's naval doctrine? Two divergent views emerged. The first view, championed by the Combined Fleet, suggested the primary way to secure victory was through a decisive battle waged against an enemy fleet. The second view, mostly favored by the Naval General Staff, focused on a defensive posture, which relied on a relatively small number of ships to act as a fleet-in-being.[19]

Until 1941, Japan's naval strategists did not study large-scale offensive fleet actions far from home waters but instead planned in terms of the fleet's subordinate service role to ground operations. Since the fleet's primary mission was to assist ground forces, there were no plans to risk ships in major naval confrontations when it was avoidable. As such, naval leaders viewed submarines and aircraft carriers as supporting weapons for Army actions, not as potent devices of offensive firepower.[20] Additionally, Japan's naval design between the world wars generally reflected the prevailing emphasis on speed and rapidity of fire rather than on armor.[21]

The signing of the Five-Power Naval Treaty in 1922 soon made it necessary for the Japanese Navy to revise its strategic thinking. The terms of the treaty allowed Japan the right to maintain a fleet of capital ships only 60 percent as large as those of either Britain or the United States.[22] With this significant limitation, Japan's naval strategists pointed out that history showed few cases where a navy equipped with a capital ship force representing less than two-thirds the tonnage of its adversary had emerged victorious in a decisive fleet action.[23] The Navy's answer to its dilemma was a submarine strategy that offset the deficiencies of the Washington treaty ratio. Accordingly, Japan sought a new method of gaining victory. In the attrition strategy that preceded interceptive operations, high-speed submarines would whittle down the enemy's fleet on its trans-Pacific passage and join fleet operations in the decisive battle.[24] As an early planning document put it, "We have no choice but to rely on submarines for some prospect of victory. It would be extremely difficult for our inferior forces to cope with the superior ones of the enemy using regular methods."[25]

In October 1941, Japan altered its naval doctrine as it planned for war in the Pacific.[26] As mandated by the London and Washington treaties, the U.S. Navy was numerically larger, so Japanese naval leaders needed a doctrine and operational plans to contend with a superior enemy.[27] They assumed the U.S. Navy would always be larger and stronger, so its strategy was simple: grind away at the U.S. fleet as it moved westward across the Pacific then, with the forces at an equivalent size, launch one grand and decisive attack. A key element of this strategy was using submarines to attack American warships.

The doctrine was deliberate and carefully drawn up. Forward patrol lines of scouting and command submarines would operate off the Hawaiian Islands, establishing contact with, and inflicting loss on, an American force moving into the western Pacific. Japan anticipated its submarines, with their high surface speed, would mount successive attacks on American battle formations. Japan would supplement initial massed destroyer attacks with assaults on the American line by midget submarines laid across the fleet's path by specially built submarine-carrying ships.[28] It, therefore, built up a large fleet of submarines, designed and trained for action against warships, and created a battleship navy, including several "super-battleships," designed for a slugging match in the open sea.[29]

Therefore, the Japanese Navy modified its strategic policy. Under this strategy, its heavy units were to remain on the defensive in Japanese home waters while other forces, including submarines, destroyers, and aircraft, would attack and reduce the U.S. fleet advancing to rescue Allied personnel in the Philippines. This diminution operation unfortunately had the effect of discouraging Japanese units from participating in any naval engagement until the main forces were ready for the decisive battle.

This strategic policy explains Japan's tenacious struggle for 78,000 tons of submarines at the London Conference in 1930, which the treaty reduced to 52,700 tons. Japan's war games had shown it needed an absolute minimum of 78,000 tons; 52,700 tons would leave it short by two squadrons, or 16 boats, of what planners considered necessary for a strategy of attrition.[30]

Decisive Battle

Prior to the 1920s, the Imperial Japanese Navy (IJN) fixated on decisive fleet engagements, as demonstrated by the decisive Battle of Tsushima during the Russo–Japanese War. During the battle, Admiral Heihachirō Togo's fleet devastated the Russian fleet, sinking 33 of 45 enemy ships during the two-day fight, at a cost of only three Japanese ships.[31] Additionally, lessons derived from the battle in 1905, and the Mahanian doctrine of the decisive battle, hardened into a dogma that continued to influence Japanese conservative strategic thinking throughout the 1930s and even beyond.[32]

Between the wars, the conviction that war with the United States was inevitable underpinned Japan's naval strategy. The Japanese naval staff had prepared their plans to meet the American "War Plan Orange," whose broad outlines had long been known in Tokyo. Drawn up in 1933, "Yōgeki Sakusen," or "interceptive operations," was the key to naval strategy that would account for the 60 percent inferiority imposed on Japan's battle fleet by the Washington treaty system.[33] Instead of building the sort of navy one might expect for an extended naval war of attrition, Japan developed one for a short, decisive, but limited war. If a decisive fleet engagement materialized, naval planners in the mid-1930s expected a devastating victory from such a scenario would damage American battleships enough to cripple America's will to keep fighting. When war came, it would feature a westward offensive by the U.S. Navy's battle fleet that would climax in a decisive fleet engagement in the western Pacific. To prevail, Japan must seek a decisive engagement early in the war.[34]

From the outbreak of World War II, the Japanese Navy had stuck to its long-cherished "one big battle" idea, in which all naval arms—surface, air, and underwater—were to be used once and for all.[35] Japanese Naval planners based their strategy on *their* perceived lessons of World War I, the importance of "quick encounter, quick showdown."[36] The basic concept of interceptive operations remained intact throughout the 1930s.[37] The traditional-minded admirals who dominated the Japanese Navy were inflexible and had a narrow perception of modern sea power. They resisted innovations in naval strategy if the results were uncomplimentary to battle fleet interests or infringed upon the strength and prestige of the Combined Fleet.[38]

The decisive victory doctrine counted Admiral Yamamoto as its most influential supporter. However, even he had mixed views towards it. On one hand, he realized the Japanese Navy could not win with a purely defensive posture because it would give the initiative to the Americans who could determine when and how to meet the Imperial Fleet. Conversely, he noted that, in previous war games, when it appeared Japanese forces would be "gradually whittled away" and a decisive victory was unattainable, naval leaders suspended the games.[39]

Japan's naval doctrine during the 1930s made no significant operational departures from the decisive-battle concept that was the fundamental basis for everything else. Japan planned for the wrong type of war.[40] The Navy designed its battle fleet to emphasize offensive firepower rather than endurance at sea. Somewhere between the Marianas and the Home Islands, the Japanese Navy would engage and destroy the U.S. fleet. Japan designed its entire naval structure to prevail in a great decisive battle somewhere in the islands of the central Pacific.[41]

This fixation blinded conservative naval officers to technological innovations rapidly transforming naval warfare and necessitating a fundamental reassessment of their strategic concepts.[42] The Japanese Navy relentlessly pursued a decisive-battle strategy from the beginning of the war until it had no more ships left with which to fight. The problem was that, except for Pearl Harbor, the battles the Japanese Navy sought and fought all turned out to be decisive defeats: Midway, the Solomons, the Philippine Sea, and Leyte Gulf.[43]

Vice Admiral Inoue Shigeyoshi, head of the Naval Affairs Bureau of the Navy Ministry, urged naval leaders to cancel their plans for the decisive battle and prepare instead for protracted air and amphibious warfare in the central Pacific, use submarines to attack enemy commerce, and build larger numbers of escort vessels to keep lines of communications open. These ideas made no impression on the Naval General Staff. Still preparing for the decisive battle in the western Pacific, hypnotized by the gigantic batteries of the "unsinkable" *Yamato*, secure in the unconquerable Japanese spirit, the Japanese Navy drifted toward war.[44]

IJN Submarine Doctrine

Before World War II, Japan's Combined Fleet admirals decided the submarine's role. Educated and trained for surface warfare, these admirals had difficulty in appreciating the potential of submarine warfare except as it could contribute directly to a successful surface engagement. Therefore, the Japanese Navy assigned its submarines roles most in keeping with the immediate concerns of the Combined Fleet. Interestingly, the Navy lacked a central operational command for its submarine force and its narrow strategic perception, in viewing its submarine arm largely as an adjunct to the Japanese surface fleet, hampered the employment of this large asset.[45]

Unlike its German allies or its American foes, Japan subordinated the war against commerce to the Mahanian doctrine established years before: to act as the eyes of the fleet and to thin down opposing forces as much as possible before bringing the two fleets together for the decisive engagement.[46] Japan's naval leaders had tied their submarines to an ineffectual doctrine.[47]

At the beginning of the Pacific War, Japan possessed a large and technically advanced submarine fleet with twice as many boats as the U.S. Pacific Fleet.[48] Expectations for the Japanese submarine service—the Sixth Fleet—were quite high. The newest submarines, the I-series, had incredible endurance, were fast on the surface, employed advanced optics, and carried excellent torpedoes that did not malfunction.[49] As in other navies, Japan's submarine force was led and manned by elite volunteers but trained for virtually its only task, attacking heavily screened American battle squadrons, in exercises so dangerously realistic they claimed several boats and crews.[50]

In their fleet support role, every time the Combined Fleet moved, submarines scouted ahead as the "Advance Expeditionary Force."[51] A focus on major American warships was at the expense of attacking the "supply train," the troop and supply ships vital for keeping any campaign fed and armed. Had this oversight been recognized and addressed, the build-up to, and the operation of, the Allied counteroffensives during the middle and later stages of the war would have been severely hampered.[52]

The directness of submarine attacks upon naval vessels possessed an attraction to the offensive-minded naval officer; the subtler and more valuable uses of the submarine did not. This led Japan to view the submarine's proper role as that of a vanguard of the fleet, whose torpedoes could soften an enemy force for the Japanese surface forces that followed.[53]

CHAPTER 3

Japanese Submarine Strategy and Tactics

> Everything in strategy is very simple, but that does not mean everything is very easy.[1]

Japan's submarine force is a story of missed opportunities. Vincent P. O'Hara, W. David Dickson, and Richard Worth, in their book *On Seas Contested*, wrote "Although Japan acquired a formidable collection of submarines whose numbers included some of the largest of their type as well as midget submarines carried aboard surface ships or larger submarines, Japanese submersibles did little to affect the course of World War II. The problem began with the Japanese Navy giving its submarine force a flawed mission: the long-distance interception of U.S. Fleet movements in the Pacific."[2] Although Japanese submarines did sink a few American warships, for example the carrier USS *Yorktown* at Midway and the heavy cruiser USS *Indianapolis* near the end of the war, American surface warships were too fast and evasive for the Japanese submarine's standard pursuit, contact keeping, and attack formulas.[3]

At the beginning of the Pacific War, Japan's submarine force held to the Navy's traditional aggressive "close-in-sure-shot" torpedo tactics rather than switch to long-distance firing (and thus was the notable exception to the Navy-wide obsession with outranging the enemy). At the same time, however, Japanese submarine commanders favored the contradictory and passive emphasis on concealment, which meant staying submerged for as long as possible and waiting for enemy fleet units to come steaming by and present themselves as targets.[4] Requirements of stealth and surprise through subsurface concealment opposed aggressive action that obliged a submarine to come at least to periscope depth where its periscope and torpedo wakes might give away its position. Forced to choose between these two, Japanese submarine commanders often chose stealth over boldness, which meant they usually failed in their missions as enemy fleet units raced by unscathed.[5]

Most lessons learned from prewar exercises greatly impacted wartime operations such as the emphasis on concealment translated during the war into extreme caution.[6] When the war began, concerns for concealment were stronger than the need for aggressive action, which, in the prewar exercises, often led to discovery by antisubmarine forces.[7] Even though prewar exercises demonstrated the basic unsuitability of Japan's submarine doctrine, Japan chose to relearn this lesson during the war, ultimately resulting in heavy losses.[8]

Commerce Raiding

The greatest waste of submarine resources by any belligerent in World War II was that inflicted upon the Japanese submarine service by its own naval command.[9] Like the U.S. Navy, at the outset of war the Japanese Navy was not prepared to cope with submarine warfare aimed at shipping. After Pearl Harbor, American submarines quickly undertook a war against the Empire's merchant marine, but Japan never faced up to the problem. It failed in antisubmarine warfare largely because the Navy disregarded the importance of attacking supply and troop ships; it assumed the role played by American submarines would be the same as that of Japan's own submarine forces and slighted the role as raiders of commerce shipping. This was difficult to explain because I-boats that reached patrol areas off California and Oregon shortly after Pearl Harbor sank several merchant vessels, alarming the entire United States' West Coast. Japan's naval leaders continued to hold to the doctrine that submarines were auxiliaries to the battle fleet.[10] Atsushi Oi explains it this way, "The Combined Fleet was the sole embodiment of the navy. The Combined Fleet, in its turn, was gripped by a single concept that fleet-versus-fleet action was the only warfare it must aim at. The task of protecting sea-borne trade was miserably slighted."[11]

The Japanese campaign plan had two parts: the attrition stage and the decisive battle stage. In the Japanese Navy Instructions for Submarine Warfare and the Decisive Battle, the first three paragraphs summarize prewar strategy:

1) Submarines are deployed effectively for the purpose of achieving their main goal: surprise attack on the enemy's main force.
2) The intent is to achieve repeated attacks on the enemy's main force. Operational preliminaries, such as types of submarines deployed, consideration of enemy intelligence, and weather conditions, are weighted carefully to help achieve these repeated attacks.
3) Except for a few submarines attached directly to the main force, most submarines constitute an advance expeditionary force. These advance submarines launch early attacks on the enemy's main force while also coordinating their operations with other Japanese units.[12]

The most glittering opportunity presented to the submarine force came early in the Pacific War: the chance for a major blow to the American conduct of the war by attacks on shipping sailing to and from the American West Coast.[13]

The I-boats failed to stop the enormous flow of scrap materials such as steel, electric cables, brass, and aluminum, left from the destruction caused by the Japanese air strike, which shipped from the Pearl Harbor Navy Yard to manufacturers in the continental United States. Japanese submarines failed to intercept vessels carrying personnel and supplies to Hawaii and torpedoed none of the crippled American combat ships sailing from Hawaii to yards at Bremerton or Mare Island.[14] More concerned about reconnaissance than combing coastal waters and attacking the numerous unescorted merchantmen, these I-boat operations were a colossal misuse of Japanese naval firepower.[15]

Submarines failed to ravage the plodding, vulnerable cargo vessels because they were perpetually stalking speedy, well-screened American task forces. The advantages gained from the occasional success hardly justified the effort expended, especially since merchant shipping presented such an attractive alternative. In the window of opportunity during the first year of the Pacific war, submarines could have made a crucial contribution to Japan's war. For as astonishing as it may seem, the submarine service never made a serious or sustained attack on American merchant shipping in the Pacific, even early in the war, when the Allied position in the Pacific was still uncertain, its supply lines most vulnerable, and its maritime resources stretched to the absolute limit. Certainly, the Americans knew this opportunity existed and were puzzled Japanese submarines never took advantage of it.[16]

The Japanese Navy paid little attention to the submarine's role as a means of attacking the enemy's sea lines of communication and the result was a dissipation of its submarine effort on a variety of piece-meal, tactical responsibilities. Accordingly, by the middle of 1942, Japan could no longer consider submarines an effective offensive branch of the Navy.[17] The fundamental reason for the failure of Japan's submarine forces in the Pacific was that staff officers in the Combined Fleet and on the Navy General Staff, those responsible for submarine tactics, did not understand the capabilities and limitations of their submarines.[18]

In the 1920s, the Japanese Navy initially built its submarine force with the intention of deploying it against enemy sea communications as well as against the enemy's main fleet in a decisive battle. However, as large as the submarine force eventually became, it was still too small to be divided between two missions and there was little interest in the doctrine advocating destruction of enemy sea communications because the destruction of the enemy's battle fleet was crucial. The Japanese did consider attacks on U.S. shipping to be an important part of a Pacific war, but only if such operations did not interfere with the primary mission of attacking the enemy's battle fleet. Once the Navy crushed the enemy's fleet, Japanese planners assumed a battle-seasoned submarine force would then find it easy to destroy enemy sea communications.[19]

Japan had no problem with unrestricted warfare. When submarines attacked merchant targets, they were effective. Japanese leadership simply failed to replace faulty strategic notions.[20] Better submarine doctrine would not have won the war for Japan, but the employment of submarines against the vulnerable supply lines would have cost the Allies in ships, goods, personnel, and effort, and delayed the outcome far more than did the fanatical last-ditch defense of indefensible islands.[21] Had the Japanese Navy concentrated its submarines in such operations in the spring of 1942, it might have set back American strategy in the Pacific by many months. However, caught up in its early victories in Southeast Asia and its fixation with the great surface battle in the mid-Pacific, the Japanese Navy let the opportunity slip by.[22] It saw commerce warfare as irrelevant to the Japanese warrior tradition. By setting aside what submarines could do to American shipping, the Navy compounded its error by failing to understand what American submarines could do to Japanese merchant shipping, a failure that was one of the major reasons for Japan's defeat in the Pacific War.[23] The Germans repeatedly tried to explain to their ally that the best hope for the Axis was to paralyze their enemies by attacks on shipping; attacks in which the possible increment provided by Japan could be of great significance[24] (see Appendix 6).

Strategy and Tactics

When Japan attacked Pearl Harbor in 1941, its submarine employment strategy had been in place for almost two decades.[25] The Japanese Navy first used submarines as an integral part of its fleet in the war with China. However, war against America would force the submarine force to change its tactical concepts four times in four years of conflict with the United States:[26]

- Phase I: "From 1931 to April 1942, submarines operated with the surface fleet; their major role was reconnaissance and attacks against warships."
- Phase II: "From April 1942 to November 1944, submarines concentrated their efforts on attacking merchant shipping."
- Phase III: "From mid-November 1942 to mid-August 1945, submarines primarily supplied bypassed island outposts."
- Phase IV: "From April 1945 to August 1945, submarines carrying Kaiten operated in groups in the open sea, primarily against tankers and troop ships."[27]

In 1938, the Japanese Navy tested their submarine force on the execution of the various tactical aspects of this mission. These exercises revealed the impractical nature of Japan's entire submarine doctrine. Three key lessons were discovered. First was the difficulty in conducting close surveillance of well-defended fleet units. Second was the vulnerability of large submarines to detection. Third was the difficulty of conducting command and control of submarines acting in concert with the battle fleet.[28] Another problem with Japanese operational control was substitution of micromanagement for commander's intent. The inclination of Japan's admirals was to centralize operational and tactical control of submarines. Instead of assigning large patrol areas in which to conduct unrestricted submarine warfare (as was the practice in the German and the U.S. fleets), naval leadership gave individual unit captains precise locations and inflexible tasking. Commanding officers obediently followed orders and rarely demonstrated initiative, cunning, or daring.[29]

In line with that thinking, submarine commanders followed a schedule for torpedo expenditure: enemy battleships and aircraft carriers were worth the firing of all torpedoes; cruisers rated three torpedoes, but a single torpedo had to suffice for destroyers and merchant ships. The disciplined Japanese followed this policy long after it had demonstrably failed. Despite the advice of their German allies, and long after Japan initiated the Phase II tactical concept, Japanese submariners remained fixated on American warships to the exclusion of merchant traffic[30] (see Appendix 6).

Operational orders unduly restricted submarines as to what they attacked while on individual patrol. During large operations, each submarine was frequently restricted to an ambush station with orders not to leave it even though a valuable target appeared outside its station limits, or even though the enemy to be "ambushed" had passed by.[31] As a rule, Japan depended more on placing its available submarines in the expected track of an American task force than on searching.[32] Paucity of operational intent, combined with timid commanding officers, effectively rendered the entire submarine force impotent.[33] In comparison, American skippers had their orders, but received considerable latitude in carrying them out.[34]

Contrary to the expectations of Japanese naval planners, the enthusiasm of Japanese submariners seemed to fade after initial submarine setbacks in the confused circumstances of the Pearl Harbor attack. Submarines failed to track down U.S. Navy capital ships and press attacks relentlessly, seemingly content with reconnaissance and harassment of their enemy.

Additionally, with the continual supply of scrap material headed to the continental United States after the Pearl Harbor attack, Japanese submarines only sank five merchant ships and damaged another five commerce vessels before the end of December 1941.[35]

Primary Tasks—Submarines

Japan's focus on the decisive battle came at the expense of the defense of sea lanes, transports, or antisubmarine warfare. This, in essence, exposed its lifelines to attack.[36] Throughout the war, submarines attacked commerce shipping only when the fighting strength of the fleet allowed it, with merchant ships becoming legitimate targets in the absence of enemy warships.[37] The Japanese Navy steadfastly clung to the notion that the "primary task of the submarines is to attack enemy heavy ships" such as battleships, battlecruisers, and aircraft carriers. Planners stated that submarines could operate against heavy and light cruisers only by "special order." These instructions reflected the prevailing view that the Navy should deploy submarines as warship killers in tandem with the surface fleet.[38] Commerce raiding required action over an extended period to be effective and Japanese decision makers were determined to achieve their goals in a short, violent war.[39]

Secondary Tasks—Submarines

At the start of World War II, Japan's naval leaders assigned their submarines various fleet support roles including scouting, screening the battle fleet, reconnaissance, and ambush missions.

Tactical Scouting. During strikes, it was customary to use submarines to scout and report on American ships and planes in bases where they could oppose the expected operation.[40] The submarines would send reports to their headquarters that in turn relayed these reports to the fleet. The carrier planes themselves made searches but did not expect assistance from submarines since the cooperation between aircraft and submarines was not satisfactory.[41]

Screening. Submarines acted as an outer screen ahead of the main body to prevent an accidental sighting.[42] A watchful vanguard of aggressive submarines would reduce the surface strength of the enemy by attrition, and the following surface units could then gain the advantage. Japan's fleet could then move into decisive battle with a fair assurance of victory.[43]

Reconnaissance. Before and during fleet operations, submarines reconnoitered the harbors or anchorages from which the U.S. fleet would sortie.[44] Then they would track and pursue the enemy fleet after its sortie, radio news of the enemy's activities to the Japanese fleet commander, and repeatedly ambush and torpedo the enemy's main force while it sailed westward to the Marianas and the decisive battle.[45]

Ambush. Ambushing was by far the most popular employment of Japanese submarines. It amounted to placing submarines in the expected path of the enemy force. Throughout the war, whenever the Japanese fleet commander expected an American task force movement, he made a well-considered guess and then rushed all available submarines to the enemy's track.[46] Japanese submarines would lie in wait for the enemy battle fleet and attack the major surface combatants with torpedoes.[47]

In April 1942, Phase II of the Japanese submarine tactics went into effect and the Sixth Fleet issued new operational priorities as most senior Japanese naval officers agreed that submarines were being improperly used. With American forces now on alert, the prewar strategy of approaching American ports to attack existing warships was extremely hazardous.[48] Japanese submarines were now to concentrate their efforts on attacking merchant shipping.

Oddly, while Combined Fleet Headquarters acquiesced to this shift in Sixth Fleet's priorities, Imperial hierarchy still felt the submarines' basic mission was sinking combatants. Japanese naval planners fashioned future operations, including Midway, accordingly.[49] During postwar interrogations, Vice Admiral Shigeyosh Miwa, Director Naval Submarine Department and Commander-in-Chief Sixth Fleet, reiterated the fundamental mission of Japanese submarines was as an auxiliary to the fleet.[50]

Japan lacked an adequate operational control system for its submarines. The Sixth Fleet Commander held operational control of all submarine squadrons and divisions as a default condition. However, when Japan planned a major offensive, operational control could take many forms.[51]

At Midway, Yamamoto held operational control throughout all stages of the battle, including preparatory reconnaissance. The Sixth Fleet's commander, usually a submariner, nominally understood the strengths and limitations of each submarine class. Not surprisingly, most successes occurred under his operational control. When another commander took control, problems quickly developed. For example, Yamamoto's submarine specialist for the Midway invasion advised him that many of the submarines intended for the mission were in unacceptable material condition. Ignoring the warning, Yamamoto ordered the submarines to assume forward reconnaissance positions. When many of them could not complete the journey to the Central Pacific, an unobstructed passage opened for the U.S. fleet to traverse.[52]

CHAPTER 4

United States Naval Doctrine

> Theory cannot be accepted as conclusive when practice points the other way.[1]

In the interwar period, the ideas of naval officer and strategist Alfred Thayer Mahan also dominated the U.S. Navy's concept of warfare at sea with emphasis placed on a single climactic fleet engagement.[2] "War Plan Orange" kept the Navy's focus on war in the western Pacific, and its Mahanian lineage justified a big fleet.[3] The Navy's existing tactical doctrine, with an emphasis on aggressive offensive action and the use of long-range fire with aerial spotting, remained staples of its doctrine through the interwar period.[4] After some refinement, the doctrine now emphasized major fleet action and relied on several fundamental principles, including tactical concentration and coordinated action against the enemy. The Navy drilled cruisers and destroyers in "night search and attack" procedures, designed to locate and damage an enemy battle fleet the night before a battle while submarines scouted ahead and attacked enemy surface vessels.[5] As the capabilities of carrier-based aircraft increased, the concept of attacking an enemy battle line with carrier planes, destroyer torpedoes, and battleship gunfire at the outset of an action became part of the Navy's tactical doctrine.[6]

Before the Pearl Harbor attack, the U.S. Navy organized the Pacific Fleet into a Battle Force and Scouting Force.[7] The Battle Force was a battleship-centric formation that, concentrated together with a large fleet train, would move as a unit, seizing objectives along its path.[8] The Navy developed three types of formations—cruising, approach, and battle—and each one had a specific role that ensured the coordinated movement of battleships and other fleet assets.⁹

When the position of the enemy was unknown and the chances of contact were slight, the Navy would employ a cruising formation, designed to emphasize security. Concentric circles of light forces around the fleet would prevent a surprise enemy contact from immediately endangering valuable ships at the center of the formation.¹⁰ By late 1941, the battleship-centric fleet was losing favor in many navies due to its vulnerability to submarines and aircraft as demonstrated by German U-boats in the Atlantic and Japanese naval aviation at Pearl Harbor. The battle fleet, the center of naval thinking and planning for over 30 years, disappeared.

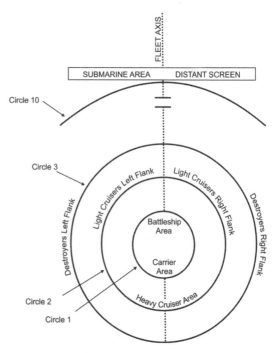

Figure 4.1: Interwar cruising formation of the U.S. fleet. (Modified from Trent Hone, "The Evolution of Fleet Tactical Doctrine in the U.S. Navy, 1922–1941." *The Journal of Military History* 67 (October 2003): 1107–48)

The Japanese attack at Pearl Harbor sank or damaged all American battleships present, forcing the Navy to reorganize into task forces and develop a new Pacific strategy with what remained.¹¹ Each task force centered on an aircraft carrier with an accompanying screen of cruisers and destroyers, with aircraft and submarines performing scouting duties.¹² Surface fleets still played their part, but the big-gun ships, though more powerful than ever, had lost their major role to the aircraft carrier.¹³ Neither the Japanese nor the Americans quite realized naval warfare was entering a new phase, one in which the seaborne aircraft of the two navies would contest for supremacy, with all other forces in a supporting role.¹⁴

Submarine Doctrine

Officially, the U.S. Navy's submarine doctrine emphasized the coordinated use of submarines with the fleet, for scouting operations ahead of the fleet's advance, and for attacks on enemy surface combatants. This doctrine specified the primary task of the submarine was to attack enemy heavy ships. It went on to define a heavy ship as a battleship, battlecruiser, or aircraft carrier. Only if authorized by special order could the target list include heavy cruisers, light cruisers, or other types of ships. In exercises, submarines did not prove particularly effective as scouts, and coordination with the main body of the fleet was very difficult. Attacks on protected warships were relatively ineffective; the slow speed of the submarines made it difficult to get into an attack position. In exercises at sea, targets were always a small fleet unit simulating a larger warship. Submarines never practiced making torpedo approaches on cargo ships, let alone firing practice torpedoes at such. Neither did they practice torpedo attacks at night on the surface, a tactic that would prove most profitable as the war progressed.[15]

Diplomatic pressure conditioned interwar development to prohibit unrestricted submarine warfare and the Navy's own vision of Mahanian sea control.[16] As late as May 1941, the Navy General Board turned down the Naval War College's recommendation that American submarines be used as commerce destroyers should there be war against Japan. Consequently, submarines conformed to the Navy's vision of a trans-Pacific war as the fallacious fleet-support doctrine continued to govern submarine operations.[17]

Submarines would be the eyes of the fleet as it proceeded across the Pacific, acting as advanced scouts and attacking enemy heavy warships as opportunities occurred.[18] In the climactic battle for sea control, submarines would play only a supporting role but would be the principal means of exercising sea control as a participant in the ensuing naval blockade of Japan.[19] In the years that followed, statements of submarine doctrine consistently stressed the use of the submarine against enemy battle forces rather than enemy merchant shipping. However, it took only a slight shift of viewpoint to use the submarine in a commerce-destroying role. The shift for America came on December 7, 1941, when Japan attacked Pearl Harbor.[20]

Submarine Skipper Problem

For at least a decade prior to the war, men who became commanding officers in submarines shared at least one common characteristic: they were superb technicians, formally trained as engineers.[21] However, it was not a good fit to have the "technical" skill in a "combat" position. When war came, it was like "relearning the business."[22] The Naval Academy curriculum centered on professional fundamentals rather than strategic concepts and the creation of an offensive mindset.[23] Prospective Commanding Officers School in New London could impart little useful combat experience and newly graduated submarine skippers entered a war for which doctrine and training had not prepared them. Moreover, these skippers would not recognize the insidious effects of an unrealistic peacetime operations and training system until the realities of combat disclosed it.[24]

In the interwar period, a submarine skipper's administrative skills, rather than his proficiency and daring in torpedo attacks, enhanced his chances of promotion. It was hardly the way to prepare for a form of warfare that demanded utmost initiative and daring.[25] Too many American submarine commanding officers, when faced with the real test, lacked aggression and confidence in their weapon. Unintended factors in the training process artificially reinforced the extreme caution built into prewar concepts of operation. The U.S. Navy conducted open-water training for Pacific submarines in waters completely different to those in which the war would be fought. The training waters lacked, for example, any of the thermal layers that would hide submarines from ever-vigilant destroyers equipped with sonar. Additionally, peacetime training exaggerated the ability of aircraft to detect submarines. The *Report of Gunnery Exercises 1940–1941* states, "It is bad practice and is contrary to submarine doctrine to conduct an attack at periscope depth when aircraft are known to be in the vicinity. Keep your periscope down in calm seas and any time within five hundred miles of an enemy airfield; stay deep; fire on sonar target data." Sonar data proved to be relatively useless. Captains had the fear of antisubmarine aircraft instilled in them. As part of their training, the Navy flew most commanding officers over a submarine operating submerged. Sometimes, under good conditions, it was visible at depths of 125 feet. Even though the published doctrine stressed aggressiveness, the submarine force deliberately hobbled itself by inculcating a culture of caution and a fear of detection.[26]

Tactical exercises also reinforced career caution. The Navy reprimanded the captain of a submarine detected while making an approach. Conversely, it commended the captain who never got to the target but was unobserved.[27] This helped produce overly hesitant thinking among submarine skippers.[28] Not surprisingly, the submarine force had too many commanders at the outbreak of the war who were unwilling to take risks where on-the-spot decisiveness was needed from the commanding officer.[29]

Early in the war, captains were technically competent but lacked a warlike attitude. Peacetime training had produced a gamesman mentality among some of the motivated officers. However, winning commendations in fleet exercises did not always translate to "shooting for blood."[30] The Navy directed prewar tactics at attacking high-speed, well-screened combat ships and trained submarine officers for a war against combat vessels, not commerce raiding. Tactics dictated commanding officers keep their submarine deep and fire at warships on sound bearings alone.[31] These conditions required extreme caution and it was this very caution that worked against skippers making attacks on merchant ships early in the war. It is no surprise that during the first year of the war, skipper performance was generally abysmal, and the Navy replaced a third of all captains for lack of aggressiveness or failure to sink ships. Additionally, early deployment of Pacific submarines reflected American inexperience with submarine operations and demonstrated that American submarines were not ready for unrestricted warfare.[32]

In wartime, submarine duty imposed psychological and physical burdens on commanders that were unforeseen in peace. There were numerous instances of submarine captains overcome by the strain of combat and turning over their commands to their executive officers.[33] Delegation of responsibility was nonexistent. The skipper was responsible for everything on his submarine and if anything went wrong, he took a career hit. Captains, growing cautious, always stayed on the bridge or in the conning tower, an endurable activity during peacetime drills, but unsustainable in combat.[34]

Interwar Tactics

The prewar U.S. Navy had outmoded tactical ideas. Dominated by the "gun club," a clique of "battleship admirals," American naval leaders stubbornly refused to acknowledge the power of carrier aircraft and submarines.[35] The fixation with decisive battleship actions distracted strategists from seriously examining alternative uses of sea power appropriate to the geographical and strategic circumstances of the situation they faced. However, the officers in charge had neither the mental preparation for such flexible thinking nor had they equipped the fleet for such alternative uses.[36] Naval leadership clung to the idea that Japanese and American Pacific fleets, two well-prepared navies, organized in similar formations, trained along similar lines, instilled with similar tactical ideas, would clash in the western Pacific.[37] However, what the "battleship admirals" did not count on was the significant effect Pearl Harbor would have on American naval doctrine and tactics.

CHAPTER 5

United States Submarine Strategy and Tactics

The most *elegant* theory is useless if it lacks practical application.[1]

In tactics as in strategy, American submarines began the war burdened by peacetime misconceptions.[2] Submarines were an important element of the Navy's plans in the interwar period and, for years, it considered them for use in major actions, but did not resolve the specifics on how to employ them. As previously stated, the U.S. Navy's main interest in submarine warfare before the outbreak of hostilities was with fleet operations. Like Japan, the U.S. Navy saw the main tasks of submarines as scouting and attacks on enemy task forces given the declared interwar policy the United States would not engage in unrestricted submarine warfare against shipping; the submarines could have no other task. However, they struggled with the mistaken mission of fleet support.[3] The U.S. Navy needed to explore the strategic potential of the submarine and, with industry, address the corresponding technical challenges. After World War I, uncertainty prevailed within the Navy and the submarine force over issues as basic as strategy and mission.[4]

In 1919, American naval officers had yet to define for themselves the proper role of the submarine. In the 1920s, Naval War College problems called for submarines to operate in direct support of the fleet, discouraging individual offense unless an exceptional opportunity presented itself. If their sea-keeping qualities allowed it, the submarine's missions were to gather intelligence, to locate enemy supply lines, and to disrupt enemy communications. The Navy never seriously considered attacks upon enemy warships or merchant vessels independent of the surface fleet or of an impending surface action. It relegated those submarines unable to keep up with the fleet to coastal defense. In general, their usefulness in fleet operations proved limited.[5]

Beginning in 1928, officers certain of the submarine's offensive potential wanted to abandon the burden of direct battle fleet support to pursue independent offensive operations.[6] Between 1928 and 1930, Commander Thomas Withers, Commanding Officer of Submarine Division Four, called repeatedly for an offensive strategy and solo tactics like those employed by the German Navy during World War I.[7] Moving to the Naval War College in 1930, Withers refined his ideas on submarine strategy. He demonstrated that working in conjunction with the fleet represented the least important of the submarine's missions and urged the Navy to permit submarines to operate independently, aggressively, and in combined attack and reconnaissance missions.[8] Rather than tying submarines directly to battle fleet support roles, strategists placed more emphasis on the idea of independent submarine patrols, offensive operations against enemy ships, and intelligence-gathering missions. The Navy General Board of senior admirals did not heed the obvious lesson of World War I that the submarine was the deadliest threat to a nation's shipping. While naval officers showed no inclination to remove submarines from the inventory, the nagging problem was how best to employ them. There were two options: the Navy could use submarines for coastal defense, or naval officers could find a way to keep them relevant to the Mahanian paradigm.[9]

Fleet exercises and war game scenarios during the late 1930s encouraged submarines to attack warships, convoy escorts, and even certain convoys themselves, when identified as critical to enemy logistical support.[10] Operating with the fleet, submarines could remain on the surface until the enemy craft were near; after an engagement, acting as a type of scavenger, they could sink disabled enemy ships that might otherwise escape.[11] Submarines were to remain submerged during daylight hours in waters where enemy air activity was likely and only minimal use of the periscope was permitted. This allowed for attacks, at depth, based on sound location and the Navy accepted the reduction of accuracy of such attacks as the price to pay for the increased chances of survival for the submarine.[12]

The most effective use of the submarine was against enemy merchant shipping. Alternative uses of the submarine for fleet support were inferior. It was a notoriously poor reconnaissance craft. It was inadequate in tracking enemy fleets, due to its low speed and endurance when submerged, that forced it to track on the surface where it was vulnerable to aircraft and escort vessels. This in turn required the submarine to keep a safe distance from enemy fleets and therefore run the risk of losing its quarry. It was a poor weapon to use against occupation forces due to the protection afforded an amphibious operation and the shallowness of the sea where such operations took place. Finally, when engaged with the fleet in close-support operations, it was subject to attack from friendly aircraft and surface vessels despite the creation of safety zones for it and the use of identification signals. Limitations experienced during early exercises transformed the fleet submarine from an extension of the battle line to an independent part of the fleet. However, while naval officers proved willing to detach the submarine from the sea-control mission, they rejected any further doctrinal development emphasizing commerce raiding. The Navy would shape the submarine into an offensive weapon commensurate with Mahanian doctrine.[13]

When Japan attacked Pearl Harbor, the U.S. Navy had 111 submarines in commission: 60 in the Atlantic, 22 in the Pacific Fleet at Pearl Harbor and 29 in the Asiatic Fleet based in Manila. The various submarine commands—at Pearl, Brisbane, and Fremantle, the latter two in Australia—ordered the boats around in helter-skelter fashion. Each of the three submarine groups administered and operated independently of the others, so there was no submarine strategy common to all.[14]

The Navy, fighting with its back to the wall, detached the submarine from fleet support and set its priority to attacks on Japanese surface combatants. Since the 1920s, this was exactly what imaginative submariners had argued should be their primary role. In the fire of emotion after Pearl Harbor, it was but a small step of operational doctrine to redefine that mission as unrestricted submarine warfare, in this case against Japanese merchantmen in a comprehensive campaign of attrition, as well as against major Japanese warships.[15]

Submarines as warships had endured a strikingly rough initiation in the Pacific encounters of December 1941 and into 1942, inflicting little harm on enemy warships.[16] A combination of poor deployment and faulty torpedoes contributed to the submarines' ineffectiveness early in the war. Although some American submarines would attack and sink any Japanese merchantmen they might come across and pull off some lucky attacks on warships, as things stood by March 1942, submarines would have little influence on the main battle.[17]

Submarine commanders using prewar concepts of operations had serious problems finding merchant ships, even with intelligence support. Moving slowly underwater, using sonar or their periscope only minimally, submarine commanders simply could not see or hear very far. Even when directed to the sector in which a merchant ship was expected, submarines could not effectively search the area before the ship had passed. Merchant ships moved faster than submerged submarines, and if the submarine missed its intercept, it could not stay submerged and hope to trail its target. Even if the submarine did contact a target, and if the commander adhered to prewar tactics and stayed submerged and invisible, he was likely to lose his target.[18]

American submarines did attack merchant shipping from the outset but were often diverted from that vital job by the temptations of enemy warships. Strangely enough, much of the distraction was caused by a top-secret asset. In September 1940, American cryptanalysts had broken the Japanese Navy code known as JN25. The resulting information on the movements of Japanese warships was priceless if wisely used. In early 1942, the U.S. Navy decided to use its submarines, aided by ULTRA intelligence, to help sink Japanese battleships and aircraft carriers.[19] However, the shore commanders sometimes forgot that battleships and carriers were faster than submarines and difficult to sink even if successfully intercepted, while cargo ships were slow and extremely vulnerable. All too often, American submarine commanders received orders to break off lucrative hunts for merchant vessels to vainly chase some distant warship. Misapplied use of radio intelligence sent the Pacific

Fleet submarines chasing over the ocean after the enemy's big warships instead of concentrating on blockading Japan's main shipping routes. Instead of proactively deploying their submarines, the Navy was reactively responding to what the Japanese were doing.[20]

The U.S. Navy established new tactics for submarines to achieve their full potential, tactics often generated on the fly or at the expense of initial failure.[21] Many submarine skippers who had excelled in the prewar service and exercises made poor showings under the harsh conditions of actual combat. Moreover, some submarines, such as those deployed at Midway, were not the best in service in many cases. For example, USS *Dolphin* was almost a decade old with a top speed of 18 knots, and only had six torpedo tubes and 18 torpedoes. USS *Cachalot* and USS *Cuttlefish* were far smaller vessels with no stern tubes, slower speed, and less endurance. Even had men and machines been up to the high standard they were ultimately to achieve in 1944–45, all their efforts would have foundered on the inadequacy of their main weapon, the Mark-14 torpedo.[22]

To the dismay of American submarine commanders, their primary weapon hardly proved to be a threat. The world's most advanced technological society was producing torpedoes that were duds. The Great Torpedo Scandal, beginning in December 1941 and lasting to August 1943, involved three distinct problems: depth control, the magnetic influence exploder, and the contact exploder. The torpedoes ran deeper than set or they exploded prematurely. Each flaw concealed the next, making it impossible to detect and correct all of them simultaneously. The deep-running torpedo hid the premature issue. Premature explosions were the product of the magnetic exploder which, when deactivated for contact detonation, uncovered the dud issue as the major problem.[23]

Naval command in Washington and the Pacific learned slowly as the dispersal of forces continued. The submarine campaign would remain unsuccessful until the Navy chose the strategy that was staring it in the face—an all-out war on Japan's commerce shipping—and until it did something to improve submarine weapons. There was apparently no attempt in early 1942 to redefine the strategic goal of the submarine force away from defeat of the enemy battle fleet towards the destruction of the Japanese war economy, to shift submarine operations to that goal, and to evaluate alternative methods of reaching that goal. Submarine skippers were told to sink ships, any kind of ships, or they would be relieved of command.[24]

Tactically, the Navy was fumbling for a submarine doctrine. In the Atlantic, Germany adopted submarine "wolf packs," attacking on the surface at night. However, in the Pacific, submarines did not implement these methods, even though the Navy had ample evidence from the British of their effectiveness. The Pacific force also clung to the sonar approach, fixing the enemy by mechanical devices rather than sighting and fixing by periscope. Prewar submarine doctrine dictated that submarines were to stalk their quarry submerged, approach quietly, and then stay as silent as possible while avoiding the attacks of surface escorts. This cautious doctrine, coupled with faulty torpedoes, reduced the combat effectiveness of even the newer American submarines at the start of World War II.[25]

Why would naval strategists refuse to heed a clear lesson of World War I and fail to develop their own submarine force as a commerce-destroying weapon if another world conflict should occur? Their answer was that the greatest effect of the submarine on naval strategy in the war was not its destruction of seaborne commerce but the changes it effected in operations of surface fleets by its reputation as a warship killer. However, could the reason also revolve around America's position against unrestricted warfare during World War I? After all, the United States could not publicly announce a war on commerce if it went to war with Japan, especially if that was one reason America declared war on Germany during World War I. It makes sense that American naval leaders adopted, at least publicly, a fleet-support role for their submarines.[26]

The submarine escaped limitation in 1922 because, as an innovative technology, the military had yet to exploit its full potential. In addition, since Japan and the United States recognized the submarine could enhance their defensive superiority in important ways, they did not agree to abolish the weapon system entirely.[27] The fact that the U.S. had signed the treaty was a symptom of its view of the submarine as a menace in enemy hands rather than an asset in her own. In any event, there was no lateral leap of imagination from the North Atlantic to the Pacific and the Navy never considered the option of a submarine campaign against merchant shipping.[28] Unrestricted submarine warfare against Japanese shipping would have brought Japan to its knees with comparatively little expense, but such use of submarines in this manner against merchant shipping had been outlawed by treaty to which the United States was a signatory, regardless of whether the enemy abided by the same treaty or not.[29] America's policy makers abhorred the unrestricted U-boat attacks that compelled the nation to fight Germany in 1917.[30] The U.S. did not want to face the same charges leveled against the Germans during the First World War.[31]

The use of submarines as commerce raiders was a sensitive topic.[32] As events escalated in Europe and Asia, how far had submarines progressed towards being useful and effective elements of the fleet? The answer depended on what the submarine's role should be. There was no doubt the potential enemy was Japan, but how would the Navy use submarines against Japan? Germany was the prime example of how effective submarines could be in destroying enemy shipping and cutting overseas lifelines.[33] German captains were much more attack minded, whereas prewar training of American commanders had not prepared them for all-out war against merchant shipping.[34] However, the submarine, which the Navy designated in 1930 for fleet support, was instantly redefined after Pearl Harbor as a weapon of unrestricted warfare against all Japanese shipping.[35] The Navy gave submarines an unplanned independent offensive mission on December 7, 1941, when, with the battle line out of action at Pearl Harbor, they were released for an unlimited war of attrition.[36] National outrage made it easy to discard prewar objections to unrestricted submarine warfare and the obvious vulnerability of Japan to such a campaign.[37]

The Navy, declaring unrestricted submarine warfare six hours after the surprise attack at Pearl Harbor, abandoned lingering remnants of prewar doctrine. Overwhelmed by reality, it also de-emphasized the decisive fleet engagement with submarine support. Yet at the outset of the Pacific War, the effectiveness of the inexperienced U.S. Navy submarine force paled in comparison with German U-boat command.[38] The U.S. Navy's submarine effort in the Pacific Campaign got off to a slow start because of poor operational doctrine, timid commanding officers, and unreliable torpedoes.[39]

CHAPTER 6

Japanese Submarine Actions at Midway

> We had no clear idea of the position of the U.S. task force, and in consequence, with the exception of *I-168*, we were unable to use our submarine strength in the Midway operation.[1]

In the spring of 1942, Japan's tactical concept for submarines shifted from warships being the primary target to a campaign against merchant shipping. However, it was still Japan's strategic concept to force the U.S. fleet into a major sea battle where, under advantageous conditions, the Japanese could inflict a decisive defeat. Following the Doolittle raid against Japan in April 1942, Admiral Yamamoto wanted to lure the U.S. fleet into that single, decisive battle and felt an invasion of Midway would draw out the American carriers in defense of the island.[2]

Preliminary to the battle, Japanese naval planners gave their submarines two primary tasks. First, Japanese submarines were to support the Second "K" Operation of early March.[3] The Sixth Fleet dispatched two 1,400-ton mine-laying submarines to French Frigate Shoals (FFS). These submarines each carried 40 tons of aviation gasoline and 12 tons of oil to service flying boats that would meet them at the shoal and make a reconnaissance of Pearl Harbor before the Midway strike.[4]

The second task required Japanese submarines to deploy in picket lines to report the approach of the U.S. fleet. Five submarines from the 3rd Submarine Squadron (SubRon 3) together with eight from the 5th Submarine Squadron (SubRon 5) were to form north–south patrol lines 200 to 400 miles north of FFS, almost halfway between Pearl Harbor and Midway, to report and attack American task forces as they sailed from Pearl

Figure 6.1: USS *Hornet* (CV-8) launches Army Air Force B-25B bombers at the start of the first U.S. air raid on the Japanese Home Islands, April 18, 1942. (Official U.S. Navy Photograph, National Archives)

Harbor to meet Japan's occupation forces. With a pre-deployed screen of submarines and the advantages of superior numbers of battleships and carriers, and with aircraft based ashore at Midway after the Occupation Force captured the island, the Combined Fleet would defeat the U.S. fleet in a decisive battle.[5]

Under Vice Admiral Teruhisa Komatsu, the Sixth Fleet's 3rd and 5th Submarine Squadrons and the 13th Submarine Division would participate in the Midway campaign. Japan's naval leaders expected their submarines, especially trained to work in conjunction with the battle fleet against enemy warships, to have an important part in the battle for Midway.[6]

Second "K" Operation

On May 19, the 24th Flotilla and the 6th Fleet, meeting at Kwajalein, came to an agreement concerning the execution of the Second "K" Operation. Two Type-2 flying boats of the 24th Air Flotilla, the 13th Submarine Division (*I-121, I-122, I-123*), and part of SubRon 3 (*I-171, I-174, I-175*) were to participate in the operation. Under the agreement, both groups scheduled the reconnaissance for May 31. If, however, conditions were unfavorable on that day, the operation would be postponed, and if reconnaissance was not possible by June 3, the operation was to be canceled.[7] Submarines *I-121* and *I-123* had their mine-storage areas remodeled to store aviation gasoline and lubricating oil, and transported teams of mechanics to service the *Emily* flying boats at FFS.[8]

The six submarines each had their specific tasks for this operation. *I-121* and *I-123*, with *I-122* as the stand-by reserve vessel, were to be on station near La Perouse Pinnacle (LPP), which is about seven miles southeast of FFS. *I-121* was 1.7 miles at 330° from LPP, *I-123* was 2.5 miles at 170° from LPP, and *I-122* was 6.5 miles at 260° from LPP.[9] Upon completion of the operation, *I-121* and *I-123* originally were to take station on Cordon A south of FFS and *I-122* would take station 60 miles north of Laysan Island.[10]

I-171, designated as the beacon ship, would transmit radio beacon signals half an hour before and half an hour after the time the flying boats were due to pass overhead. *I-174* was to cruise in the waters

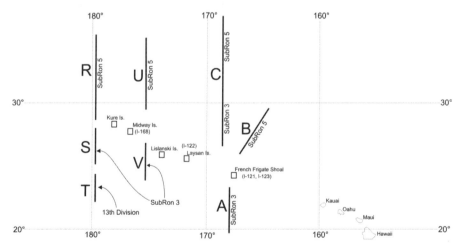

Figure 6.2: Japanese submarine dispositions throughout the battle. Each patrol line (A, B, C, etc.) indicates the position over time as Japan used its submarines reactively to locate and attack the American carriers.

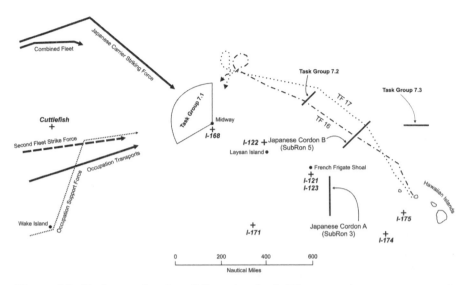

Figure 6.3: Battle map showing all forces involved. Of note are the separate approach directions of the Japanese Striking Force and Occupation Force. Task Group 7.1 is set up in a defensive arc northwest of Midway while Japanese submarines are between Midway and Hawaii in their failed attempt to intercept the American carriers.

southwest of Hawaii to rescue the aircrews in the event they had to make an emergency landing. *I-175* was to be in position 80 miles southwest of Oahu to report weather conditions, wind force and direction, and type and height of waves in the Pearl Harbor area to the commanding officer of the 24th Air Flotilla. By May 20, all submarines participating in the operation departed Kwajalein and by May 30 had reached their designated stations.[11]

Submarine *I-121* arrived off FFS on May 27. The flying boats were to rendezvous with the boat between May 25 and June 1 for fueling. However, when *I-121* arrived at FFS, an American seaplane tender was at anchor with seaplanes coming and going. *I-121* reported the situation and waited. On May 31, *I-123* reached FFS, found two enemy ships lying at anchor, and reported enemy flying boats near the entrance to the shoals.[12] American intelligence had reported the planned submarine-to-aircraft refueling operation so Admiral Nimitz reacted swiftly by sending a seaplane tender to the crucial area to prevent the Japanese activities.[13] Vice Admiral Eiji Gotō, 24th Air Flotilla commander at Kwajalein and responsible for directing the Second "K" Operation, ordered a 24-hour postponement, instructing *I-123* to keep watching the shoals in the hope the enemy ships would depart.[14]

On May 31, Gotō officially canceled the seaplane reconnaissance from FFS and reassigned the six submarines. Through some failure in communication, the submarines did not receive the cancellation order. *I-121* had no direct radio communication with the flying boats and since the planes did not appear during the time he spent in the vicinity of FFS, the commanding officer of *I-121* assumed Vice Admiral Gotō had canceled the operation.[15]

With the suspension of the Second "K" Operation, Teruhisa Komatsu ordered *I-171*, *I-174*, and *I-175* of SubRon 3 to take station on Cordon A and *I-121*, *I-122*, and *I-123* of the Attached Submarine Group to patrol the neighborhood north of Laysan Island and FFS. *I-121*, *I-122*, and *I-123* commenced a retirement westward toward Laysan.[16]

Gotō promptly communicated these developments to Admiral Yamamoto on the battleship *Yamato*. During the afternoon of June 4, Yamamoto modified this directive and ordered *I-121*, *I-122*, and *I-123* to proceed to a position south of Laysan Island "because of the need of guarding the south of the archipelago." However, it seems these submarines had already, apparently on their own initiative, proceeded in this direction. They joined up south of Laysan Island on June 4 and scouted westward throughout the day. *I-122* carried out a reconnaissance of both Laysan and Lisianski Islands much further west along the chain, closer to Midway itself.[17]

The failure of the Second "K" Operation meant it was impossible to know American naval strength present at Pearl Harbor. Nevertheless, Combined Fleet Headquarters still hoped that if the U.S. fleet did sortie from Pearl Harbor to oppose the Midway invasion, Vice Admiral Komatsu's submarine cordons, scheduled to be on station between Hawaii and Midway by June 1, would suffice to provide advance warning as well as knowledge of the enemy's strength.[18] With Combined Fleet Headquarters not considering the failure of the Second "K" Operation a major problem and conveying confidence the submarine patrol lines would provide them with ample warning and details, Japan sent an Advanced Expeditionary Force of submarines to scout ahead of the Combined Fleet.[19]

The disposition of the Advanced Expeditionary Force of Japanese submarines deployed for the Midway operation varies from author to author. Some discrepancy exists as Fuchida and Okumiya omit *I-174* from SubRon 3 and *I-164* from SubRon 5. Bates leaves *I-162* off SubRon 5. Morison omits *I-166* from SubRon 5. Boyd and Yoshida omit *I-165* from SubRon 5 and do not include *I-122* in the Second "K" Operation. However, they do include *I-164*, sunk by the submarine USS *Triton* on May 17 near Kyushu.[20] Additionally, Japan intended to deploy midget submarines for fleet action and island defense. These midget submarines sailed on board two converted seaplane carriers, *Chiyoda* and *Nisshin*, sailing with the Midway invasion fleet. However, there also exists discrepancy surrounding midget submarines. Padfield states there were eight Type As, whereas Morison indicates there were two motor torpedo boats and six midget submarines. Orita states the converted seaplane carriers had 24 on board. Carpenter and Polmar indicate *Chiyoda* carried eight Type As and *Nisshin* carried five motor torpedo boats. Boyd and Yoshida state *Chiyoda* and *Nisshin* each carried several two-man midget submarines. Parshall and Tully also had *Chiyoda* carrying submarines while *Nisshin* carried motor torpedo boats. However, since Japanese surface forces never got within sight of Midway or the U.S. fleet, Japan never launched these midget submarines and torpedo boats.[21]

Cordons

Admiral Yamamoto assigned over 200 vessels for the Midway operation, 16 of which were submarines.[22]

He placed considerable reliance on the submarine force to watch and report U.S. movements. Yamamoto concluded the most effective use of the submarines would be cordons, some already alluded to above, covering the approaches toward the Midway and Aleutians invasion points. Yamamoto's Midway plan directed the submarine force to station two cordons. Each would be populated by a squadron (Cordon A—SubRon 3, Cordon B—SubRon 5), placed northwest and west of Hawaii. Both cordons were about halfway between Hawaii and Midway

Japanese Order of Battle—Submarines, Advance Expeditionary Force		
3rd Submarine Group, 3rd Submarine Squadron, Rear Admiral Chimaki Kono	5th Submarine Group, 5th Submarine Squadron, Rear Admiral Tadashige Daige	Attached Submarine Group, 13th Submarine Division
I-168	I-156	I-121
I-169	I-157	I-122
I-171	I-158	I-123
I-174	I-159	
I-175	I-162	
	I-164	
	I-165	
	I-166	

and were to be in position by June 1. About May 25, SubRon 5 submarines and *I-169* of SubRon 3, all anchored at Kwajalein, had orders to sail immediately to the line of deployment to assume their assigned positions along the route between Pearl Harbor and Midway.[23] Cordon A consisted of four submarines that were to be on station by June 1. (See Figures 6.2 and 6.3)

Seven submarines established Cordon B, northeast of Cordon A. These submarines were also to be on station on June 1 in a line roughly southwest to northeast.[24] (See Figure 6.2) Cordon A submarines were in a north–south line, with a geographical position of Lat. 20°00′ N., Long. 166°20′ W., and Lat. 23°30′ N., Long. 166°20′ W., between Midway and the approaches from Hawaii south of FFS. Cordon B was a geographical position between Lat. 28°20′ N., Long. 162°20′ W., and Lat. 26°00′ N., Long. 165°00′ W. The delay and cancellation of the Second "K" Operation meant *I-121* and *I-123* would be late on station at Cordon A, not reaching it until June 3. As previously stated, *I-121* and *I-123* may not have even reached their patrol lines, either due to Yamamoto's order to proceed westward or possibly by their own initiative to head in that direction.[25]

SubRon 5

From the Japanese perspective, SubRon 5, stationed across the path any American forces would take when proceeding from Oahu to Midway, held the key role in the plans for the Midway battle.[26] Cordon B was the vital "sentry line" group of submarines, important in the battle because it was supposed to provide the Japanese any knowledge of American forces nearing Japan's aircraft carriers. However, SubRon 5 was comprised of outdated boats, each at least a dozen years old and scheduled for retirement into the training service. Commander Shojiro Iura of the Naval General Staff protested the decision in selecting SubRon 5, explaining to Yamamoto's chief of staff that its submarines were too old and too slow for the planned mission.[27] The staff of the submarine force fully understood the unsatisfactory condition of SubRon 5 before the battle. Inexplicably, naval leadership still assigned this crucial assignment to SubRon 5, a "second-line unit" under Rear Admiral Tadashige Daigo.[28] Iura realized every available warship must be committed to this operation, but he warned the Combined Fleet staff officers they were taking too much for granted when they stationed such a worn-out group of submarines in the path the U.S. fleet was most likely to use. His warning went unheeded and Combined Fleet approved the plan unchanged so far as the use of submarines.

Extensive repairs to SubRon 5 submarines, plus the participation of SubRon 3 in the canceled Second "K" Operation, put deployments behind schedule.[29] SubRon 5 was to be on station by June 1 but failed to reach the assigned patrol area on time due to overhaul delays that postponed its departure from Japan.[30] Furthermore, the boats stopped to refuel at Kwajalein, were again late departing for their assigned area, and consequently reached their picket line, Cordon B, on June 3.[31] In addition, a typographical error in their orders delayed some of the Japanese submarines, starting them off towards the wrong location.[32] With the cordons not yet established, Yamamoto and his staff remained completely in the dark regarding U.S. activities. Commander Iura was correct in his assessment of SubRon 5's shortcomings. First, their overhauls in Japan took too long, causing the submarines to arrive later than expected at Kwajalein. This, in turn, pushed the refueled submarine's departure date back to between May 26 and 30. Additionally, longer daylight hours combined with increasing American patrol activity, meant that SubRon 5, with limited time during the night to maneuver on the surface, traveled mostly submerged while avoiding American scout planes from Midway.[33]

Once on station, Japanese submarines remained submerged during the day and surfaced at night, never relaxing their lookout for American forces coming from Pearl Harbor. The skippers patiently scanned the empty ocean, but they had arrived too late. It was while SubRon 5 slowly approached its patrol line that the American carriers reached their positions northeast of Midway unseen, to lie in wait for Japan's Combined Fleet, completely upsetting Yamamoto's plan.[34] Aboard *Yamato* and the carrier *Akagi*, admirals Yamamoto and Nagumo, respectively, waited for the submarine contact reports in vain.[35] If the submarine cordons had sighted the American task forces, Yamamoto and Nagumo would have had both actionable information and the time to make last minute adjustments to their operational plans. As it was, they received neither.[36] Even if SubRon 5 had been on time, arriving on station by June 1, it would have made no difference as the American carriers had long since passed the positions of the cordons and moved far to the northwest.[37]

Midway Island Reconnaissance

Part of the submarine force (*I-168* and *I-169* of SubRon 3) was to reconnoiter Midway from the end of May to the first part of June. Afterwards, both submarines would move southeast and take positions, with *I-171*, *I-174*, and *I-175*, on Cordon A after these submarines had carried out their portions of the Second "K" Operation. However, *I-168* was undergoing repairs in Japan and sailed independently from *I-169*. *I-168* did reconnoiter near Midway, keeping it out of any action, but the submarine would be near Midway when Japanese occupation forces landed as intended. Also, *I-169* seems to have proceeded directly to its assigned patrol area on Cordon A and did not perform any reconnaissance of Midway.[38]

On May 31, *I-168* arrived at Kure Island, 110 miles west-northwest of Midway. Part of the overall strategy required seizing the island for

Figure 6.4: Japanese submarine *I-68* underway in March 1934, probably during trials. This submarine was renamed *I-168* in May 1942. It torpedoed USS *Yorktown* (CV-5) on June 6, 1942, causing damage that led to the carrier's sinking the following morning. (National Archives)

a seaplane and midget submarine base.[39] On June 1, *I-168* arrived at Midway and observed no craft other than a picket submarine south of Sand Island. *I-168* did report an intensive air patrol was in force southwest of Midway to a 600-mile limit, that strict air alert was in place with numerous aircraft on patrol night and day, and the presence of many construction cranes on Midway suggested American activity on the island. This report from *I-168* was the only reconnaissance information of any importance a Japanese submarine reported throughout the engagement.[40] *I-168* remained in the vicinity of Midway from June 1 until it attacked the crippled American carrier USS *Yorktown* a few days later.[41]

Japan's "N" Day

On the morning of June 4, Japan's submarines continued their scouting and reconnaissance assignments in accordance with Yamamoto's plan as Japanese carriers launched the first air attack on Midway. Japanese search planes soon sighted American forces about two hundred miles east of the Japanese Striking Force and it was immediately apparent to Yamamoto that his submarines were now out of position.[42] At 1220, Yamamoto dispatched DesOpOrd Number 155 to all commanders with new tactical positioning which also included moving the submarine cordons westward.[43] From Kwajalein, Vice Admiral Komatsu ordered all fleet-type submarines to move their picket lines and establish a Cordon C by the morning of June 5.[44] (Figure 6.2) The shift westward of submarine picket lines to Cordon C occurred after the American attacks on the Japanese carriers. Japanese thinking appears reactionary instead of proactive.

In the immediate aftermath of the attack on the Japanese carriers, and before canceling the operation, Yamamoto ordered a naval bombardment of Midway.[45] The bombardment may have been in preparation for the invasion, or at least to ground American land-based planes. It seems Yamamoto was not merely attempting to boost morale but was quite serious in intending to continue with the attack on Midway. In accordance with DesOpOrd Number 158, at 2030 on June 4, *I-168* was to shell Midway until 0200 when cruisers from the Occupation Force would relieve the submarine. This was a futile tasking for a submarine with a single 3.9-inch gun and no accurate range finder.[46]

Admiral Nobutake Kondo detached the four heavy cruisers *Kumano*, *Suzuya*, *Mikuma*, and *Mogami* from his Occupation Force, along with escort destroyers *Asashio* and *Arashio*, to carry out Yamamoto's orders for a night bombardment. All four cruisers were armed with ten 8-inch guns, however, Vice Admiral Takeo Kurita's position was 400 miles west of Midway when he received his orders, which virtually insured he could not arrive at Midway before sunrise.[47] At 2120 on June 4, Yamamoto canceled the scheduled shelling of Midway and ordered all units to proceed to the Main Unit's scheduled position.[48] By the time Kurita, in command of the 7th Cruiser Division, received his orders, he was within 90 miles of Midway where, at 0215, the American submarine USS *Tambor* spotted the Japanese heavy cruisers.[49]

The only shells fired at Midway that night were six to eight rounds from *I-168*, all of which landed harmlessly in the lagoon.[50] As soon as *I-168* fired its first round, the alerted shore batteries came to life with searchlights and return fire.[51] Counter fire quickly convinced Lieutenant Commander Tanabe Yahachi that such an operation did not fall within the proper roles and missions of his submarine and, after only three minutes of shelling, *I-168* submerged and resumed routine patrolling.[52] The brief exchange of shots between Midway and *I-168* resulted in no damage to either side. Yamamoto made the decision to abandon Operation "MI" by midnight on June 4 but hoped that submarines could still deliver a decisive blow against American carrier forces around Midway. Because of heavy losses to Japanese carriers, Yamamoto suspended the invasion of Midway and ordered all forces, except submarines, to withdraw westward.

At 0652 on June 5, a seaplane from *Chikuma* found the abandoned USS *Yorktown* approximately 150 miles northeast of Midway; Yamamoto ordered *I-168* to find and sink the American carrier.[53] During the afternoon of June 5, fearful that American carriers were pursuing him, Yamamoto ordered all submarines around Midway to shift their deployment west of Midway.[54] Komatsu ordered all Cordon C submarines westward, instructing them to form Cordons R, S, and T.[55] (Figure 6.2)

Figure 6.5: USS *Yorktown* (CV-5) being abandoned by its crew after being hit by two Japanese Type 91 aerial torpedoes, June 4, 1942. USS *Balch* (DD-363) is standing by at right. Note oil slick surrounding the damaged carrier, and inflatable life raft being deployed off the stern. (Official U.S. Navy Photograph, National Archives)

On June 6, *I-168* spotted *Yorktown* and its screen at a range of 11 miles. The submarine negotiated the American destroyer screen 2,000 yards from the carrier, approaching *Yorktown* off its starboard quarter, and carefully moved to reach an ideal firing position. At 1336, Tanabe fired four torpedoes at the carrier. One ran under the ship and narrowly missed the destroyer USS *Benham*. Another ran shallow and sliced through USS *Hammann*, breaking its back, and causing the ship to sink in three minutes. *Yorktown* took two hits opposite the June 4 hits made by *Hiryu*'s torpedo bombers, destroying what remained of the carrier's mid-length compartmentalization.[56] At 0501 on June 7, *Yorktown* slid beneath the surface of the Pacific.[57] Depth-charge attacks by American

Figure 6.6: USS *Hammann* (DD-412) sinking with stern high, after being torpedoed by *I-168* in the afternoon of June 6, 1942. Photographed from the starboard forecastle deck of USS *Yorktown* by Photographer 2nd Class William G. Roy. Angular structure in right foreground is the front of *Yorktown*'s forward starboard 5-inch gun gallery. Note knotted lines hanging down from the carrier's flight deck, remaining from the initial abandonment on June 4. (Official U.S. Navy Photograph, National Archives)

Figure 6.7: Diorama by Norman Bel Geddes, depicting the torpedoing of USS *Hammann* and USS *Yorktown* by *I-168*, during the afternoon of June 6, 1942. (Official U.S. Navy Photograph, National Archives)

destroyers only succeeded in damaging *I-168*, which later limped back to Kure for repairs.[58]

SubRons 3 and 5, heading west to close the pursuing American carriers, took up station on June 8 on Cordons R and S, whereas Submarine Division 13 took up station between June 10 and June 11 on Cordon T.[59] (Figure 6.2) All the submarines, except *I-168*, had now moved westward where the U.S. fleet might be located. However, they did not encounter a single American ship upon arrival at Cordons R, S, and T.[60]

The submarines patrolled their respective cordons until June 12 when the Combined Fleet Headquarters received new information that American carriers were still east of Midway. Komatsu ordered SubRons 3 and 5 east to form Cordons U and V and search for the carriers. (Figure 6.2) Komatsu discontinued the search on June 15 as it was too late to entrap USS *Hornet* and USS *Enterprise* as they had escaped to the safety of Pearl Harbor.[61]

It seems Japanese high command was a victim of its own indecision. Another high-speed dash to intercept the elusive American forces would have been impossible for most of the submarines because of insufficient fuel supply after earlier maneuvers. Thus, submarines assigned to the original picket lines, except for two sighting reports, accomplished nothing of consequence during the Midway Operation. Of note, *I-169* sighted American forces northeast of Midway on the night of June 7 but could not launch an attack and eventually lost contact. Just after sunset on June 6, the commanding officer of *I-121* sighted a surfaced American submarine, more than likely USS *Dolphin* on the 12-mile circle, southwest of Lisianski Island, heading northeast. *I-121* could not attack the American submarine due to its payload of aviation gasoline; no torpedoes were on board.[62]

All forces that participated in the Midway campaign, except the submarine force, returned to their respective home bases around June 15. The submarines began withdrawing on June 15 when Komatsu ordered them to leave the battle area. SubRon 3 and SubRon 5 returned to Kwajalein about June 20 and Submarine Division 13 returned to Yokosuka and Sasebo in the latter part of June.[63]

CHAPTER 7

United States Submarine Actions at Midway

Fleet opposed invasion—Midway![1]

Admiral Yamamoto did not know how well-informed Admiral Nimitz was. Through the efforts of Commander Joseph J. Rochefort and his code breakers, Nimitz knew the broad outline of Yamamoto's plan.[2] On May 21, Rochefort was able to give an accurate outline of the Japanese plan, identifying two elements, one to attack the westernmost Aleutian Islands and one to strike at Midway. The Aleutian plan was a diversionary operation; Midway was the main objective.[3]

On May 25, American code breakers broke the Japanese Navy's date cipher that contained much of the battle order of the Japanese fleet and the date and positions from where they would launch their attacks.[4] By May 27, Rochefort and the intelligence staff had almost all of the Japanese Order of Battle—dates, times, places, ships, rendezvous, plans,

Figure 7.1: Lieutenant Joseph J. Rochefort, September 1934. (Naval History and Heritage Command)

and intentions.⁵ American intelligence pieced together a remarkably complete estimate indicating the Midway expedition was composed of a striking force centered around four front-line carriers, a support force, and an occupation force.⁶

By applying the decrypts to old intercepts, Rochefort established the Japanese would attack the Aleutians on June 3, would launch a strike at Midway at 0700 on June 4, and he discovered the planned invasion. Rochefort showed Fleet Intelligence Officer Edwin T. Layton a partially decrypted message containing the words *koryaku butai*, meaning "invasion force." The geographic designator "AF" in a signal referring to the "forthcoming campaign" followed the message containing "invasion force." Rochefort told Layton that the Japanese used *koryaku butai* during the invasions of Rabaul, Java, Sumatra, and Bali. Rochefort knew the Japanese intended to invade "AF" which he convincingly proved was Midway.⁷

Rear Admiral Robert H. English commanded the U.S. Navy's submarine force in the Pacific Theater of Operations early in World War II. From his headquarters at Pearl Harbor, English was responsible for submarine deployment. With Rochefort's intelligence, English began planning how to deploy his submarines for the coming Japanese attack. In May 1942, there were at least 48 submarines in the Pacific Theater. Eight were at Fremantle in Western Australia, another 11 were on patrols beginning at Fremantle and ending at Pearl Harbor. At sea, there were four submarines from Pearl Harbor on patrols, scheduled to end at Fremantle. The remaining 25 submarines were immediately available to Admiral English.⁸ However, six of these accompanied the Aleutians Force, leaving 19 to cover the approaches to Midway. Three remained out of the Midway battle. USS *Thresher* and USS *Argonaut* were undergoing overhaul and English ordered USS *Silversides* to continue patrolling the Kii Suido entrance to Japan's Inland Sea. A fourth submarine, USS *Triton*, which made a fruitless pursuit of the damaged Japanese carrier *Shōkaku* after the Battle of Coral Sea, sank submarine *I-164*, part of SubRon 5. *Triton* was returning from the South China Sea too low on fuel and torpedoes to divert to the Midway area.⁹

Admiral English immediately recalled six submarines on distant patrols. The submarines, if they had sufficient fuel and torpedoes, were to return to Pearl Harbor via Midway and search for and attack Japanese ships withdrawing after the battle.[10] Submarines USS *Drum*, USS *Pollack*, USS *Tuna*, and USS *Pompano* headed east from Japanese waters. USS *Greenling* was coming from a patrol in the Carolines and Marshalls, and USS *Porpoise*, due a stateside overhaul, was heading for Pearl from Fremantle.[11]

The number of separate invasion, carrier-strike, and covering forces in the complex Japanese plan complicated the problem of deploying the submarines even though English had ample time to draw in distant units for the defense of Midway.[12] He formed the available 19 submarines into a single organization, Task Force 7, and divided them into three groups to support the forces at sea and at Midway.

American Order of Battle—Submarines, Midway Campaign under Rear Admiral Robert H. English, Commander Submarine Force, Pacific Fleet, at Pearl Harbor			
Task Group 7.1 Midway Patrol	Task Group 7.2 Roving Short Stops	Task Group 7.3 North of Oahu	On Patrol
7.1.1 *Cachalot*	7.2.1 *Narwhal*	7.3.1 *Tarpon*	*Drum*
7.1.2 *Flying Fish*	7.2.2 *Plunger*	7.3.2 *Pike*	*Greenling*
7.1.3 *Tambor*	7.2.3 *Trigger*	7.3.3 *Finback*	*Pollack*
7.1.4 *Trout*		7.3.4 *Growler*	*Pompano*
7.1.5 *Grayling*			*Porpoise*
7.1.6 *Nautilus*			*Tuna*
7.1.7 *Grouper*			
7.1.8 *Dolphin*			
7.1.9 *Gato*			
7.1.10 *Cuttlefish*			
7.1.11 *Gudgeon*			
7.1.12 *Grenadier*			

Among the 19 submarines available for the Midway engagement, six had never made a war patrol (USS *Flying Fish*, USS *Gato*, USS *Grouper*, USS *Nautilus*, USS *Trigger*, and USS *Finback*) and four of these (*Flying Fish*, *Grouper*, *Trigger*, and *Finback*) were newcomers from the West Coast and had no time for combat training at Pearl Harbor. Eight of the 19 (USS *Cachalot*, USS *Grayling*, USS *Gudgeon*, USS *Tambor*, USS *Trout*, USS *Plunger*, USS *Pike*, and USS *Tarpon*) were just in from patrol and needed repair.[13]

English next worked on positioning each submarine task group along likely Japanese approach routes to Midway. Four submarines (USS *Cuttlefish*, USS *Dolphin*, USS *Grenadier*, and USS *Gato*) had either just departed on routine patrol or were at the point of departure when English ordered them to Midway. English assigned these four patrol areas farthest from Midway because, being ready for a routine patrol, they were fully fueled and carried a full complement of torpedoes.[14] English then ordered *Cuttlefish* to a position farther west where intelligence believed certain enemy ships would rendezvous before the battle.

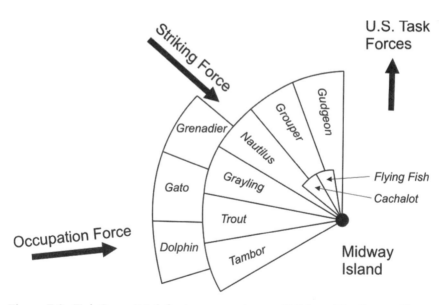

Figure 7.2: Task Group 7.1 defensive arcs northwest of Midway. The diagram illustrates how USS *Nautilus* was the only American submarine in position to intercept the Japanese Striking Force.

Admiral English deployed the majority of Task Group (TG) 7.1 in arcs west of Midway. Submarine placement was as follows: *Dolphin*, *Gato*, and *Grenadier* were 200 miles from Midway between bearings 240° and 310°. *Tambor*, *Trout*, *Grayling*, *Nautilus*, *Grouper*, and *Gudgeon* were 150 miles from Midway between bearings 240° to 360°. *Flying Fish* and *Cachalot* were on station patrol 50 miles from Midway between bearings 310° and 350°. *Cuttlefish* was on station patrol 700 miles due west of Midway.[15] (see Figure 6.3) Except for *Flying Fish* and *Cachalot*, all submarines patrolled 20° sectors and were to operate within a circle of 20 miles of the midpoint of their sector chords. Initially, submarines of the three task groups were to operate on the surface, but English apparently modified this order on May 30, ordering them to patrol at periscope depth during daylight hours and to remain ready to surface and pursue the enemy when they received a contact report.[16]

English stationed TG 7.2, comprised of *Narwhal*, *Plunger*, and *Trigger*, 420 miles east of Midway and 200 miles north of French Frigate Shoals. TG 7.2, northwest of Japan's Cordon B, was to provide support for TG 7.1 or, if needed, support retreating American carriers of Task Force 16 and 17. (See Figure 6.3) He stationed submarines of TG 7.2 at 30-mile intervals on a northeast–southwest line bearing 045°–225°. If the American carriers were forced to pull back, the plan was to allow them to withdraw over this patrol line if needed. However, *Plunger* was unable to move to its allotted station in time for the battle; it was able to leave Pearl Harbor on its second war patrol on June 9, when it set out for Shanghai. *Plunger*'s patrol report (Appendix 2) verifies the June 9 departure date but makes no mention of Midway activities.[17]

English stationed TG 7.3—*Tarpon*, *Pike*, *Finback*, and *Growler*—on an approximate east–west line about three hundred miles north of Pearl Harbor with orders to conduct station patrols, guarding against the possibility of a Japanese diversionary raid against Pearl Harbor. (See Figure 6.3) The distance between submarines is unknown but was probably in the same range of those in TG 7.2. This task group was down a submarine as *Growler* missed the battle, unable to leave Pearl Harbor until June 20, when it set out for Alaskan waters via Midway. *Growler*'s patrol report (Appendix 3) makes no mention of Midway activities.[18] The positioning of Task Force 7 took place between May 21 and May 24; all submarines of the Midway defense force were on their assigned stations and patrolling their assigned sectors by the morning of June 3.[19]

On May 27, the Japanese Striking Force left its anchorage in the Inland Sea and headed for Midway. Components of the Midway Occupation Force sortied from Saipan and Guam a day later, taking circuitous routes to deceive any spying American submarines.[20] After May 29, once both the Striking Force and Occupation Force had set sail towards Midway, the Japanese reported at least 16 enemy submarines, including six near Japan, four northeast of Wake Island, and four around Truk. Japanese intelligence overestimated the number of American submarines, as there were only four left in Japanese waters: *Pollack*, *Silversides* (guarding Kii Suido), *Drum* (off Tokyo Bay), and *Triton*.[21]

Japanese intelligence likely received multiple contact reports on the same four submarines. For example, on May 29, Japanese intelligence reported six American submarines in Japanese waters just outside the Bungo Straits. This, however, was *Pollack*, the only American submarine then in the vicinity of Bungo Suido. As previously mentioned, on May 16, *Triton*, under the command of Lieutenant Commander Charles C. Kirkpatrick, spotted the Japanese carrier *Shōkaku* with two escort destroyers south of Shikoku returning from the battle of the Coral Sea; *Triton* was unable to intercept the fast-moving ships. On May 17, it sighted the Japanese submarine *I-164* cruising eastward on the surface south of Kyushu. Kirkpatrick fired his last bow torpedo at the rising sun flag painted on the Japanese submarine's conning tower, sinking *I-164*. This attack was the opening shot of the Midway engagement as *I-164* was part of SubRon 5.[22]

By June 2, evidence the enemy had discovered or strongly suspected a Japanese advance toward Midway mounted sharply. First, from May 30 through June 2, the Japanese sighted four American submarines about five hundred miles northeast of Wake Island, indicating the possible existence of an American submarine patrol line some 600 miles southwest of Midway. The sighting of "four" enemy submarines northeast of Wake Island, was actually just one—*Cuttlefish*.[23] Second, Japanese radio intelligence noted a marked increase of communications traffic out of Hawaii; 72 out of 180 intercepted messages were "urgent," indicating an

Figure 7.3: USS *Cuttlefish* (SS-171) at the Philadelphia, Pennsylvania, Navy Yard on November 15, 1943. (National Archives)

unusually tense situation.[24] At this point, the Japanese somehow estimated a dozen or more enemy submarines were keeping track of the Japanese fleet's progress. More than likely this was again multiple contact reports on *Cuttlefish*.[25]

On June 4 at 0214, Pearl Harbor received a transmission from *Cuttlefish* reporting contact with, and an attempted attack on, a Japanese tanker traveling on course 060°, about five hundred miles northeast of Wake Island and 600 west of Midway. Approaching daylight and enemy warships forced the submarine to submerge, however, *Cuttlefish* had located the Japanese Occupation Force. It changed course to stay between the tanker and the main body, but subsequently lost contact with the former. At 0925, English gave all submarines the position, course, and speed of the Occupation Force.[26]

Cuttlefish was west of the International Date Line, therefore the June 5 contact report from the submarine (as written in the patrol report) was June 4 for Midway and Pearl Harbor. *Cuttlefish*, moving eastwards, would cross the date line on June 6. A little more than an hour before this sighting, at 2100 on June 4, Admiral English ordered *Cuttlefish* to close Midway and search for a burning battleship. This ship had been reportedly set on fire at 1639 by B17 bombers attacking the Occupation Force. *Cuttlefish* proceeded toward Midway as directed until spotting the tanker. *Cuttlefish* never located a burning battleship, but this contact report from Midway would mark the beginning of several instances where English sent TG 7.1 submarines on searches for non-existent ships based on reports from Midway patrol planes.[27]

The Japanese Occupation Force detected the urgent transmission and correctly guessed an enemy submarine was tracking its progress.[28] Matome Ugaki, Chief of Staff of the Combined Fleet, was nervous about American submarines. He would later write, "According to radio interception, an enemy sub supposed to be either ahead or in the vicinity of our Transport Force dispatched a long, urgent message to Midway. If the dispatch message was a report of discovering our force, it would surely serve to alert the enemy, thus contributing to making our game in battle heavier."[29] The Japanese were unable to decipher the coded message and Admiral Yamamoto apparently never considered the Americans might deduce the purpose of the transport convoy as an invasion of Midway.[30] The Combined Fleet, full of confidence, followed a zigzag course and proceeded along its plotted route with Yamamoto failing to realize the mere presence of submarines meant the enemy had some foreknowledge of the movement toward Midway.[31]

Early on the morning of June 4, as *Cuttlefish* was in contact with the Japanese Occupation Force, the Strike Force carriers were approaching Midway from the northwest. As the carriers closed to within 200 miles, a search plane from the Japanese cruiser *Tone* reported two surfaced submarines. It had spotted *Grouper* and *Nautilus* patrolling submerged in their assigned patrol zones. When looking at the locations of submarine placement west of Midway, *Grouper* and *Nautilus* were the only two defending submarines near the position reported by the Japanese search plane. (Figure 7.2) Both reported sighting planes on the horizon and then being strafed and/or bombed while submerged at periscope depth.[32] The presence of these submarines does not appear to have alarmed Admiral Nagumo, Commander Mobile Force, feeling his antisubmarine defenses, including a destroyer screen, an antisubmarine air patrol, and his speed and maneuverability were adequate protection. His plot of their position, which placed them about fifteen miles from his planned track, seemed to indicate his force would pass clear of the American submarines. He therefore maintained his current course.[33]

The carrier air battle developed on the morning of June 4, northwest of the main arc of submarines. At 0720, an American search plane sighted the Japanese Striking Force. When Admiral English learned of the Japanese carrier's location, he ordered all submarines in the Midway defensive screen to attack the Japanese carriers. Only *Cuttlefish*, *Cachalot*, and *Flying Fish* were to maintain their stations while the others headed for the carriers at best speed. The *Grouper* did sight enemy planes and ships but was unable to attack enemy shipping because aircraft and depth-charge attacks kept the submarine submerged below periscope depth.[34]

Figure 7.4: USS *Nautilus* (SS-168) at Mare Island, California, on April 15, 1942. (National Archives)

Only Lieutenant Commander William H. Brockman, Jr., in command of *Nautilus*, managed an attack on the enemy fleet. Brockman intercepted a contact report of Japanese carriers and proceeded towards their reported location. Between attacks by Midway-based aircraft, Brockman raised the submarine's periscope in the middle of the Mobile Force and fired two torpedoes at 0825, setting off a grand confusion of circling destroyers and exploding depth charges.[35] Although unsuccessful, this attack had a crucial effect on the battle. Shortly after Brockman fired his torpedoes, the Japanese changed course northward, preparing their own assault on the American carriers, and left the destroyer *Arashi* behind to keep *Nautilus* pinned down.[36]

Figure 7.5: Lieutenant Commander William H. Brockman, Jr., after being presented with the Navy Cross for his performance while in command of USS *Nautilus* during the Battle of Midway in June 1942. Photographed during the awards ceremony at the Pearl Harbor submarine base, November 7, 1942. (Official U.S. Navy Photograph, National Archives)

Arashi continued to depth charge *Nautilus* for about thirty minutes and then returned to its proper defensive role with the Carrier Striking Force. Two dive-bomber squadrons from USS *Enterprise*, led by Lieutenant Commander Wade McClusky, spotted *Arashi* charging at high speed back to the Japanese carriers. McClusky altered his course to follow *Arashi* and, within a few minutes, he spotted the Japanese carriers.[37]

At 1029, Brockman in *Nautilus* sighted four columns of grey smoke on the horizon which, based on an intercepted radio message, was coming from damaged Japanese carriers.[38] Brockman took his time to reach a good firing position undetected and, between 1359 and 1405, he fired three torpedoes from a distance of 2,700 yards at a target he identified as a stricken Japanese Sōryū-class carrier.[39] Witnesses on *Kaga* sighted a

Figure 7.6: a) Japanese aircraft carrier *Soryu* running trials in January 1938; and b) *Kaga* at sea following its 1934–36 modernization. Brockman indicated he attacked a Soryu-class carrier, which was later identified as *Kaga*. (National Archives)

periscope a few thousand yards from the ship, and minutes later spotted the wakes of three torpedoes approaching the carrier. Two torpedoes narrowly missed *Kaga*; the third hit but failed to explode, glancing off the side and breaking into two parts. The warhead sank, but the air cylinder continued to float, spinning slowly. Several of *Kaga*'s crew, who were in the water, grabbed the floating section and used it as a support while awaiting rescue.[40]

Discrepancy exists concerning the torpedoes *Nautilus* fired and the ship attacked. Captain Takahisa Amagai, *Kaga*'s air officer, who was in the water when *Nautilus* fired its torpedoes, said he saw one broach, hit the hull, fail to explode, and ricochet away. The other two found their mark.[41] Captain Keizo Komura of the cruiser *Chikuma* said he witnessed all three torpedoes hit and explode.[42] The version that matches the patrol report states *Nautilus* closed the *Kaga* and fired three torpedoes; two missed and the third was a dud.[43] This also matches the accounts of the Japanese sailors in the water that witnessed the event.[44] Admiral English, at the time, credited Brockman with sinking *Sōryū*, but postwar analysis identified the ship as *Kaga* and that Brockman's torpedoes caused no additional damage to the Japanese carrier.[45] The patrol report indicates Brockman identified it as a Sōryū-class carrier, not the *Sōryū* itself.[46] The Navy awarded Brockman the Navy Cross for actions during the Battle of Midway (see Appendix 7).

At 1525, and despite four Japanese carriers burning, English believed a landing attempt on Midway was still possible. After much discussion, and with the approval of Admiral Nimitz, at 2315 English ordered all submarines of TG 7.1 to redeploy in a tightened protective arc 100 miles west of Midway. English assigned each submarine, except *Cuttlefish*, a 10-degree sector spanning the arc 230° to 350° from Midway. All were to arrive on station and dive before dawn to guard against the possible advance of the Occupation Force. Submarines of TG 7.2 and TG 7.3 remained on station patrol and had not moved from their original locations during the battle.[47]

Unknown to English, Yamamoto had ordered the bombardment mission of Midway. Yamamoto assigned the four heavy cruisers under command of Rear Admiral Takeo Kurita to a dawn bombardment as a prelude to the seizure of the island. However, around midnight on June 5, Yamamoto issued orders for a general withdrawal. Upon receiving the withdrawal order, Kurita's cruisers were only about ninety miles from Midway. They withdrew as ordered but, not long afterward, they sighted *Tambor*.[48] However, *Tambor* had already spotted them.

At 0215 on June 5, Lieutenant Commander John W. Murphy Jr. in *Tambor* saw small, dark bumps on the horizon but could not identify the ships. Just after 0300, he radioed a brief contact report to Midway, reporting "many unidentified ships," but did not provide their type,

Figure 7.7: USS *Tambor* (SS-198) at Mare Island, California, on December 6, 1943. (National Archives)

number, course, or speed.[49] *Tambor*'s unidentified ships were the four Japanese cruisers and two destroyers scheduled to relieve *I-168* from its bombardment duties. In the confusion, and maneuvering to avoid *Tambor*, cruisers *Mogami* and *Mikuma* collided, damaging *Mogami*'s bow and rupturing one of *Mikuma*'s fuel tanks, spilling fuel into the ocean.[50] Without firing a shot, *Tambor* had indirectly caused significant damage to two heavy cruisers. The influence of the submarine's encounter also affected crucial decisions made by Admirals Spruance and English.

At 0400 on June 5, English received *Tambor*'s report of "many unidentified ships." English now consulted with Nimitz and, for over three hours, both commanders believed a Japanese occupation force was approaching Midway. Therefore, at 0845, English released a dispatch that directed all submarines of TG 7.1 to take station on a five-mile radius circle from Midway, but to remain in their previously assigned sectors.[51]

Figure 7.8: Japanese heavy cruiser *Mikuma*, photographed from a USS *Enterprise* (CV-6) SBD Dauntless during the afternoon of June 6, 1942, after it had been bombed by planes from *Enterprise* and USS *Hornet* (CV-8). Note the shattered midships structure, torpedo dangling from the aft port-side tubes, and wreckage atop the number four 8-inch gun turret. (Official U.S. Navy Photograph, National Archives)

With the two Japanese cruisers out of range, *Tambor* surfaced and sent a full and accurate contact report giving the enemy's course. Both Pearl Harbor (at 0608) and Midway (at 0617) received *Tambor*'s report which stated the two Mogami-type cruisers were damaged and proceeding west at 17 knots from a position of 272° (T), 115 miles from Midway. A PBY patrol aircraft confirmed this sighting but identified the ships as two battleships. Commander, Naval Air Station (CNAS) Midway, acting on the second contact, directed a strike at the retiring cruisers. It was unfortunate that Murphy waited until after 0600 to make this report because for three hours no one knew whether the enemy force was advancing from the west or withdrawing from the previous day's battle area.[52]

Even Murphy's more specific report of two damaged cruisers limping away from Midway could be consistent with an invasion. Given these circumstances, Admiral Raymond Spruance, in command of Task Force 16 and its two carriers USS *Enterprise* and USS *Hornet*, acted cautiously. Mindful of Nimitz's instructions to apply "the principle of calculated risk," he did not pursue the damaged cruisers, but gave priority to his basic mission: the protection of Midway. Spruance placed his carriers 100 miles northeast of Midway to strike a Japanese occupation force, which also kept *Enterprise* and *Hornet* out of harm's way. This action was more important than even Spruance knew. He was unaware that to the west lay the super-battleship *Yamato*. Had he continued to the west during the night of June 6/7, he would probably have run into the superior Japanese forces the next morning. Murphy's initial vague report helped keep Spruance from blundering into range of *Yamato*'s big guns. Had the battleship sunk the lightly armored *Enterprise* and *Hornet*, Yamamoto would have salvaged a draw from defeat.[53]

At Pearl Harbor, there was considerable apprehension the Japanese would still go ahead with their invasion plans. English needed to reposition TG 7.1 and TG 7.2 to better defend against the anticipated invasion fleet. English ordered submarines of TG 7.1 to move to the 12-mile circle and return to their original defense sectors west of Midway.[54] TG 7.2 was to proceed west at best speed to designated points on the 100-mile circle north of Midway, search for survivors, and then leave the search area in time to arrive on the 12-mile circle from Midway by the following dawn.[55] TG 7.3 was to take station on the 250-mile circle northwest of Oahu, because the locations and intentions of the enemy were not yet clear, and the possibility existed of a raiding force proceeding towards Oahu.[56] Additionally, English ordered *Cuttlefish* to search for stragglers at its 1809 position, which was about three hundred fifty miles from Midway. This order was received 11 hours after English sent it. By that time, *Cuttlefish* was too far east to be of any use in the chase for stragglers.[57]

Because of *I-168*'s brief bombardment, CNAS Midway reevaluated the situation and concluded *I-168* was following the original plan to create a diversion for a landing party. However, in view of Japan's losses, he believed that, when no further attacks developed, the Japanese were retreating, and *I-168*'s commander did not receive the order. English apparently did not arrive at this same conclusion for another 24 hours as he retained his submarines on the 12-mile circle from Midway until dawn on June 6.[58]

Tambor's sighting of Cruiser Division Seven was the last submarine contact with Japanese surface ships during the battle. When it was apparent the Japanese fleet was withdrawing, English sent submarines in pursuit, but, by June 5, all Japanese ships were outside the reach of Midway submarines. Reports of damaged Japanese ships came in and the remainder of June 5 involved TG 7.1 submarines chasing down more sighting reports (many several hours old) by Midway search planes, none of which were successful. For example, at 1224, English ordered *Tambor*, *Trout*, and *Grayling* to sink a damaged enemy battleship in position bearing 264°, 125 miles from Midway. At 1809, English ordered *Grouper*, *Flying Fish*, and *Gudgeon* to search for two battleships, three heavy cruisers, about ten destroyers, and two burning carriers reported in a position bearing 310°, 200 miles from Midway. These were either mythical or inaccurate.[59] English continued to send information and positions of Japanese ships to submarines approaching Midway from their patrol areas. Such contact reports on fast-moving surface ships were useless to distant, slow-moving submarines, since it was impossible to make accurate estimates of the enemy's course or destination. Despite considerable scurrying about, there were no further submarine contacts with the Japanese fleet.[60]

At midnight on June 6, *Narwhal*, *Trigger*, *Dolphin*, *Gato*, *Grenadier*, *Gudgeon*, *Nautilus*, and *Cachalot* were on the 12-mile circle from Midway. *Grouper* was on station on the 5-mile circle from Midway, and *Tarpon*, *Pike*, and *Finback* were on station northwest of Oahu. *Tambor*, *Trout*, and *Grayling* were searching for the damaged battleship last reported in position bearing 264°, and *Flying Fish* was searching for the Mobile Force last reported as 200 miles from Midway.

At 0855, English directed TG 7.3 to return to Pearl Harbor and dispatched orders at 0905 for *Gato*, *Grenadier*, and *Narwhal* to do the same. At 1255, he told *Cuttlefish* that if it did not make contact prior to dark, the submarine was to return to Pearl Harbor. Likewise, at 1320, he gave similar instructions to *Flying Fish*, *Grouper*, and *Gudgeon*.[61]

At 2015, English directed *Dolphin, Nautilus, Cachalot,* and *Trigger* to form on a 25-mile circle from Midway between bearings 200° and 350° as a precaution against a "small landing attempt by a small unlocated unit."[62] At 2300, English directed *Cuttlefish* to intercept an apparently damaged and abandoned battleship that was most likely *Mikuma,* which had probably sunk by time of the message. At 2325, English received a report from *Grayling* of being bombed by three B-17s who mistook the surfaced submarine for a Japanese cruiser. *Grayling* quickly submerged and escaped unscathed.[63]

At midnight on June 7, *Dolphin, Nautilus, Cachalot,* and *Trigger* were on the 25-mile circle from Midway while *Narwhal, Gato,* and *Grenadier* were proceeding to Pearl Harbor. *Gato* and *Grenadier* arrived on June 10; *Narwhal* on June 12. TG 7.3 was northwest of Oahu heading towards Pearl Harbor. *Tambor, Trout,* and *Grayling* were searching for two enemy heavy cruisers and two destroyers as *Flying Fish, Grouper,* and *Gudgeon* were still pursuing the Mobile Force to the 500-mile circle from Midway. English directed *Tuna,* returning from operations in Japanese waters, to assist *Cuttlefish* in locating reportedly abandoned battleships.[64]

At 1250, English ordered *Cachalot, Nautilus, Dolphin,* and *Plunger* to return to Midway, the four arriving there the same day. At 1325, he directed *Trigger* to return to Pearl Harbor; the boat arrived on June 12. At 2100, English directed *Flying Fish* and *Grouper* to return to Midway—they arrived on June 9—and ordered *Gudgeon* back to Pearl Harbor, arriving on June 14. All submarines were now heading to Pearl Harbor or Midway except *Tambor, Trout, Grayling,* and *Cuttlefish.*[65] At 2145, English directed *Trout* and *Tuna* to pass through a large area covered with wreckage and to obtain any material of value for identification of ships. The reported wreckage location was at Lat. 28°-52' N., Long. 173°-18 E. Two hours and 15 minutes later, English received a report from *Tuna* of a large amount of oil in this area. This oil and wreckage appear to have been all that remained of the sunken Japanese cruiser *Mikuma.*[66]

During the afternoon of June 9, *Trout* rescued two survivors of *Mikuma*'s crew: Chief Radioman Katsuichi Yoshida and Third Class Fireman Kenichi Ishikawa.[67] At 2342, Admiral English directed *Tambor, Trout,* and *Grayling* to return to Pearl Harbor; they arrived on the 16th.

This ended American submarine activities during the Battle of Midway. By June 10, there was nothing for English to do but proceed with the redeployment of his submarines to carry on with their war of attrition against Japanese shipping.[68]

CHAPTER 8

Analysis: Undersea Warfare at Midway

> The dispositions of a thoughtful commander ensue from correct decisions derived from correct judgements [sic], which depend on a comprehensive and indispensable reconnaissance. A careless commander bases his military plan upon his own wishful thinking.[1]

Japanese and American naval leaders gave their respective submarines prominent roles at the Battle of Midway. However, the overall perception to submarine operations before, during and after the battle was that both sides failed to use them effectively.[2]

As stated in Chapter 2, in the first decade of the 20th century, Japanese naval strategists mapped out the basic contours of Japanese naval strategy. A blend of Mahan's doctrines and traditional Chinese and Japanese military concepts, their thinking emphasized the subjugation of the enemy through maneuver, strategy, and attrition, rather than by strict quantitative superiority.[3] Almost everything that occurs within a naval battle is tactical, from ship-to-ship fighting to the movement of ships in the presence of the enemy, in order to gain battle advantage.[4] For the Japanese, surprise was essential, and they sought to fold into their operational plans the best and most significant elements of the "Sun Tzu" style of war fighting: surprise, secrecy, and deception.[5]

Battle Preliminaries

Like Pearl Harbor, Midway was an operation mounted on Admiral Yamamoto's insistence. He imposed it upon a reluctant and skeptical Naval

General Staff, and he decided its timing. The General Staff favored an offensive in the southwest Pacific, with the strategic objective of isolating Australia from the United States. Yamamoto, in contrast, was resolved upon returning to the Central Pacific.[6] One factor in persuading the General Staff to Yamamoto's view was the Doolittle Raid in April 1942. With the Doolittle Raid, America pierced the Empire's innermost defenses. Japan had to respond. The raid on Tokyo ended the General Staff's opposition to Yamamoto's Midway plan.[7]

For attacks to be successful they do not necessarily have to attack a physical weakness; they can be psychologically based, directed at the mind and morale of the enemy. Sun Tzu wrote:

> Therefore, determine the enemy's plans and you will know which strategy will be successful and which will not; *agitate him* and ascertain the pattern of his movement. Determine his dispositions and so ascertain the field of battle. Probe him and learn where his strength is abundant and where deficient.[8] [Emphasis added]

The lesson to learn is that even though an attack may not inflict major physical damage, the attack can manipulate the enemy's emotions. If aroused enough, these emotions will overcome logic and negatively affect strategy. The Doolittle Raid produced such an effect in Yamamoto. The result was that he changed his strategy from invading Hawaii and Australia to destroying American naval power in a decisive battle at Midway.[9]

Yamamoto conceived an idea that would attempt to tilt the odds heavily in Japan's favor. He said, "Our best course of action is to deliver a knockout blow to the U.S. Fleet at the very start." Yamamoto was convinced that, to win the war, he must destroy the U.S. fleet in 1942. He believed an attack on Midway would force his enemies to undertake measures for its defense and thus enable him to crush them.[10]

Statements from various officers associated with the battle verify that their *perceived* intention of the battle was to capture Midway (see Appendix 5). One such quote stated, "The purpose of the operation is to capture Midway, to advance our positions in order to check enemy activities from that direction, and to destroy the enemy fleet which might launch an attack otherwise."[11] However, Yamamoto's real target was not Midway, it was the destruction of the American carrier strength.

His primary plan in occupying Midway was to force the Pacific Fleet's carriers to give battle and destroy them, thereby completing the task left unfulfilled in December 1941. He also intended to secure an advanced outpost that would, among other things, reduce the prospect of a repetition of the American air raid on the Home Islands in April. The Carrier Striking Force would bomb Midway and be prepared to attack the U.S. fleet, should it come out. With the enemy weakened, Battleship Division 1 of the main body would hurry to the battle area to finish off the enemy task force.[12]

For Japan, Midway proved to be a case of third time unlucky. With their reconnaissance (and, to a much lesser extent, their strike) arrangements, the Japanese made the mistake of trying to repeat once too often a formula that in the past had worked despite its weaknesses.[13] From the tactical standpoint, the Midway plan illustrated an adherence to the outmoded doctrine of the battleship advocates, which was difficult to reconcile with Yamamoto's supposed understanding of the role of air power. He expected to destroy the American carriers and his surface forces would engage and destroy what remained in the decisive battle he was seeking. However, based on Yamamoto's operating plan, it seems as if he was expecting to face only one or possibly two American carriers. Additionally, the man who conceived the carrier strike on Pearl Harbor seemed slow to institute sweeping changes in fleet organization and tactics to make air power the central core of the combat forces.[14]

Yamamoto was obviously unaware of American carrier strength due to the cancellation of the Second "K" Operation and the erroneous belief that Japanese forces sank USS *Yorktown* at the Battle of the Coral Sea. Coupled with the inadequate air search on the day of the battle, Yamamoto had no indication three enemy carriers were nearby and no idea there were more than he anticipated.[15]

When Yamamoto planned the Midway campaign in detail, the Japanese Navy's previous successes led him to neglect some basic rules of warfare.[16] Perhaps the most telling comment on the Japanese arrangements for Midway is that during a battle that saw the Combined Fleet deploy 24 submarines, 109 surface units, and 433 aircraft, the Japanese managed to attack exactly one American warship while losing four fleet carriers and a heavy cruiser.[17]

The most remarkable part of Japan's plan for Midway was the complexity involved to establish themselves in the Central Pacific and annihilate the Pacific Fleet.[18] The complex plan illustrates a fundamental defect in Japanese naval strategy in that whenever Japanese planners had sufficient strength, they divided forces and drafted an elaborate plan. Successful execution required a tactical competence rare at any time in any navy and needed the enemy's passive acceptance of their role. Additionally, two of Yamamoto's experienced fleet commanders, Vice Admirals Nobutake Kondō and Chūichi Nagumo, were absent during the Midway planning phase. As a result, staff members, who had no first-hand knowledge of the capabilities of these forces, drew up the plans.[19]

To pull off his Midway strategy, Yamamoto also needed luck. His intricate battle choreography required his opponents move according to predicted positions; one false step or foreknowledge of the plan could throw the entire operation into disarray. Yamamoto's plan was based on the supposition Nimitz and his forces would behave exactly as he planned they should. Nimitz, however, placed his naval forces to contest control of Midway and, in doing so, caught the Japanese carrier force providing support for the operations against Midway itself, instead of preparing to fight a carrier battle.[20]

Yamamoto expected the invasion to draw out the Americans, the submarine pickets would alert the Japanese Striking Force, which would defeat the American carriers "once and for all" as they steamed up into the trap. The Japanese assumption that Operation "MI" would catch the U.S. fleet by surprise led them to believe their amphibious forces would be able to transit to Midway before any American counter-response could take shape.[21] The trouble lay in the fact the entire Japanese invasion plan was based on the assumption tactical surprise would be achieved and the enemy fleet would not get under way until *after* the assault on Midway began.[22] The failure to weigh the enemy's capabilities was the basis for the tardiness of the planned submarine cordon and for the breakdown of the Second "K" Operation. Given a little less complacency, prompt and effective reconnaissance almost surely would have enabled the Japanese to pinpoint the American sorties, their strength, their course, and destination, and be prepared to attack.[23]

At the very time when Yamamoto could have brought about the decisive battle he longed for, he chose to disperse his ships, in what appears to be an attempt at deception, to pursue different objectives. For example, a major part of the air formation destined for Midway to provide a critically important shore-based air capability in the battle expected to develop when the Americans responded to the occupation, was embarked in the two carriers directed to the Aleutians. Clausewitz wrote, "The best strategy is always *to be very strong*; first in general, and then at the decisive point. There is no higher and simpler law of strategy than that of *keeping one's forces concentrated*. No force should ever be detached from the main body unless the need is definite and *urgent*." (Emphasis in original)[24]

Mahan would have applauded the objective of engaging the American carriers, but he would have admonished Yamamoto: "Never, never divide the fleet."[25] Japan's Navy, with Mahanian intellectual roots, prepared tardily and insufficiently for an onslaught not directly related to the decisive battle.[26] With the ships available, Yamamoto's fleet was more than strong enough to defeat the smaller American forces.[27]

Yamamoto's Operational Plan

The common theme throughout historical texts is that Japan's forward submarine screens failed to execute their primary function of interception, warning, and attrition. Most accounts of Japan's defeat at Midway frequently cite the weakness of I-boat deployment as a major factor. For example, Wheeler puts significant blame on SubRon 5, writing "Among the several factors that contributed to the Japanese disaster at Midway, the failure of SubRon 5 took high place." Bates leans more towards the delay getting on station. He says, "This delay in stationing submarines is considered to be a major flaw in the Japanese plan." Despite where blame is placed, none of the substantial number of Japanese submarines in the vicinity of Midway was able to locate the American carriers prior to the main fleet engagement.[28] The accusations against the submarine screens, in particular Cordon B, emanate from military analysts, Japanese submarine captains, and Yamamoto himself. However, was the late arrival of SubRon 5 a significant contributor to Japan's defeat at Midway, as most historians imply, or was the defeat a result of Yamamoto's flawed tactical and strategic plan?

The admiral approved plans that were flawed on several counts.[29] He endorsed a reconnaissance plan that assigned submarines of both cordons fixed positions, rather than patrol boxes in which they could freely operate. Scouting lines consisted mostly of gaps that lacked overlapping fields of vision.[30] Even if the submarines had conformed to Yamamoto's schedule, there is some question whether they could have succeeded in sighting the U.S. fleet due to their assignment to static, fixed positions.[31]

However, there appears to be some type of command disconnect or miscommunication between what Yamamoto wanted and what happened. In an interview, Captain Yasuji Watanabe recalled Yamamoto consoling Admiral Kameto Kuroshima, who was taking the defeat heavily. Watanabe indicated Yamamoto said, "It was a big mistake that the submarine sweep was not well done."[32] To what "sweep" is Yamamoto referring?

His plan called for static lines of deployment, not sweeping action. Did deployment plans change without Admiral Komatsu's knowledge? Was it a breakdown in communication? It seems initial expectations were for submarines to sweep along the line northeast of Midway southeast towards Hawaii.[33] Japan used the successful tactic during the attack on Pearl Harbor where 10 submarines cruised line abreast 300 miles ahead of Nagumo's strike force with three more just 50 miles ahead of Nagumo. If Yamamoto repeated this simple tactic during the approach to Midway, with the line of submarines swinging to the east on Nagumo's flank, surely some would have sighted the American carriers.[34] Apparently, Komatsu made no effort to employ the submarines as scouts on the approach to their stations. According to Parshall and Tully, Komatsu, who admired Yamamoto, had such confidence in the Midway operation that in his opinion the battle was as good as won. His confidence was so great that he focused on post-battle follow-up plans to attack the Panama Canal and western North America and therefore paid little attention to the details of submarine deployment against Midway.[35]

The initial failure to provide a reconnaissance force for the carriers was rather strange as submarines always led the fleet to sea and covered its withdrawal. Writing up the submarine portion of such orders was a responsibility of Commander Arima Takayasu, Yamamoto's submarine officer. However, for some reason, Admiral Kuroshima told Takayasu they had no need to do so. This rather incredible oversight meant the Japanese submarines were committed to action without a workable operational plan. Submarine participation appeared as an afterthought to the Midway operation and the cordon details never appeared in the official orders.[36]

Orders rectifying this situation were issued during the second week of May when war games played at the beginning of the month showed the carriers needed an advance guard. This left several Japanese submarines involved in the operation with about two weeks to complete arrangements, put to sea, and take up station in front of the carrier force. Additionally, the task assigned to the submarine force was basically reconnaissance and destruction. However, there does not appear to have been sufficient submarines assigned to effectively carry out their mission in this operation, as operational plans for submarine deployment required 15 in the Midway area on both combat and logistic missions, four in the Aleutians area, and two off Seattle.[37]

The Japanese, expecting to have the element of surprise during their Midway attack, based their submarine deployment plan on the expectation the enemy would behave predictably and that American forces would sortie from Pearl Harbor *after* the Japanese assault on Midway began.[38] Yamamoto anticipated submarines of Cordons A and B would intercept the American carriers heading towards Midway *after* June 4, and this would bring on the decisive engagement. The Japanese placed great reliance on their submarines sighting the American forces coming up from Pearl Harbor. The I-boats would be able to pinpoint the Americans for air strikes and the submarines might get in a torpedo attack on the approaching U.S. fleet.[39]

The tight timetable meant there was simply not enough time for most submarines to be on station by June 1. With some submarines undergoing overhaul and others at sea when they received their orders, it was improbable for all submarines to be in their assigned positions by the appointed hour. Moreover, these submarines would be unable to provide the "sweeping" action Yamamoto and others mentioned.

The most plausible explanation is that Yamamoto most likely changed his orders from a static disposition to a sweeping one; however, the orders never reached Admiral Komatsu. In addition, since submarine cordon details were not in the official orders, Komatsu deployed his submarines along their static patrol lines per Yamamoto's previous instructions.[40]

From sweeping to static cordons, from operational plans to tight timetables, why were submarines not used properly in the first place since they held the actual key to success at Midway?[41] The reason that Japanese submarine commander Admiral Komatsu did not properly estimate the situation and make provision for an earlier and more complete employment of the submarines is obscure. More than likely, he either lacked the freedom to make significant alterations to Yamamoto's plan, or he deployed the submarines in agreement with Yamamoto's plan, a plan that depended on the U.S. fleet not moving towards Midway before June 1.[42]

Because Japanese submarines failed to detect American naval forces, Japanese forces, to a large degree, operated blindly until it was too late to change the course of the battle.[43] Perhaps some submarines were not even in the right place.[44] Captain Keizo Komura, commanding officer of the cruiser *Chikuma* at Midway, revealed in 1967 that a typographical error in the orders had sent submarines to the wrong positions. Combined Fleet attempted to conceal the blunder, but Komura learned of it soon after the battle from an officer on Yamamoto's staff.[45]

Captain Yasuji Watanabe commented that the submarine line (Cordon C) was too far east to locate the U.S. fleet. Watanabe stated this "error in positioning" and inadequate air search were the two reasons for the loss at Midway (see Appendix 5). As opposed to a typographical error sending submarines to the wrong position, this error in positioning seems more like bad strategic guesswork. Whether these are the same or separate incidents is unclear. Either Komatsu redeployed submarines of Cordons A and B to the wrong positions or Yamamoto's dispatch told Komatsu the location of Cordon C and Komatsu ordered the submarines to relocate to those positions. Yamamoto sent a dispatch (DesOpOrd Number 155) which included orders for submarines to move west, requiring Komatsu to move submarines from Cordons A and B to Cordon C. Regardless of who made the error, Cordon C submarines were too far east to intercept the American carriers.

Japanese Submarines

Japanese submarines did not fail to execute their primary function at Midway. By June 3, the greater parts of SubRon 3 and SubRon 5 reached their assigned stations along Cordons A and B, respectively. According to the Combined Fleet's original plan, these submarines were to be on station by June 1, about five days before the Occupation Force arrived at Midway.[46] Japanese planners predicted the U.S. fleet would arrive at Midway sometime between June 7 and June 13, several days too late to stop the invasion and occupation.[47] Even if SubRon 5 had arrived on station by June 1, these submarines would have still missed the American ships as the three carriers had already passed through the area.[48]

The question then becomes, if Japan's submarines were on station by June 3, and Yamamoto did not expect the U.S. fleet until at least June 7, why do most historians conclude the submarines failed in their task? Granted, the submarines did arrive after the American carriers had passed but, according to Yamamoto's strategic plan, submarines of Cordons A and B were in place four days *before* the anticipated sortie of the U.S. fleet. There is no basis to blame the Japanese defeat at Midway on the late arrival of SubRon 5. Yamamoto bears responsibility since the Combined Fleet staff conceived, prepared, and finalized the operational plan for the Midway campaign which produced the defeat.[49] The late arrival of SubRon 5 was a by-product of Yamamoto's poor strategic planning in conjunction with an apparent breakdown in communication between him and Komatsu.

American Fleet Situation

Within days of the Pearl Harbor attack, Admiral Husband Kimmel, wrote: "The losses of battleships commit us to the strategic defensive until our forces can again be built up. A very powerful striking force of carriers, cruisers and destroyers survives. These forces must be operated boldly and vigorously on the tactical offensive in order to retrieve our initial disaster."[50] With the balance of forces favoring Japan, and with no prospect of the United States matching Japan's numbers before the end of 1942, the U.S. could not risk a head-on fleet engagement. Rather, it had to employ what Admiral Ernest J. King called "strong attritional tactics," meaning opposing the enemy with a combination of submarines, land-based air power and carriers, with the fleet handling carriers in a tactically defensive manner that minimized the risks to themselves and their escorting cruisers.[51]

King's "strong attritional tactics" involved submarines and carriers as the striking element of his fleet-in-being. The fleet-in-being concept dictates the use of aggressive mobility and the exploitation of opportunities presented by an enemy to overcome a temporary strategic defense and ultimately obtain command of the sea.[52] The concept allows the use of a naval fleet in a way that avoids a decisive action by strategic or tactical activity until the situation develops in the fleet's favor. Julian S. Corbett, in his book *Principles of Maritime Strategy*, explained it this way, writing "The idea was to dispute the control by harassing operations, to exercise control at any place or at any moment as the opportunity presented itself, and to prevent the enemy exercising control in spite of his superiority by continually occupying his attention. The idea of mere resistance was hardly present at all. Everything was counterattack, whether upon the enemy's force or his maritime communications."[53]

On February 8, King explained his logic to Navy Secretary William Knox by noting a static defense in the Pacific was not possible. Any effective defense in the future required a "defensive offensive" now, a strategy to "hold what you've got and hit them where you can, the hitting to be done not only in seizing opportunities but by making them."[54] King therefore instructed Nimitz to employ strong attrition tactics and not to unnecessarily risk the carriers and cruisers.[55] Consequently, Nimitz impressed upon Admirals Fletcher and Spruance that they were to engage the Japanese only if they had a good chance of inflicting disproportionate damage. Nimitz said, "You will be governed by the principle of calculated risk, which you shall interpret to mean the avoidance of exposure of your force to attack by superior enemy forces without good prospect of inflicting, as a result of such exposure, greater damage on the enemy."[56]

American Submarines at Midway

At the beginning of the Pacific war, the American submarine fleet was just beginning to mount its offensive against Japanese merchant shipping. At this same time, the U.S. Navy was retreating in all areas. The U.S. Pacific Fleet spent virtually all its energy checking the Japanese advance and wresting back the strategic and operational initiative.[57] With the Battle of Midway on the horizon, Nimitz used all available American submarines to support fleet operations.[58] Postwar criticism questioned the act of pulling submarines away from commerce raiding. A common criticism was that this wholesale withdrawal of submarines, to perform reconnaissance and attack roles at Midway, was a wasteful deployment. Another was that while one could argue the Americans had their backs against the wall at Midway, how do you justify committing half of the American submarine force in the Pacific to the battle, where submarines played only a tangential role in the action.[59] Nimitz had to husband scarce resources to support the defense against Japanese advances. At Midway, this forced him to use all his available resources, requiring submarines to adapt to a new, but temporary role of fleet support. Commerce raiding was set aside as Midway's defense took a higher priority.[60]

Combined surface, air, and submarine operations demanded close coordination in the Midway area.[61] Therefore, Nimitz retained overall command so that he could, if necessary, coordinate the movements of submarines, the carriers, and Midway's aircraft.[62] Admiral English wanted to use submarines offensively in long-range search-and-destroy missions. Nimitz overruled him, leaving those missions to aircraft from Midway, which were better suited to carry out that role than the slower submarines. Nimitz was determined to deploy the submarines defensively in front of Midway.[63]

Acting on Nimitz's instructions, and as a part of Nimitz's overall strategy, English deployed the majority of Task Group (TG) 7.1 in defensive arcs west of Midway.[64] Because Nimitz knew the basic form of Japan's campaign, they were able to tie the submarines to a defensive role in the hope the enemy's advance to Midway would take him over the patrol lines placed in his path. Clausewitz wrote, "In a defensive battle, we can employ our divisions offensively. So, the defensive form of war is not a simple shield, but a shield made up of well-directed blows."[65] This decision is key to understanding the role of American submarines at Midway.

With apparent disregard for anything but the Japanese carriers, most historians criticize Nimitz for not placing American submarines in the path of the advancing Japanese Striking Force and making massed submarine attacks. The problem is these historians almost exclusively think in offensive terms. After all, Nimitz had a good idea where the Japanese carriers would appear. Historians conclude he stationed the submarines too close to Midway and not at locations where they could attack the Japanese Striking Force. For example, Tuohy writes, "U.S. submarines had been poorly deployed to intercept the Japanese fleet attacking Midway. They were too close to the island. They needed to be much farther away to spot, report and attack the Japanese carriers heading for Midway." Holmes stated, "Whoever created the submarine plan, it was bad. Most of the submarines were disposed for a concentrated defense close in to Midway, instead of being offensively placed farther out where they may have had an opportunity to torpedo a Japanese carrier before the decisive battle." Padfield added:

> The disposition of the main group, 7.1 has been criticized as being too close to Midway, for most boats were inside the distance at which the Kido Butai would launch its strike on the island; had they been grouped further to the west they might have had a chance of sighting and attacking the Japanese carriers before they reached their attack position.

These are just three examples out of many.[66]

These statements are standard conclusions most historians make when evaluating the role American submarines played at Midway, citing a failure in strategy and improper deployment. For example, Thomas G. Hunnicutt wrote:

> The placement of submarines at Midway and poor command and control by the CINC and ComSubPac precluded their massing to attack in concert with Midway based and carrier-based aircraft. Better placement of the arcs further out would have reduced submarine transit time as well as allowed the submarines to attack and disrupt the force before the arrival of American aircraft.[67]

However, we find the answer to submarine positioning in the one question no one seems to ask: what was the operational plan for the submarines at Midway? If the intended use of American submarines was to attack the Japanese Striking Force as most authors conclude, then why did Nimitz and English deploy them in defensive arcs west of Midway when intelligence knew exactly where the Japanese carriers would be? Ultimately, there was more to American submarine deployment plan than most realize or understand.

Intelligence

At Midway, Nimitz was to "hurt" the Japanese carriers and "frustrate" the invasion attempt.[68] He intended to use his intelligence advantage to make up for numerical inferiority so he could concentrate his carrier strength to blunt the spearhead of the Japanese attack.[69] Carrier aircraft can isolate and neutralize the enemy and conduct Combat Air Patrols to achieve air superiority and suppress enemy air defenses. Air superiority is usually vital for the success of amphibious operations. Without the air support to ensure sufficient sea control, the amphibious operation would be fatally compromised.[70] Despite the remarkable intelligence available to Nimitz, he knew the operation they had embarked upon was an enormous gamble and a great deal could go wrong.[71] All he and English could do was to deploy their forces according to their best calculation of enemy positions and intentions.[72]

Nimitz knew carrier-borne air power was the decisive naval weapon, and that the Japanese Navy's operational center of gravity was their carrier force. Without the carriers, Nagumo could not eliminate Midway's ground and air defenses; neither could he provide a concentration of air power great enough to cover other components of his fleet. Nimitz knew that, to defend Midway against invasion, he would have to destroy the Japanese carriers.[73]

He ordered "Fleet opposed invasion—Midway" three weeks before the anticipated invasion of the island.[74] Nimitz had great faith in his intelligence team. He staked all his chips on Commander Joseph Rochefort's analysis, committing all his forces to the defense of Midway including Task Force 16 (USS *Hornet* and USS *Enterprise*), Task Force 17 (USS *Yorktown*), and a submarine screen west of Midway to detect the approach of the Japanese Striking Force and Occupation Force.[75]

At 0700, June 3, Nimitz received the first piece of tactical intelligence that reflected successful planning for the Midway operation. A Midway-based PBY reconnaissance plane reported, "Main body...bearing 262, distance 700 miles...eleven ships, course 090, speed 19 knots." The PBY spotted the Occupation Force exactly where it was expected.[76] The second piece of tactical intelligence came when USS *Cuttlefish*, on station 700 miles west of Midway, spotted Japan's Occupation Force right where Rochefort correctly anticipated the Japanese would rendezvous.[77] Nimitz could plan his counterstrategy to "hurt" the Japanese carriers, dictated by the need to avoid a one-to-one match with a numerically superior enemy.

Invasion

Once American forces eliminated the Japanese carriers and their aircraft, Nimitz and English turned their attention to "frustrating" the Midway invasion attempt. After consultation with Nimitz, and believing a landing attempt by Japanese forces proceeding toward Midway from the west was still possible, English ordered TG 7.1 submarines to form on the 100-mile circle from Midway by dawn, June 5, and TG 7.2 submarines to proceed west at best speed.[78] At 0630 on June 5, Nimitz and English received USS *Tambor*'s contact report of "many unidentified ships," 90 miles from Midway.[79] After consultation with Nimitz, and believing that some of the Japanese forces were still attempting to get in position to make a landing on Midway, at 0845 English directed TG 7.1 submarines to remain in present assigned sectors but to close Midway to a radius of 5 miles.[80] As a result, TG 7.1 submarines and Task Force 16 closed Midway to oppose the apparent landing. Nimitz and English remained concerned the Japanese would go ahead with their invasion plans. However, at 0900, *Tambor*'s second report indicated damaged Japanese cruisers retiring westward. At 1153, English ordered TG 7.2 submarines to the 100-mile mark north of Midway. At 1159, he ordered TG 7.1 submarines to form on the 12-mile circle from Midway and to return to their original defense sectors to act against a possible invasion.[81]

The destruction of the Carrier Striking Force rendered the amphibious operation untenable. The main reason for the failure of the amphibious operation was the Japanese inability to secure sea control before the amphibious task group reached Midway.[82] It becomes obvious that, by the placement and movement of submarine assets between June 4 and June 5, the role Nimitz gave his submarines was the defense of Midway. In fact, this appears to be his intent all along by stating "[submarines] might well have played the decisive role in the battle had the Japanese Fleet pushed in to Midway and attempted a landing."[83]

English told the submarine commanders that he expected a full-scale invasion of Midway, and the Japanese force would probably consist of an invasion convoy backed up by aircraft carriers, cruisers, and destroyers.[84] On June 4, English ordered all TG 7.1 submarines except for USS *Cachalot*, USS *Flying Fish*, and USS *Cuttlefish*, to attack the enemy carriers. Why would he have to order TG 7.1 submarines to intercept and attack the Japanese Striking Force if that was their primary task? The answer is that offensive actions were not the primary role of American submarines at Midway. English changed submarine orders to "offensive action" once the location of the Japanese carriers was known. After American carrier aircraft sank the Japanese carriers, English reassigned the submarines to their defensive sectors and moved them in closer to Midway to repel an anticipated invasion. This suggests defense against invasion was the primary role for most of these submarines.

By examining the geometry of the Midway submarine deployment (see Figure 7.2), only two of all the defending submarines had any chance of getting into action against the Japanese carriers: USS *Grouper* and USS *Nautilus*. If Nimitz's goal for TG 7.1 was the destruction of the Japanese Striking Force, he would have initially vectored them to the anticipated location Rochefort designated. However, Nimitz placed his submarines in defensive arcs west of Midway, which indicates the submarines' priority was to patrol their assigned sectors and defend Midway against a Japanese invasion, and then attack the Japanese fleet if the opportunity presented itself.[85] Ironically, most historians note the fact that Nimitz and English placed their submarines into defensive arcs west of Midway, but do not make the connection that Nimitz was defensive minded with orders to hold Midway. Some historians claim American submarines were to scout and report the location of the Japanese ships, and to intercept and attack, with the objective of inflicting maximum damage on the enemy.[86] At Midway, this is inconsistent with TG 7.1 patrol reports (see Appendix 1). Task Group 7.1 submarines were patrolling their assigned sectors until the morning of June 4 when, at 0716, English ordered them to intercept and attack the Japanese Striking Force.

CHAPTER 9

Midway Submerged: Conclusions

> Know the enemy and know yourself; in a hundred battles you will never be in peril. When you are ignorant of the enemy but know yourself, your chances of winning or losing are equal. If ignorant both of your enemy and of yourself, you are certain in every battle to be in peril.[1]

The U.S. and Japanese navies did not expect to imitate the German submarine war against commerce. Instead, both attempted to find a role for their submarines in the prevailing prewar strategy that involved decisive clashes between the main battle fleets as articulated by Alfred Thayer Mahan.[2] For the United States, Pearl Harbor changed that. Together, submarines and aircraft carriers became the striking weapons of the American fleet.[3]

The Japanese Navy contributed to some of their own disappointments. The prewar obsession with the decisive battle and the consequent over-specialization in design and training had stifled initiative from top to bottom. The Japanese were prepared neither to wage a submarine campaign of attrition nor defend themselves against such undersea warfare. In the decisive, total war Japan wanted to wage, a country must fight with everything it has, including its supply line. The United States realized this; Japan never did. The United States' weakness was its merchant shipping. If Japanese submarines had attacked American merchant shipping, the United States would have drawn escort resources to defend the supply line. Japan missed its opportunity; damaging enough merchant shipping early in the war would have delayed the American advance across the Pacific.[4] Japan developed its naval forces in line with a single plan for waging war, each unit of the fleet designed to fill a specific slot in the overall strategy against Allied units in the Pacific.[5]

One of the principles of Mahanian strategy was concentration of strength for the decisive blow.[6] From the outbreak of the war, Japan's Navy stuck to its long-cherished "one big battle idea," in which all naval arms, surface, air, and underwater, were to be used once and for all.[7] However, at no time did the Japanese Navy strike with its fully concentrated force, nor did it strike in a manner that effectively combined its air and surface units or push on to decisive results when they were within reach. A crucial part of the carrier arm was missing at Midway, and a substantial force diverted to the Aleutians, while the powerful supporting surface units operated so far away from the carriers that they were unable to join the battle or even contribute their own antiaircraft and reconnaissance assets to the operation.[8]

Japanese Submarines

The Japanese Navy came to Midway with a flawed doctrine.[9] An invasion of Midway would force the U.S. Pacific Fleet to counterattack, where submarines and air strikes would weaken it and then Yamamoto's Main Body battle line would move in to destroy whatever remained.[10] Despite all its excellent qualities, the Japanese Navy was an outdated and flawed instrument, designed for a type of war that had already passed into history.[11] Despite criticism, Yamamoto's division of his force makes it plausible Japanese command thought it held the advantages of both superior strength and complete surprise.[12] Yamamoto's plan showed signs of overconfidence—of a dangerous contempt for the enemy—the Japanese best described as "victory disease."[13]

Why did such a vast armada fail to accomplish its mission? There is no doubt American intelligence of Japanese plans was a decisive factor. However, the most obvious reason for the miscarriage of the plans of the Japanese was their failure to achieve the surprise on which they counted. Prior to Midway, every Japanese operation had gone exactly according to plan, and it seemed their High Command expected that same good fortune in this campaign; the bombing of Midway would bring the

U.S. fleet out of Oahu, and the Japanese scouting line of submarines to the north of Oahu would detect and report that movement. However, Yamamoto's battle plan was flawed and did not consider contingencies such as the Americans being aware of the invasion plan. The Japanese chose to ignore warning signs that indicated American naval leaders might be aware of their plans. These contingencies did not fit into Yamamoto's plan, which depended too much on the U.S. fleet reacting exactly the way the Japanese expected.[14]

If Yamamoto's plan proved mistaken or outmoded by technology, as it did, or if American naval leaders reacted in unexpected ways, as they did, the whole structure was bound to collapse and the over-specialized units, unfit for other roles, would inevitably flounder.[15] For example, Nobutake Kondo said:

> In past operations, Japan succeeded in launching surprise blows upon the enemy, because Japan only attempted to advance operations, either under the cover of her air forces or after having gotten at least approximate information about the enemy. In the case of Midway Island, however, it was utterly different. We met with fiasco because we did not get any sign of the existence of an American task force near Midway Island. It was our great regret that we lacked sufficient measures in establishing guard screens by means of submarines both ahead and to the sides of our fleet, as well as the fact that we failed to have some submarines go to Midway Island beforehand to get some information.[16]

Lieutenant Commander Tanabe in *I-168* reported intense American air activity with an average of 90 to 100 flights from the island's airstrip each day and reconnaissance planes spending most of the daylight hours in the air, suggesting they were patrolling to at least 700 miles out. Additionally, Japanese intelligence missed several important red flags such as the submarines sent to refuel flying boats reporting enemy activity at French Frigate Shoals, traffic analysis that American submarines had sighted the Occupation Force, and that U.S. carriers were north of Midway. That Japanese intelligence did not see the red flags was due to the divisions in command organization and intelligence staff. As the Japanese later discovered, the intelligence from their carrier task force staff was so bad that one wonders if they were functioning at all. Every estimate was bad, every guess was wrong. Undoubtedly, the serious intelligence failure played almost as large a part in the American victory as the brilliant feats of Rochefort's team at Pearl Harbor.[17]

It would have been so easy to have had a better submarine cordon, a stronger air search, an extra carrier on the scene.[18] Ito later stated, "It is hard to believe that the same men who had done the careful intelligence work for the Pearl Harbor attack could have done the haphazard job of the Midway operation."[19] The Japanese force was a formidable one, but it was nevertheless only a portion of their whole fleet. Spruance struck with all the strength he had on the spot, and which could be rushed to the spot, and that strength proved to be sufficient to administer a severe defeat to the Japanese. Had they come in much greater strength, American opposition could not have been greater than it was. Since the Japanese squadron included four battleships and four aircraft carriers, they were already risking a force whose loss would have been a catastrophic blow to their naval position in the Pacific.[20]

Many claim that one of the more serious mistakes of the Japanese was in their handling of their submarines. Much of Japanese plans in the Central Pacific depended on their success at Midway. However, they would not realize this dream, chiefly because, as Orita stated, "… use of our submarines in the Midway operation was so poor. Perhaps Combined Fleet had a low opinion of submarines, which had not sunk many enemy ships in the war's first months."[21]

The Midway plan assumed the American carriers would remain in port until the threat to Midway was recognized. When the flying boats were unable to refuel at FFS, due to American activity there, the operation to confirm whether or not the carriers were still at Pearl Harbor failed to deliver. There was no backup plan. The carriers crossed the Japanese submarine patrol line before it was populated; *Hornet* and *Enterprise* on May 29 and *Yorktown* on the night of May 31. Just as Admiral Nimitz hoped, the carriers took their positions northeast of Midway and waited. Orita claims they were able to reach their hiding position safely, and remain undetected there, because the sentry line of SubRon 5 arrived on station too late.[22]

As much as historians would like to place at least partial blame for the Japanese defeat at Midway on this fact, Japanese submarines were still on station by June 3, four days before Yamamoto's plan expected the U.S. fleet to sail. Even if SubRon 5 was on station by the appointed date of June 1, these submarines would still have missed the American carriers. The cause of the defeat, even partially, is not due to the late arrival of SubRon 5 or the individual submarine commanders of those submarines. The blame lies elsewhere.

During the battle, with the exception of *I-168*'s sinking of *Yorktown* and USS *Hammann*, Japanese submarines sailed the distant peripheries in idle frustration, sighting little and sinking nothing.[23] In using submarines like chess pieces, moved according to predetermined plans, or in reaction to American movements, the Japanese pressed them into roles for which they were unsuited and failed to develop them as well as the Americans did for the role to which they were suited. Orita said, "Had our submarines been used properly and effectively, the history of the Pacific naval war might have been written quite differently."[24]

Orita's statement is true to a point, as commerce raiding would have delayed America's Pacific war effort. However, within the Japanese Naval Command (JNC) hierarchy, there was too much mismanagement and micromanagement. For example, the JNC dictated the number of torpedoes submarines could fire per orders: full salvoes were permitted only against capital units such as aircraft carriers and battleships; three torpedoes were allowed against cruisers, but only one against destroyers and merchantmen. JNC never changed these priorities except for specific commerce raiding missions in the Indian Ocean. Submarines did not perform sustained attacks on American supply convoys across the Pacific and they passed up valuable targets because they did not belong to the force or category specified in the mission orders. Lessons were not learned or, if learned, not acted upon because the necessary staff organization did not exist.[25]

The fault lies with Yamamoto and the strategic plan to invade Midway that he forced on the General Naval Staff. Operation "MI" required the Americans to react in a certain way for which he made no contingencies if they did not. Yamamoto's intelligence indicated the possibility that American submarines were aware of the Occupation Force, yet he did not react accordingly. Radio silence prevented Nagumo from knowing that

Gotō canceled the Second "K" Operation, and the whereabouts of the American carriers was unknown. Then there was the mismanagement of the submarines and the apparent breakdown in communication between Yamamoto and Komatsu that either delayed submarine deployment or initially sent them to wrong locations.

Finally, and possibly more important, what was Yamamoto's goal for the Midway operation? Was it the occupation of the island as seen in statements of various personnel (Appendix 5) or was it the destruction of the U.S. fleet? It seems Yamamoto's goal was the latter, and the threat of invasion of Midway was a lure. However, Bates makes an interesting statement along these lines:

> It is possible also that [Yamamoto] had hoped, in line with the thought that it might be possible to bring about a fleet action, to present to the enemy what seemed to be an important, vulnerable target. Although not mentioned in his Operation Order, he may have believed that the Midway Occupation Force would be considered such a target by the American Commander, who would be lured into attacking it. This would indicate why the Midway Occupation Force was so far to the south in generally good weather, whereas the Mobile Force was well to the north in generally bad weather.[26]

Was Yamamoto using the Occupation Force as bait? If so, his subordinates did not realize this as they were under the impression they were to capture and occupy Midway. (Appendix 5) However, this would explain several things such as why Yamamoto did not seem worried about American submarines spotting his Occupation Force, the need for radio silence, and mismanagement of Japanese submarines. Other problems, such as the extreme failure of Japanese intelligence and the difference in strategic plans between the Pearl Harbor attack and the Midway operation, become bigger issues than initially thought.

American submarines spotted the Occupation Force and sent several contact reports. Yamamoto seemed unfazed by this. Additionally, if he counted on American forces spotting his Occupation Force and anticipated the U.S. fleet would sail to attack it, then he would have known the need for a submarine sweep, or even static lines, was not a priority. This may explain the omission of submarines from the operation's orders and would help clarify issues surrounding Japanese submarine deployment, redeployment, and the issuing of wrong locations.

If Yamamoto did capture Midway, Bates states his goal was to use the island as a base for long-distance reconnaissance planes to alert him of any actions taken by the Americans.[27] This is a more reasonable plan since long-term occupation of Midway was not realistic, it being nearly impossible to maintain a supply line from Japan. It is quite probable Yamamoto never intended to occupy Midway. Japanese Monograph 110 clearly states that, after the completion of the operation, and even after the withdrawal of surface forces, submarines were to continue operating around the Midway and Hawaii areas.[28] If Yamamoto's intent was to occupy Midway, why would he withdraw surface forces? This act would make it easy for American forces to retake the island.

Occupation of Midway does not make strategic sense from Japan's viewpoint. Yamamoto's strategic plan, built on the pretense a threat to Midway would stir the U.S. fleet to react, may have had nothing to do with occupying the island. It would almost seem that Yamamoto's real objective was to use his Occupation Force to lure out the U.S. fleet so he could strike and destroy the American carriers while they were preoccupied. Not only does it appear that Yamamoto places significant, although as we have seen unwarranted, blame on his submarines for the defeat, could this blame be an attempt to shift focus away from the fact he was willing to sacrifice his Occupation Force? The evidence points that way, or at least hints at a cover up by the Combined Fleet. However, we may never know.

American Submarines

Between World War I and World War II, American naval leaders employed submarines in the scouting line of the battle fleet with plans to sweep the sea of Japanese destroyers and allow the U.S. fleet to engage the enemy fleet.[29] Additionally, the Navy envisioned American submarines ambushing warships near their bases or in advance of a sea battle. However, after Pearl Harbor, naval command could not execute unrestricted submarine warfare against Japan as no attack plan existed. With war forced upon America, it was necessary to radically change all ideas, doctrines, and training procedures and convert a peacetime-trained submarine force into one capable of waging unrestricted and unlimited warfare.

Prior to the war, the United States labored under a very false idea that submarines would operate with the fleet. The net result was that, while it had a few submarines which were materially correct and whose personnel were well trained, there was no solid background or correct concept of the proper employment of the individual submarine in unrestricted and unlimited warfare against the enemy.[30] The Navy removed the cautious, prewar mandate. However, for the first two years of the war, submarines went on patrol with defective torpedoes, and they were given patrols that did not utilize them for what they were best suited—commerce raiding.[31]

Critics of submarine usage at Midway suggest the results of American submarines in the battle was disappointing. Confusion, indecision, and poor contact reporting limited them to making only negligible contributions to the American victory.[32] Advanced warning of Japanese intentions and the availability of submarines provided a perfect opportunity to use them decisively. Additionally, for several days after the battle, Admiral English gave submarines near Midway, and those coming in from patrol, several contact reports concerning damaged Japanese vessels in retreat, yet they attacked or sank nothing.[33] In their defense, these reports came from aircraft and were often erroneous, misleading, or several hours old and pursuing submarines were unable to overtake or make contact. *Mogami* and *Mikuma* were the only crippled Japanese vessels sighted as others were well to the west.

Various historians have said that, despite the exploits of USS *Nautilus*, American submarines contributed nothing at Midway; the decisive input had come from Rochefort, Spruance made the battle-winning decision, and Yamamoto and Nagumo made fatal mistakes.[34] In hindsight, when historians make these types of criticisms regarding the defensive deployment of Task Group 7.1, the question is whether they think more attacks by submarines with malfunctioning torpedoes would have resulted in greater damage to the Japanese. The answer, based on the example set by *Nautilus*, is "no."

For submariners, the Battle of Midway was a new experience, being the only defensive battle of the Pacific War that extensively used submarines.[35] Their influence on the battle certainly helped turn the tide. For example, submarine sightings forced the Japanese task groups to move with caution after the first submarine alert. USS *Tambor* set in motion a chain of events that brought disaster on two Japanese heavy cruisers. *Nautilus* disrupted the maneuvers of the Strike Force, threw a battleship out of the line, created day-long pandemonium, and attacked, unsuccessfully due to faulty torpedoes, the Japanese carrier *Kaga*.[36] Other submarine successes include *Nautilus* and the Japanese destroyer *Arashi*. Without *Arashi* staying behind to keep *Nautilus* submerged, and then racing at high speed back to the Striking Force, it is highly unlikely McClusky and his dive bombers would have found the Japanese carriers. Two other events include USS *Triton* sinking *I-164*, which was part of SubRon 5, and USS *Cuttlefish* spotting the Occupation Force. Finally, on June 9, USS *Trout* rescued two Japanese sailors, survivors of *Mikuma* and the first Japanese prisoners of war taken by an American submarine.[37]

The Battle of Midway demonstrates that even possession of the best intelligence does not guarantee victory. Nimitz, Spruance, and Fletcher had the enemy's plans laid clear before them, or as clear as the obscurities of war will ever allow, thanks to the relentless intellectual effort of Rochefort and his fellow cryptanalysts. They had, all the same, nearly lost.[38] Submarine deployment in close-in defensive positions in a battle fought in daylight left few attack opportunities and seriously curtailed their mobility.[39] However, the opposite is also true in that placing the submarines in the *anticipated* location where the Striking Force was to appear was just as likely to fail. Rochefort's prediction was "five minutes, five degrees, and five miles out."[40] Five miles is a significant distance to cover in a short amount of time for a submerged submarine. Unless the Striking Force ran right up on a submerged, slow-moving submarine, it is highly unlikely the submarine could have attained an attack position on the fast-moving carrier task force. Moreover, if by chance an American submarine did attain an attack position, what guarantee was there the highly suspect American torpedoes would explode upon hitting the target?

The risk of failure in using submarines as offensive weapons was too great. Furthermore, if Nimitz and English had decided to place all their submarines at the anticipated location of the Japanese Striking Force, this would have left them with nothing in the way of a defensive screen in which to spot and oppose the anticipated Occupation Force they knew was heading toward Midway. Nimitz realized these facts, which explains why he assigned scouting and reconnaissance to carrier and Midway-based aircraft and used his submarines as a defensive screen.

After the battle, Nimitz wrote the following in his after-action report:

> Above everything else, a submarine is an offensive weapon that must be employed aggressively and boldly. Although there were some critical mistakes by individual commanding officers, as a group the submarines were handled well, supplied important information, and filled an essential need in the strategy of the operations by providing both a secondary scouting and a strong close-in striking force. They might well have played the decisive role in the battle had the Japanese fleet pushed in to MIDWAY and attempted a landing.[41]

English, also writing in his after-action report, made a similar statement:

> The submarine is primarily an offensive weapon and should usually be employed only on offensive missions. This particular engagement, where the known objective covered a very small area, represents a particular case where submarines may be employed efficiently as a defensive weapon. It is believed that the submarines would have given a very good account of themselves if a landing had been attempted. Submarines are under a great handicap when chasing damaged enemy units within the range of our own aircraft since it is often necessary for them to submerge to avoid attack, thus greatly reducing their mobility.[42]

Nimitz and English both stated the submarine was an offensive weapon. However, Nimitz adhered to Admiral King's "defensive offensive" strategy. With timely intelligence, Nimitz believed Japan's plan was to invade Midway. He developed an offensive strategy to attack the Japanese carriers with naval aircraft and a defensive strategy to oppose the anticipated invasion by modifying the role of submarines from commerce raiders into a defensive screen. This defensive strategy prohibited sending submarines on hit-and-run missions as English wanted; besides, Nimitz knew they were unsuited for that task.[43]

Nimitz did not assign submarines strike missions due to mobility issues and it was still anyone's guess where the Japanese fleet would appear. If carrier and Midway-based aircraft had trouble finding the Japanese Striking Force, and they could cover a significantly bigger expanse of ocean, why would anyone think a submarine, using the very same intelligence, would have any better luck finding the Japanese fleet?

Historians, when researching the Battle of Midway regarding submarine deployment, need to think defensively. Nimitz brilliantly employed King's "defensive offensive" at Midway. He succeeded in both attacking the Japanese Striking Force and defending Midway from invasion by correctly assigning his available assets to their proper role. Historians also need to realize Yamamoto's perceived strategy called for the occupation of Midway, which, he reasoned, would draw out the U.S. fleet. Even though most think of the Battle of Midway as a carrier vs. carrier battle, the goal, as understood by Nimitz, was the invasion and occupation of Midway, so he deployed his submarines accordingly.

In terms of strategy, Yamamoto got it wrong, and it was his strategic plan, not the actions of a handful of Japanese submarines, which lost the Battle of Midway. Nimitz, on the other hand, got it right. He used his submarines in a way to ensure victory, not as offensive weapons, as Admiral English preferred and a decision many historians have disagreed with ever since, but as a defensive screen against a Japanese amphibious assault. Nimitz understood that destroying the Japanese carriers would ensure American air superiority, which in combination with the defensive screen of submarines would prevent the Japanese occupying the island.

By his own words, Nimitz assigned the task of "secondary scouting and close-in strike force" to his submarines. With this strategic and tactical understanding, it is obvious American submarines succeeded in their assigned "defensive" role during the Battle of Midway, and that historians should no longer deem their contributions as a failure. Furthermore, Nimitz made the correct assessment of his available assets in defending Midway. He had a few weeks to make a strategic decision based on limited information. Historians have had decades to evaluate and re-evaluate volumes of data Nimitz never had. He got it right and his strategy was successful. We should give Admiral Chester W. Nimitz the benefit of the doubt that he knew what he was doing.

APPENDIX I

Patrol Reports of U.S. Task Group 7.1 Submarines

USS *Cachalot* (SS-170): First/Second War Patrol[1]

Patrol report indicates *Cachalot* ended first war patrol on March 18, 1942, at Pearl Harbor. Patrol report indicates *Cachalot* departed on second war patrol from Midway on June 9, 1942. Patrol report does not contain any information on Midway activities.

USS *Cuttlefish* (SS-171): Second War Patrol[2]

30 May 1942

1230 (L)	Received orders to patrol point —. Reported time of arrival on station, fuel, etc. to CTF7. Changed course for new assignment.

31 May 1942

0804 (L)	Sighted 3 Type 96 Navy Heavy Bombers about 5000 yards on port quarter on northerly course and flying very low. Lat 26-18 N Long 169-43 E. Submerged to 150 feet and changed course. Four people reported orange markings as plainly visible and individually identified planes as above (Aircraft Contact #1).
0900 (L)	Surfaced and resumed course and speed.
1047 (L)	Sighted one bomber similar to those previously sighted coming in fast on port bow. Submerged

	to 150 feet and changed course. Two bombs were dropped as we were submerging, without causing damage to the vessel. (Aircraft Contact #2, Air Attack #1) Lat 26-34 N Long 169-55 E. Since we were but 25 miles from station remained submerged and conducted periscope patrol enroute. It is believed that these planes are operating from Wake (470 miles) as it is not thought that carriers would fly them off for scouting purposes.
1845 (L)	Surfaced and sent contact report.
1 June 1942	Conducted periscope patrol at point —.
0930 (L)	Sighted unidentified seaplane thought to be PBY. He ran west of us for 5 or 6 miles, commenced zigzagging at very low altitude and disappeared on bearing 200° (T) (Aircraft Contact #4).
3 June 1942	Conducted periscope patrol at point —.
0930 (L)	Sighted unidentified seaplane believed to be PBY which did not approach close enough for positive identification (Aircraft Contact #5).
4 June 1942	Conducted periscope patrol at point —.
1000 (L)	Sighted plane tentatively identified as PBY (Aircraft Contact #6).
1040 (L)	Sighted same or similar plane on northerly course passing 3 or 4 miles away identified by silhouette as PBY (Aircraft Contact #7).
2100 (L)	Received orders to close Midway and search for burning battleship. Due to inability to copy NPM on loop this was our first indication any contact. Later rigged portable lead to radar antenna for listening submerged and this worked fairly well if sufficient mast was exposed. Changed course for last reported position of BB.

2320 (L)	In Lat 27-00 N Long 170-02 E sighted large darkened ship broad on starboard bow. (Contact #10, Attack #5) Changed course toward and closed to 6000 yards. Vessel was identified as large heavily laden tanker similar to KUROSHIRO MARU on course 060° speed 11 knots, angle on the bow 090° port, changed course to 060° and increased to full speed to gain attack position.
5 June 1942	Continuing attack on tanker. Due to low speed differential it was not until 0214 that we had gained sufficient bearing to commence attack. Due to bright moonlight it was planned to run in on a normal approach course until range was 6000 yards and distance from track 3000 then continue submerged and fire on 110° track from 800 to 1000 yards.
0214 (L)	Commenced swing to normal approach and saw target change course to left. He finally steadied on 300° (T) leaving us 8000 yards on his starboard beam. Started chase all over again but was forced to dive by approaching daylight before we could attack. Sent contact report and commenced trailing submerged, changing course to north to remain between tanker and main body.
1332 (L)	In Lat 27-35 N Long 170-40 E picked up by sound a peculiar clomping noise at about 60 beats per second. (Contact #11). Due to reported submarine in vicinity attempted to develop bearing without success. QB out of commission and bearing was never good enough for attack without echo ranging. Stopped all machinery and eliminated this vessel as source. Relative bearing changed with course changes but true bearing varied little. Sound finally faded out to

	north after getting quite loud and broad. Possible submarine contact.
2100 (L)	Received order to take station 100 miles from Midway. Increased speed to 12 knots.
6 June 1942	Running on surface en route Midway.
0650 (M)	Received message to report position and complied. Suggested patrol for cripples present position.
1800 (M)	In Lat 27-35 N Long 175-00 E began passing a considerable amount of wooden gear—among it was a mess bench and a boom crutch, the latter with Japanese characters painted on it over the numeral 2. There were faint traces of oil slicks but apparently quite old.
6 June 1942	[*Author's note: Crossed International Date Line*].
0430 (Y)	Received orders to patrol present position. This message was missed on its first transmission and not received until eleven hours after time of origin. We were of course 100 or more miles too far east to be of any use in the chase for stragglers. It is believed that the reason for the failure to receive the message earlier is due to fatigue of radio personnel. The requirements of radio, sound, and radar, along with constant maintenance work on sound and radar gear, have about worn the radiomen out and resulted in missing or badly garbled messages.
0500 (Y)	Sent position report to CTF7 and submerged for periscope patrol, guarding NPM on our jury rigged radar antenna.
0730 (Y)	Sighted PBY going west (Aircraft Contact #8).
1200 (Y)	Received CTF7's EUROPE but could not decode it. Surfaced and asked for repeat which we received at 1235. Plot shows forces to be 135 miles due

	west making 15 knots so no attempt was made to intercept. Missing the message yesterday has put us out of the fight completely.
1356 (Y)	Made quick dive on radar indication at 12 miles. Planes not seen and not identified. Must have been a large formation to give us a 12 mile indication. (Aircraft Contact #9) Lat 27-40 N Long 176-50 E.
1415 (Y)	Made quick dive on radar indication at 6 miles. Sighted 4 B-17 Bombers going west before leaving bridge (Aircraft Contact #10). Flare failed.
1700 (Y)	Received CTF's SAVAGE—garbled.
1750 (Y)	Received orders to patrol to westward and return to Pearl if no contact were made before dark. Patrolled to westward at 12 knots.
2000 (Y)	Set course for Pearl in accordance with instructions.
2130 (Y)	Reported course and speed to CTF7 requested repeat on SAVAGE (garbled) and FARMER (missed).

7 June 1942

0145 (Y)	Received orders to search for abandoned battleship. Changed course to 298° (T) and speed to 12.2 knots.
0815 (Y)	In Lat 27-27 N Long 176-20 E sighted PBY bearing 270° (T) distant 5 or 6 miles on southerly course. Attempted to establish communications but was unsuccessful, getting only a few unintelligible blinks before he disappeared astern to reappear at 0840 on starboard quarter on northerly course about 7 or 8 miles away. Again could not establish communications (Aircraft Contact #11).
0900 (Y)	Worked out probable drift of abandoned battleship and changed course to 300° (T) for point estimated as best for intercept.
1100 (Y)	Radar out of commission.

1255 (Y)	In Lat 28-00 N Long 175-20 E bomber with red wing markings appeared out of rain squall and banked for attack. OOD dove upon sighting markings. Two bombs were dropped while we were submerging without damage to the vessel. Two lookouts also reported red markings, the third saw no markings at all. All identify plane as Type 97 Heavy Bomber. The bombs were much closer or much larger than the last ones (Aircraft Contact #12, Air Attack #2).
1330 (Y)	Came to periscope depth and attempted to tune radar.
1340 (Y)	Sighted PBY going east (Aircraft Contact #13).
1415 (Y)	Put a bubble in safety and sent a contact report.
1500 (Y)	Radar in commission. Surfaced and continued assignment.
2325 (Y)	Receive orders to discontinue search in morning. Commencing to rain, overcast, sea picking up, no fix since noon.

8 June 1942

0500 (Y)	Arrived at best estimated position of BB. Visibility 300 to 4000 yards, continuous heavy rain, rough choppy sea. Making 7.7 knots. Wind picking up from SW. It doesn't appear that a badly damaged ship could last long in this weather. Received CTF7's UNITY repeated asking for acknowledgement. Reported conditions, fuel remaining, etc.
0800 (Y)	Some improvement in conditions, rain has become squalls with fair visibility between. Wind and sea still rising.
1000 (Y)	Sighted PBY on northerly course between rain squalls. Attempted to communicate but was unsuccessful (Aircraft Contact #14).

1030 (Y)	Received orders to return to Pearl. Since we have air search in area, requested results of search prior to my departure.
1123 (Y)	Lookout reported periscope two points abaft port beam, distant 500 yards. Lat 29-08 N Long 173-08 E. OOD turned away preparatory to firing stern tubes in accordance with standing instructions but nothing more was seen or heard and no one but lookout saw anything. Possible, but doubtful submarine contact (Contact #12).
1250 (Y)	Another submarine contact in Lat 28-52 N Long 173-18 E which was developed into debris. Commenced running through several square miles of wreckage and debris including almost anything that will float. Airplane fending off spars, furniture, bedding, sea chests, lockers, floor boards, cans, firkins, boards, cork lagging, burned and charred fragments of wood, timbers, spars, 2×4's [sic], benches, doors, buoys, life rings, etc. Attempted to pick up life ring but broke stud on port engine while maneuvering to do so. Since it was too rough to send men on deck, except for something vital, and since no markings were observed, contented myself by running through the stuff, changing course to look at likely objects until 1430 when suction was lost on port reduction gear pump putting the whole port side out of commission. Since this is usually a long job, and since Japanese air reported in vicinity and in view of the possible submarine contact, submerged to complete repairs.
1500 (Y)	Surfaced, having found the casualty to be a simple loss of suction, and resumed search through wreckage. The only markings seen were Japanese characters on a broken soap box.

1600 (Y)	Ran out of wreckage and set course for Pearl. Reported position of abandoned battleship and 5–6 miles south of my estimated position. The wreckage was spread over a considerable area—about a mile wide and 8 or 10 miles long. The down wind debris was that which had the most sail area, that upwind consisting mostly of stuff which floated without much showing above the surface, indicating a common origin. It was too concentrated to have been discarded by a ship underway but there was no evidence as to whether it was flotsam or jetsam. It is unfortunate that no conclusive evidence of sinking could be discovered and salvaged.

USS *Dolphin* (SS-169): Second War Patrol[3]

14 May 1942

0900 (VW)	Underway in accordance with Commander Submarines, Pacific Fleet Operation Order No. 50-42. U.S.S. LITCHFIELD escorting until darkness.
1700 (VW)	Made Trim dive, everything satisfactory.
1715 (VW)	LITCHFIELD dropped two 300 lb. depth charges, range 675 yards, depth setting 50 feet. DOLPHIN at 50 feet.

15 May 1942

0703 (WX)	Sighted PBY, exchanged recognition signals, had to use flare as plane evidently couldn't read Aldis lamp.

16 May 1942

0842 (X)	Sighted PBY, distance seven miles, was not challenged.

APPENDIX I • 111

1108 (X)   Sighted PBY, distance about ten miles, was not challenged.

17 May 1942

1222 (X)   Starboard lookout sighted periscope and feather momentarily (Contact #1) bearing 070° relative, distance about 400 yards. O.O.D. changed course to left to bring stern tubes to bear and increased speed to open range. Periscope was again sighted momentarily on the starboard quarter, midway of the turn, after this brief sighting contact was lost. At first sighting submarine was apparently on parallel course. Sent report to Commander Submarines, Pacific Fleet.

1615 (X)   Submerged to allow submarine to overtake us in case she was trailing.

1820 (X)   Surfaced, nothing sighted.

19 May 1942

1422 (X)   Exercised gun crew at Battle Surface, fired 10 rounds of target ammunition from deck gun.

30 May 1942

0849 (M)   Sighted PBY distance about seven miles, was not challenged.

31 May 1942

0330 (M)   Submerged, commenced high periscope patrol.

1 June 1942

0558 (M)   Sighted PBY, distance about five miles.

4 June 1942

2000 (M)   Received first contact report from Comtaskfor Seven (040841)

5 June 1942

0810 (M)	Surfaced after receiving Comtaskfor Seven 041843. Proceeding at full speed to intercept Carrier Group.
1132 (M)	Sighted PBY bearing 270° relative.
1710 (M)	Changed course to proceed to new patrol station, assigned by Comtaskfor Seven 050325.
1900 (M)	Above message canceled, changed course to proceed to original patrol station.
2056 (M)	Changed course to proceed to patrol station assigned by Comtaskfor Seven 050629.

5 June 1942   [*Author's note: Crossed International Date Line*].

0353 (Y)	Submerged, commenced high periscope patrol on new station.
0743 (Y)	Surfaced, proceeded to patrol station assigned by Comtaskfor Seven 051909.
1459 (Y)	Sighted periscope dead astern, distance 2000 yards.
1510 (Y)	Arrived on station, commenced patrol.

7 June 1942

1700 (Y)	Received Comtaskfor Seven 080341 directing entry Midway to receive fuel and provisions.

8 June 1942

0715 (Y)	Moored port side to U.S.S. CACHALOT at dock, Midway.

USS *Flying Fish* (SS-229): First War Patrol[4]

4 June 1942

1917–2053 (Y)	60 miles from MIDWAY, on bearing 338°T. Heard a total of 10 explosions just about sunset, the last one farther away than the others, which had been heard in groups of two to three. The depth when

APPENDIX I • 113

	the first series were heard was 55 feet, with periscope and submerged antenna exposed. Increased depth temporarily, and surfaced at 2000 (Y). 8 minutes after surfacing sighted a low flying plane, burning running lights, broad on the port beam, estimated range 1500 yards, altitude 200 feet, and a zero angle on bow. Dove and surfaced 25 minutes later.
2100 (Y)	On station, 60 miles from MIDWAY. Radio intercepted a despatch from a plane stating that it had to make an emergency landing, followed up immediately by another despatch stating that it had landed safely. Simultaneously a glow was picked up from the bridge which lasted for only a short time. Believing it could have been the aircraft's landing flare, a course was set for its bearing and ran down that line for 13 miles without sighting anything.
2240 (Y)	Departed for new patrol station, 100 miles from MIDWAY, on the arc prescribed by CTF 7's despatch orders.
5 June 1942	
0310 (Y)	On 100 mile circle from MIDWAY. Sighted darkened ship in bright moonlight estimated range 5000–6000 yards and submerged for periscope approach. Upon closing the range identified target as U.S. submarine, patrolling at slow speed. Increased the range and when clear surfaced for morning sights. Morning fix shows ship to be in GUDGEON's area at the time of contact.
0753 (Y)	On 100 mile circle from MIDWAY. Surfaced and went to full power on four engines, closing MIDWAY in accordance with despatch orders from CTF 7.

1020 (Y)	50 miles from MIDWAY. Sighted Task Force 16 bearing 050° (T), distance 12,000 yards and passed it to port. Established emergency recognition with planes from that Force.
1300 (Y)	Arrived on station, 12 miles from MIDWAY and submerged to periscope depth until darkness. At 2340 (Y) received CTF 060609 directing change in station. Proceeded on four engines, opening distance from MIDWAY.

6 June 1942

0905 (Y)	Receive despatch orders from Task Force Commander to maintain prescribed course until 500 miles from MIDWAY, and continued at 3 engine speed upon reaching 200 mile circle. 1030 (Y) crossed International date line cruising west.

7 June 1942

2020 (M)	Lat. 31-31-00N., Long. 178-09-25E. Retired toward MIDWAY at dark, as directed by radio from the Force Commander. Nothing sighted before or after dark.

8 June 1942

0035 (M)	Retiring toward MIDWAY, course 130° (T). Reversed course in accordance with CTF 070700, and proceeded on two engines.
0804 (M)	Lat. 31-36-00N., Long. 177-47-30W. Sighted planes and masts of ships. Submerged but was unable to close the range. Surfaced, went to 4 engines to get in better attack position, and subsequently identified force sighted as Task Force 16. Exchanged calls with CTF 16 at 8,000 yards bearing 030° (T).
2135 (M)	Lat 31-14-10., Long. 177-06-00E. Set course for MIDWAY, as directed by CTF 7 despatch orders.

9 June 1942

2020 (M)	Lat 30-14-00N. Crossed International date line, cruising east.
1300 (Y)	Entered MIDWAY Lagoon. Ships present: NAUTILUS, GROUPER, CACHALOT, PLUNGER, and DOLPHIN.

USS *Gato* (SS-212): First War Patrol[5]

25 May 1942

0011 (L)	Changed course to take station off MIDWAY as directed by ComSubPac.

26 May 1942

1413 (L)	En route MIDWAY patrol station. Sighted airplane (Par. 6, No. 14). Radar contact which led to plane being sighted. Submerged until 1531 (L).

27 May 1942 (L) to 28 May 1942 (Y)

1412 (Y)	Enroute MIDWAY Patrol station, sighted airplane (Par. 6, No. 14).

29 May 1942

0352 (Y)	Arrived on patrol station west of MIDWAY.

30 May 1942

1517 (Y)	Sighted airplane (Par. 6, No. 15).

31 May 1942

0042 (Y)	Set course for MIDWAY to obtain fuel in accordance with ComTaskFor 7 instructions.
0527 (Y)	Sighted three airplanes (Par. 6, No. 16).
1114 (Y)	KURE ISLAND bore 000°T, 5 miles.

1521 (Y)	Secured at Pier, MIDWAY and commenced fueling.

1 June 1942

0519 (Y)	Underway from MIDWAY en route to patrol station.
1900 (Y)	Arrived on station, sighting numerous PBY's [sic] and B-17's [sic] patrolling out of MIDWAY while en route.

2 June 1942

	Patrolling in assigned sector on 200 mile circle west of MIDWAY.
0607 (Y)	Sighted airplane (Par. 6, No 17).

3 June 1942

	Patrolling in assigned sector on 200 mile circle west of MIDWAY.
0552 (Y)	Sighted airplane (Par. 6, No 18).
1410 (Y)	Sighted airplane (Par. 6, No 19).

4 June 1942

	Patrolling in assigned sector on 200 mile circle west of MIDWAY.
0745 (Y)	Surfaced and proceed at full power on course 080°T to close enemy forces located northwest of MIDWAY as directed by ComSubPac.
0935 (Y)	Radar contact airplane distance 12 miles.
1500 (Y)	Changed course to 320°T. No further reports of reports of position of enemy forces received and considered no contacts likely west of MIDWAY this late in the day.
1546 (Y)	Sighted airplane (Par. 6, No. 20). By flashing light obtained information from this plane that enemy forces bore 338°T from MIDWAY.
1555 (Y)	Sighted airplane (Par. 6, No 21).

1620 (Y)	Sighted airplane (Par. 6, No 22).
1720 (Y)	Changed course to 180°T and proceeded to station in sector on 100 mile circle west of MIDWAY.
5 June 1942	Patrolling in sector on 100 mile circle west of MIDWAY.
0405 (Y)	Sighted two DD's [*sic*] (Par. 5, No 34) angle on bow 000.
0410 (Y)	One of above DD's turned searchlight on GATO as we attempted to get on port beam. Submerged. No attempts made to search or A/S measures.
0526 (Y)	Sighted airplane (Par. 6, No 23).
0611 (Y)	Sighted airplane (Par. 6, No 24).
0723 (Y)	Surfaced. Proceeded at full power to station 5 miles west of MIDWAY as directed by ComSubPac.
0743 (Y)	Sighted flight of airplanes (Par. 5, No. 25). Submerged.
0817 (Y)	Surfaced.
0819 (Y)	Radar contact airplane 8–9 miles.
0859 (Y)	Radar contact airplane 18 miles.
0902 (Y)	Sighted flight of airplanes (Par. 6, No. 26). Submerged.
0931 (Y)	Surfaced.
0934 (Y)	Sighted airplane (Par. 6, No, 27).
0937 (Y)	Sighted airplanes (Par. 6, No 28). Cruiser type planes headed for GATO. After this vessel submerged enemy planes chased PBY for several miles then returned and patrolled in general location of this vessel for about 45 minutes.
1055 (Y)	Surfaced. Sighted airplane (Par. 6, No. 29). No opportunity to identify ship so submerged.
1116 (Y)	Surfaced.
1530 (Y)	Arrived on station 5 miles off MIDWAY. Modified to 12 mile circle during night.

6 June 1942	Patrolling in sector on 12 mile circle west of MIDWAY.
0946 (Y)	Proceeded to Pearl as directed by ComSubPac
1530 (Y)	Sighted airplane (Par. 6, No. 30).
1935 (Y)	Sighted vessel (Par. 5, No. 35). Maneuvered to clear area as own forces were known to be en route MIDWAY.

USS *Grayling* (SS-209): Second/Third War Patrol[6]

Patrol report indicates *Grayling* ended second war patrol at Pearl Harbor on May 16, 1942. Patrol report indicates *Grayling* departed on third war patrol from Pearl Harbor on July 14, 1942. Patrol report does not contain any information on Midway activities.

USS *Grenadier* (SS-210): Second War Patrol[7]

29 May 1942

1600 (Y)	Underway in accordance with despatch order from ComTaskForce 7, proceeding via assigned route to patrol station on the 200 mile circle bearing 310–330T from Midway, in addition to taking on fuel, water and provisions at Midway, made repairs to #1 electric still and renewed one cylinder liner in #3 engine.

31 May 1942

0400 (Y)	Arrived on station and took up patrol, running submerged during daylight.

1 June 1942

0930 (Y)	Patrolling on station.
	Sighted PBY plane patrolling on northwesterly course from Midway. Completed repairs to #3 engine and put it back in commission.

2 June 1942

0045 (Y)	Set course 225°T, shifting station in accordance with despatch instructions to patrol sector bearing 290°–310°T from Midway and to remain within 20 miles of center of sector chord.
0420 (Y)	Arrived on new station and took up submerged patrol.
0651 (Y)	Sighted PBY plane on patrol.
1440 (Y)	Sighted PBY plane on patrol.

3 June 1942 Patrolling on station.

0645 (Y)	Sighted a PBY plane patrolling on northwesterly course, well clear.

4 June 1942 Patrolling on station.

0615 (Y)	Intercepted plane contact report on enemy. 2 CL's [sic] and 1 BB bearing 320° distance 170 miles from Midway, course 135°T, speed 25 knots. Since this force was already beyond us, continued submerged patrol looking for other enemy units.
0744 (Y)	Sighted unidentified aircraft bearing 043T on southwesterly course. When plane turned and headed toward GRENADIER went to deep submergence.
0837 (Y)	Surfaced and proceeded toward Midway but was chased down by unidentified plane flying toward ship at 0855 (Y). When area was clear of aircraft, surfaced and continued on course toward Midway, hoping to intercept retiring enemy units.
1420 (Y)	Changed course to 0901T passed about 60 miles north of the island after intercepting a despatch from USS PORTLAND that she had been attacked 150 miles north of Midway. This was the first

	indication received as to where the action was taking place.
1539 (Y)	Forced down by large seaplane, probably a PBY, flying toward this ship. Continued surface running when area was clear.
2030 (Y)	In accordance with instructions from ComTaskForce 7, set course for new patrol station on the 100 mile circle from Midway, the sector bearing 290–300T.
2355 (Y)	Arrived on station.
5 June 1942	Patrolling on station.
0502 (Y)	While submerged at periscope depth, felt a strong explosion which seemed fairly close but nothing was sighted.
0848 (Y)	Surfaced and began retiring along median of section toward Midway in accordance with instructions.
1450 (Y)	Commenced patrolling on the 12 mile circle from Midway. Several PBY planes were sighted while enroute but all kept well clear.
6 June 1942	Patrolling on station.
0220 (Y)	Started shifting to new patrol station on sector bearing 250–260T from Midway.
0545 (Y)	Dived during morning twilight and resumed in and out patrol on surface.
1154 (Y)	Set course 132T, heading for Pearl, in accordance with despatch instructions from ComTaskForce 7.

USS *Grouper* (SS-214): First War Patrol[8]

4 June 1942

0331 (Y)	Dived expecting to sight the enemy at any moment.
0716 (Y)	Received message from CTF Seven giving position of enemy carriers and main body and ordering task group 7.1 less CACHALOT, CUTTLEFISH and FLYING FISH to go after them. Our position

	looked good so we remained submerged taking a course to intercept at 6 knots.
0726 (Y)	Manned battle stations.
0731 (Y)	Sighted a number of planes on the horizon bearing 210°T. The distance was too great to tell much about them but they appeared to be taking off from a carrier.
0751 (Y)	We were machine gunned and then bombed while running at 55 feet with 12 feet of periscope exposed in order to sight enemy carriers. I could see numerous splashes all around the ship and the last few bombs were quite heavy. Increased depth to 140 feet.
0807 (Y)	Bombed again. Very close. Changed course.
0818 (Y)	Heard a large number of explosions at a greater distance believed, at the time, to be our own planes bombing enemy carriers.
0830 (Y)	Came up to periscope depth.
0832 (Y)	Sighted anti-aircraft bursts from three ships, over the horizon, bearing 255°T to 263°T. No explosions could be heard.
0839 (Y)	Sighted a large number of various type planes scattered throughout the sky between bearings 255°T and 263°T. Numerous dog fights appeared to be going on in and out of the light clouds. Changed course to close the firing ships.
0855 (Y)	Sighted a large number of planes, not in formation, bearing 216°T. Some appeared to be bombers but no time was wasted with a periscope exposure to merely identify planes as the Japs were too good at spotting submarines and the sea was glassy calm with bright sunlight and a few scattered clouds in the sky.
0856 (Y)	Raised periscope again to find a Type "O" fighter diving into the upper window with a machine gun and cannon firing. The cannon shells were

	heard exploding very close to the conning tower. Ordered 140 feet.
0858 (Y)	Bombed again on the way to 140 feet.
0917 (Y)	A series of 10 to 12 heavy explosions resembling depth charges were heard close aboard. I had been making a quick sweep in low power each time the periscope was exposed using the remainder of the exposure in high power to search for the carriers ahead. Nothing had been sighted astern and nothing had been heard on the sound equipment. Depth was increased to 250 feet as it seemed the planes could see us at 140 feet.
0930 (Y)	We were depth charged from 0930 to 1114. From 10 to 12 charges were dropped on each attack. Attacks took places at 0930, 0936, 0940, 1010, 1011, 1014, 1019, 1020, 1027 and 1114. At 1005 we started for periscope depth to see if we were being bombed or depth charged and to take a shot at any one that was depth charging us. We could hear nothing on the sound equipment. On reaching 140 feet the explosions became so close that depth was again increased to 250 feet.
1140 (Y)	Came up to periscope depth and sighted smoke from two burning ships bearing 311°T to close and sink the burning ships which were believed to be carriers.
1141 (Y)	Bombed again. Increased depth to 140 feet and continued closing burning ships.
1314 (Y)	Heard several heavy explosions and changed course to 290°T thinking the range to the first burning ship might have been underestimated and we did not want it to blow up and sink on top of us. Did not come up to check position as we did not desire to attract any more bombs and also had hopes of arriving at a position between the ships so we could sink them both with one trip to periscope depth.

1410 (Y)	Started for periscope depth to check position of burning ships.
1420 (Y)	Started a quick sweep in a low power and the first thing sighted was a HIBIKI class DD close aboard on the starboard quarter. The DD was picking up speed and turning towards us. Ordered 250 feet. No time to make a set up or to fire circulars.
1422 (Y)	Destroyer passed over ship. Depth charge pattern five starboard and six port. Propeller noises very loud for a few seconds throughout the ship. Sound picked him up about the same time as I did and reported that he slowed down as soon as he crossed over. We were then depth charged until 1927. Four or five charges being dropped at each of the following times: 1429, 1446, 1504, 1615, 1705, 1725, 1732, 1750, 1835, 1917, 1925 and 1927.
1930 (Y)	Decided to come up to 120 feet and fire circulars. 120 feet seemed just as safe at 180 feet and I was sure of better torpedo and tube performance at that depth.
1959 (Y)	Fired right circular, as slow speed, from bow tubes.
2004 (Y)	One explosion that sounded like a torpedo hit.
2016 (Y)	Fired right circular, at slow speed, from stern tubes.
2231 (Y)	Surfaced and proceeded to eastern part of sector to get in a battery charge before we had to dive again.
2313 (Y)	Received message from CTF Seven directing GROUPER to take station for periscope patrol in sector 310°T to 320°T distance 100 miles from Midway. Proceeded to assigned station at 17 knots.

5 June 1942

0730 (Y)	Received message from CTF Seven ordering task group 7.1 to surface and proceed to 5 mile circle from Midway remaining in same sectors. Surfaced and proceeded at 19 knots.

0845 (Y)	Sighted plane on horizon.
0850 (Y)	Unable to identify plane. Dived to 150 feet changing course on the way down.
0917 (Y)	One heavy explosion astern. Bomb or depth charge dropped in position where we dived. Decided to remain submerged thinking the enemy force must be headed for Midway along our track and if we stayed down we could avoid air screens and get in an attack.
1118 (Y)	Sighted PBY headed for Midway and decided enemy must not be in vicinity or there would be some fighters after the PBY. Surfaced and proceeded at 19 knots.
1207 (Y)	Sighted two fighters diving out of the clouds above and astern of us. Dived to 200 feet.
1245 (Y)	Heard echo ranging and came to periscope depth. Sighted friendly task force making high speed range 7000 yards.
1325 (Y)	Own forces clear. Surfaced and proceeded at 19 knots.
1347 (Y)	Sighted 7 heavy or medium bombers coming out of the clouds overhead. Dived. Ship seemed to hang at 160 feet and the diving officer flooded more water into auxiliary thinking air pockets in the main ballast tanks, that would give our position away if vented, were holding the ship up. Negative had already been blown. About this time both torpedo rooms and the air manifold station reported sea pressure gauges approaching 200 lbs. At the same time the needles of the deep reading depth gauges in the control room swung around and hit the pegs. The diving officer reported we were below 500 feet. All tanks were blown. All sea pressure gauges were well beyond the 200 lb. calibration. We came up at full speed with about a

	30° up angle until bow buoyancy could be vented and the air to the forward group of tanks secured. The depth charge switch was in and kept the overload relays from kicking out. Leveled off at 230 feet and surfaced slowly. No planes in sight. The best estimate of maximum depth reached is 600 feet aft, where sea pressure gauges in the after torpedo room and maneuvering room hit the stops at about 260 lbs. Proceeded at 15 knots, inspecting for damage. A number of electrical cables had been pushed in a couple of inches, the cast iron plugs in the water manifolds for the generator coolers had been flying around the engine room like machine gun bullets, large quantities of water had been taken in through the stern tubes and everyone had a few more gray hairs. No other serious damage noted.
1455 (Y)	Made test dive to 200 feet to check cable leaks that had been tightened.
1536 (Y)	Surfaced and proceeded on assigned mission at 19 knots.
1848 (Y)	Arrive on station. Sighted four friendly submarines.
6 June 1942	
0140 (Y)	Received message from CTF Seven to proceed 200 miles bearing 310°T from Midway looking for 2 BBs 3 CAs 10 DDs and 2 burning CVs. Proceeded at 17 knots.
0324 (Y)	Lookout sighted a periscope on the port beam distance about 2 miles. Lookout conned ship to place periscope astern until it was picked up by O.O.D. and C.O. Propellers were stopped in order not to increase the range too much.
0833 (Y)	The O.O.D. and I both sighted the periscope and one torpedo was fired from the stern tubes set to run at slow speed. Periscope disappeared shortly

	after firing. No explosion noted. Proceeded on assigned mission notifying a passing PBY of the submarine's presence. The PBY informed us there was a plane down five miles astern. Returned to investigate and sighted what appeared to be a plane sinking. It came up again as a large whale. Resumed course along assigned route.
1005 (Y)	Received message from CTF Seven to continue another 300 miles on three engines.
7 June 1942	
1538 (M)	Received message from CTF Seven to retire toward Midway if no contacts made by dark.
1946 (M)	Reversed course and slowed to 14 knots.
8 June 1942	
0148 (M)	Received message from CTF Seven to continue chase. Reversed course.
9 June 1942	
0000 (M)	Received message from CTF Seven to proceed to Midway for fuel and stores in preparation for a patrol.

USS *Gudgeon* (SS-211): Third War Patrol[9]

26 May 1942	
0900 (VW)	Underway in accordance with Comtaskfor Seven dispatch 060015 May 1942. Picked up escort at entrance buoys and proceeded toward Kauai Channel.
0945 (VW)	Sighted large U.S. task force of two carriers, several cruisers and destroyers and maneuvered to avoid. Hot stern tube gland prevented speeds in excess of 12 knots.

1246 (VW)	Made trim dive in center of Kauai Channel in company with escort. Went to 150 feet, no leaks.
1418 (VW)	Surfaced. Zig zagging in company with escort until dark.
1800	Changed time to zone plus 11.
27 May 1942	Uneventful day spent running in engines, stowing gear and field day. Sighted patrol plane (PBY) which kept well clear.
28 May 1942	
0458 (X)	Made training dive and cruised at 55 feet testing loop and vertical antenna reception.
0900 (X)	Made battle surface and fired 5 practice rounds. Results indicated more practice needed.
1311 (X)	Sighted patrol plane (PBY) who turned to attack course. Exchanged identification but he persisted on attack course. When he had closed to two miles dove to 100 feet and remained for one hour.
1454 (X)	Surfaced and continued on mission.
29 May 1942	
0757 (X)	Made training dive to 250 feet, no appreciable leaks.
1017 (X)	Surfaced in sight of patrol plane (PBY) he stayed well clear. Did not exchange identification signals.
30 May 1942	
0600 (X)	Dove to 55 feet and stayed submerged to kill time. Due to change in orders by CTF 7 262158 of May 1942 calling for periscope patrol instead of surface patrol on station decided not to enter sector until after dark.
1400 (X)	Held battle surface and fired 5 practice rounds of 3" ammunition. Much improvement noted.

1700 (X)   Held 50 caliber machine gun practice and fired several bursts. Practiced with sub-machine guns.

31 May 1942

0000   Changed time to zone plus 12 time.
0330 (Y)   On station patrolling sector chord.
0430 (Y)   Dove, sighted many U.S. aircraft patrols during day.
1935 (Y)   Surfaced.

1–3 June 1942   Uneventful patrol. Sighted usual aircraft patrol. CTF 7 020303 changed station to circle in center of chord.

4 June 1942

0410 (Y)   Dove on station.
0715 (Y)   Received CTF 7 041843 of June 1942 indicating contact on enemy carrier.
0744 (Y)   Surfaced and proceeded on course 170°T at full speed to intercept. Continuous radar plane contacts from 10 to 30 miles. It is believed that a directional radar could have led me to the carriers for large formation plane contacts are plainly discernible. Decided to dive for planes within 10 miles. Planes reported at 8 miles. Decided to dive when planes within six miles.
0842 (Y)   Sighted large heavy tops of two vessels bearing 020°T on course 250°T, turned to normal approach course and studied them. Appearance indicated two Japanese BB's similar to Haruna with heavy forward tower, one stack close behind and stick mast aft. Dove to attack at full speed. First periscope observation showed many planes conducting dive bombing attack. Closed on normal approach course for 45 minutes, did not sight targets again. Did not see anti-aircraft bursts.

0938 (Y)	Sighted large formation of Japanese planes in three layers proceeding toward area from south (20 to 30 planes, did not count them). They turned and headed west. Decided my area might be rendezvous point for returning planes and carriers due to these two contacts and decided to stay submerged and await developments. Heading on course 350°T speed 2 knots. Plenty of visual evidence that U.S. planes had made these contacts so decided not to send in contact reports.
1130 (Y)	No carriers. Felt I should proceed to a better station but had no idea which way to go. Decided to await a new contact report. Only missed 10 messages on schedule so far. Continuous plane contacts made surfacing dangerous unless an attack is foreseen.
1400 to 1600 (Y)	Sighted several single Japanese dive bombers on course west. They passed close aboard. Believed them to be strays from Midway attack.
1600 (Y)	Back on station and undecided as to next move. Could hear bombs exploding at great distance through hull.
1925 (Y)	Just before surfacing and cruising with vertical antenna up got plane contact on radar, distance decreasing fast. Decided it was too dark for him to see us and left vertical up to catch long message coming in.
1928 (Y)	Bomb exploded fairly close aboard. Sounded like a Japanese bomb. Went to 100 feet and stayed for 30 minutes.
2028 (Y)	Surfaced on station.
2100 (Y)	Proceeding to new station on 100 mile circle.

5 June 1942

0222 (Y)	Arrived new station.
0335 (Y)	Dove to 55 feet.
0532 (Y)	Sighted PT boat and usual morning patrol planes.

0720 (Y)	Received orders to new station.
0725 (Y)	Sighted PT boat.
0730 (Y)	Surfaced and proceeded to new station, 12 miles bearing 345 from Midway.
1000 (Y)	Six U.S. dive bombers dove at us from the sun. Too late to dive, pulled flare. Planes acknowledged and proceeded to eastward.
1030 (Y)	Sighted large U.S. force of two carriers, 5 heavy cruisers and several destroyers, exchanged identification with one carrier and they proceeded westward.
1315 (Y)	Exchanged calls with N.A.S. Midway.
1326 (Y)	Pulled identification flare and dove on new station and patrolled on course 345–165°T on a four mile leg.
1920 (Y)	Surfaced lying to on course 345°T charging batteries. Ready battery motors.
2145 (Y)	Large bomber with running lights on heading directly for this vessel and Midway. Do not believe he saw me but he turned on landing lights which might have picked me up. Fired Very star of proper color. Plane veered away, circled close aboard and proceeded to Midway to land. Recognition signals have been invaluable this trip.

6 June 1942

0000 (Y)	Received CTF 7 0606069 June. (It was noted that six hours elapsed between originating time and TOR).
0005 (Y)	Went ahead full speed for new station, 200 mile circle bearing 310 from Midway.
0945 (Y)	Went to 3 engine speed proceeding 500 mile circle on same bearing. Sighted many patrol planes and exchanged identification with light.
1132 (Y)	Crossed 180th meridian. Changed date June 7.

1932 (M)	In accordance with CTF 7 070035 retired at two engine speed, course 130°T.

8 June 1942

0100 (M)	Received CTF 7 070700 of June 1942 (also six hours between time originated and TOR. 18 hours of advancing the search were thus lost.)
0117 (M)	Changed course to 320°T and continued search.
0552 (M)	In latitude 31-26N, longitude 178-47E sighted unidentified vessel on horizon bearing 240°T, dove and closed to identify. Observed two U.S. destroyers of 398 class, apparently echo ranging on course 320°T, retired on course opposite to theirs for two miles then on course perpendicular for two miles.
0839 (M)	Surfaced, nothing in sight. Continued search on course 320°T.
1530 (M)	Received CTF 7 080217 of June 1942, later part could not be decoded. Sent position and fuel report.

9 June 1942

0000 (M)	Received CTF 7 080730 ordering this vessel to return to Pearl Harbor, T.H.

USS *Nautilus* (SS-168): First War Patrol[10]

4 June

0420 (Y)	Submerged on course 040°T.
0544 (Y)	Intercepted message that many planes were headed for Midway from a point 320°T from Midway distance about 150 miles. This was on the northern boundary of NAUTILUS area and we were close to this point. Swept horizon continuously.

0658 (Y)	Sighted a formation of air planes resembling Army Flying Fortresses dead ahead.
0710 (Y)	Sighted bombing on bearing 331°T. NAUTILUS position Lat. 30-00 N, Long. 179-25 W. Changed course to 340°T and went to battle stations submerged.
0755 (Y)	Saw masts over horizon. While making this observation we were strafed by aircraft. Changed depth to 100 feet. Echo ranging first heard at this time.
0800 (Y)	Sighted a formation of four ships. One battleship of ISE class and one cruiser drew toward the starboard bow, two other cruisers toward the port bow. Decided to attack the battleship and changed course to draw ahead. Sighted and bombed by plane. A cruiser of the JINTSU class approached to attack with depth charges. At least two ships were echo ranging on the NAUTILUS.
0810 (Y)	JINTSU class cruiser dropped pattern of 5 depth charges followed seven minutes later by a pattern of 6 depth charges.
0819 (Y)	Went to 90 feet to avoid scouting planes. Nine depth charges dropped at distance of about 1000 yards. When attack ceased, planed up to periscope depth to observe.
0824 (Y)	The picture presented on raising the periscope was one never experienced in peacetime practices. Ships were on all sides moving across the field at high speed and circling away to avoid the submarine's position. Ranges were above 3000 yards. The JINTSU class cruiser had passed over and was now astern. The battleship was on our port bow and firing her whole starboard broadside battery at the periscope. Flag hoists were being made; searchlights were trained at the periscope.

APPENDIX I • 133

	The exact position of the NAUTILUS may have been known by the enemy at this time because #9 deck torpedo was running hot in the tube as a result of the shearing of the torpedo retaining pin during the depth charging. Periscope estimate was made on the battleship and put on the Torpedo Data Computer. Range estimated at 4500 yards, angle on the bow 80° starboard, speed 25 knots.
0825 (Y)	Fired #1 tube at battleship followed by #2 tube with a 1° right offset. After firing #2 it was found that #1 had not fired. Battleship changed course to the left and headed directly away. Range to battleship had now increased to 5000 yards and track was 180°. Held further fire. During this time echo ranging by surface ships was continuous and accurate. Immediately after our firing at the battleship, the JINTSU type cruiser headed for NAUTILUS.
0830 (Y)	Went to 150 feet. Depth charge attack began.
0846 (Y)	Ordered periscope depth. Battleship and other accompanying ships, except JINTSU type cruiser, were well out of range. Echo ranging by cruiser was still accurate.
0900 (Y)	Raised periscope and sighted aircraft carrier bearing 013° relative. Carrier was distant 16,000 yards and was changing course continuously. She did not appear to be damaged, but was overhung by anti-aircraft bursts. NAUTILUS was on a converging course. While making this observation the JINTSU type cruiser began to close again at high speed.
0910 (Y)	When cruiser reached 2500 yards fired #2 torpedo tube. Cruiser was observed to change course.
0918 (Y)	A cruiser attacked with 6 depth charges. These were more accurately placed than previous charges.

	Went to 200 feet, used evasive tactics at slow speed, but continued advance to close the carrier. Cruiser continued echo ranging and at 0933 two of her depth charges landed close.
0955 (Y)	Echo ranging ceased. Ordered periscope depth to estimate the situation. On looking found that the entire formation first seen, including the attacking cruisers had departed. The carrier previously seen was no longer in sight.
1029 (Y)	Saw 3 masts on the horizon bearing 005°T distance 10 miles. Changed course to 005°T. Raised the vertical antenna and intercepted a radio message stating that a CV was damaged. Large clouds of grey smoke were seen at four places over the horizon. The nearest cloud of smoke had not previously been sighted, so continued to close it at the best speed that the condition of the battery and probable future operations for the day would allow.
1047 (Y)	Sighted three planes approaching. Lowered periscope and vertical antenna and continued approach at periscope depth.
1145 (Y)	Identified the source of smoke as a burning carrier. The carrier was still about 8 miles away and was in latitude 30°-13' N., Longitude 179°-17 W. Decided to overtake if possible and to attack.
1224 (Y)	Range not having decreased appreciably changed speed to two-thirds ahead on both motors after estimating that sufficient battery capacity just remained for operations until night fall.
1253 (Y)	Range decreased. Sighted two cruisers escorting the carrier. Tentatively identified CV as a carrier of the SORYU class. The carrier was on even keel and the hull appeared to be undamaged. There were no flames and the fire seemed to be under control. Accompanying cruisers were about two miles ahead of the carrier.

1300 (Y)	The CV, which had been making 2–3 knots when the approach began, was now stopped. At closer range it was seen that efforts were being made by boats under her bow to pass a towing hawser and many men were seen working on the forecastle.
	The decision had to be made in which order to attack the targets presented. Attack on the cruisers and later on the carrier was considered, but the remaining capacity of the battery would not allow a further chase of several miles to catch the moving cruisers, even if it were possible to overtake them. The decision was therefore made to complete the destruction of the CV before she could be repaired or taken in tow. Approach continued at periscope depth. An apparent course was chosen to give torpedo hits on the starboard or island side of the carrier. During the next hour a repeated check was made of the silhouettes of American and Japanese carriers in order to be certain of the identity of the target. The target was a carrier of the SORYU class.
1359 (Y)	Fired three torpedoes at the carrier from periscope depth. Attempts to fire the 4th torpedo were unsuccessful. Immediately prior to firing each torpedo, the Torpedo Data computer generated bearing was checked by periscope bearing. Mean run of torpedoes was 2700 yards. The wakes of the torpedoes were observed through the periscope until the torpedoes struck the target. Red flames appeared along the length of the ship from the bow to amidships. The fire which had first attracted us to the attack had been underneath the demolished after flight deck and was nearly extinguished by the time the NAUTILUS reached the firing point.

	This fire again broke out. Boats drew away from the bow and many men were seen going over the side. All 5 officers in the conning tower observed the results of the torpedoing.
1405 (Y)	Fired last of three torpedoes at the carrier. Cruisers began reversing course at high speed and started to echo range.
1410 (Y)	Cruiser passed directly over the top of the NAUTILUS. Changed course to 190°T and went to 300 feet. A prolonged depth charge attack now began.
1610 (Y)	Came to periscope depth. Saw carrier, but the escorting cruisers were no longer in sight. They had abandoned the carrier and she was afire along the entire length.
1800 (Y)	Heavy black smoke enveloped the carrier and formed a cloud over the ship to a height of a thousand feet. The officer making this observation compared the cloud to the oil smoke which arose from the U.S.S. ARIZONA when that ship burned at Pearl Harbor, T.H., December 7–9. Nothing could be seen of the carrier's hull.
1840 (Y)	Heard heavy subsurface explosions and went to depth charge stations. A search by periscope failed to reveal any object in the vicinity except the still greater cloud of black smoke from burning oil. If the carrier was not found by patrol planes which searched the vicinity the following morning, the Commanding Officer believes that she was destroyed at this time by fire and internal explosions. He did not however actually see her sink.
1941 (Y)	Surfaced with exhausted battery and returned to NAUTILUS patrol area. Five torpedoes expended, forty-two depth charges received. On surfacing no smoke or flame of any sort was seen.

5 June 1942

0414 (Y)	Submerged.
0720 (Y)	Surfaced in accordance with orders and proceeded at best speed for Midway.
0906 (Y)	Driven down by enemy plane.
1133 (Y)	Driven down by enemy plane.
1520 (Y)	Driven down by enemy plane.
1745 (Y)	Arrived on station.
6 June 1942	Uneventful.
7 June 1942	Received orders to proceed Midway for fuel and provisions. Arrived at 1930 (Y).

USS *Tambor* (SS-198): Third War Patrol[11]

21 May 1942

1400	Underway from Submarine Base, Pearl Harbor, T.H. in accordance with operation order.
1508	Formed cruising formation with GRAYLING and TROUT. Guide center in TAMBOR. WASMUTH and LAMBERTON joined formation as A/S screen. Proceeded to northwestward through KAUAI Channel.
1900	Made trim dive.
1938	Surfaced. Dismissed escorts. Directed TROUT and GRAYLING to proceed independently in accordance with operation order.
2000	Position Lat. 21-3904 N. Long. 158-38 W. Weather cloudy. Wind N. force 2 visibility good, sea E. force 2.

22 May 1942

0800	Position 23-49 N. Long. 159-56.5 W. Course 332 T. speed 15 knots.

0900	Set clocks back ½ hour to zone +10 time, changed course to 294 T.
1200	Position Lat. 24-08.3 N. Long. 160-35 W. Since departure Pearl average speed 12 knots distance made good 270.1 miles.
2000	Position Lat. 24-49.2 N. Long. 162-17.2 W.

23 May 1942

0800	Position Lat. 25-55.4 N. Long. 164-58.8 W.
0900	Set clocks back ½ hour to zone +10½ time.
1035	Made training dive. Exercised at battle stations submerged.
1200	Position Lat. 26-10 N., Long. 165-47 W. Distance last 24 hours 308 miles. Average speed 12.6 knots.
1313	Fired 4 rounds from 3" gun and exercised machine guns.
2020	Position by D.R. Lat. 26-43 N., Long. 167-22 W. Weather overcast, wind NW, force 3, visibility fair, sea NW force 3.

24 May 1942

0800	Position by D.R. Lat 27-50 N., Long 169-55.5 W.
0900	Set clocks back ½ hour to zone +11 time.
1045	Made training dive. Exercised at battle stations submerged.
1200	Position by D.R. Lat. 28-15 N., Long. 170-53 W., Distance made good last 24 hours 301½ miles. Average speed 12.3 knots.
1411	Task Group 7.1 augmented and now composed as follows: Six SS on 150 mile circle between bearing 240 T and 360 T. from Midway. Four SS on 200 mile circle between bearings 250 T and 330 T from Midway. Two SS on 60 mile circle between 315 T and 338 T. from Midway. Names and task group numbers of additional SS not furnished.

2000	Position by D.R. Lat. 29-01 N., Long. 172-42 W. Weather overcast, wind variable force 2, visibility fair, sea NE, force 3.

25 May 1942

0536	Changed course to 270 T.
0800	Position Lat. 30-02 N., Long. 175-33.3 W. Weather cloudy. Sea Moderate.
0900	Set clocks back ½ hour to zone +11½ time.
1046	Made training dive. Exercised at battle stations submerged.
1200	Position Lat. 30-03 N., Long. 176-32 W., Distance made good last 24 hours 330 miles. Average speed 13.4 knots.
1739	Changed course to 214 T.
2000	Position Lat. 29-31 N., Long. 178-23 W.

26 May 1942

0500	Arrived on station. Commenced surface patrol at 5 knots, courses 340 and 160. Mid point of patrol being point 150 miles bearing 250 from Sand Island Light, Midway Islands.
0800	Position Lat. 27-24.1 N., Long. 180-00 W. Weather fine. Sea calm.
0900	Set clocks back ½ hour to zone +12 time.
1034	Made training dive. Exercised at battle stations submerged.
1200	Position Lat. 27-34 N., Long. 179-53 W.
2000	Position Lat. 27-17.2 N., Long. 180-00 W.

27 May 1942

0800	Position Lat. 29-24.2 N., Long. 179-58 E. Noted current 258 T. set .53 knot. Weather clear. Sea calm.
1034	Made training dive. Exercised at battle stations submerged.

1200	Position Lat. 27-22 N., Long. 179-57 E.
1445	Sighted two Catalina patrol planes.

28 May 1942

0705	Sighted Catalina patrol plane out from MIDWAY.
0800	Position Lat. 27-16 N., Long. 179-52 E.
1031	Made training dive. Exercised at battle stations submerged.
1101	Exercised at battle surface. Fired two rounds from 3" gun.
1200	Position Lat. 27-20 N., Long. 179-58.2 E.
2000	Position Lat. 27-27 N., Long. 179-57.5 E.

29 May 1942

0715	Sighted Catalina patrol plane out from Midway
0800	Position Lat. 27-16 N., Long. 179-52 E. Weather clear. Sea calm.
1041	Made training dive. Exercised at battle stations submerged.
1116	Exercised at quick emergence and machine gun attack. Fired .50 cal., .30 cal. and submachine guns.
1200	Position Lat. 27-25.6 N., Long. 179-58.5 E.
2000	Position Lat. 27-28.4 N., Long. 179-56.0 E.

30 May 1942

0639	Sighted two Catalina patrol planes out from MIDWAY.
0800	Position Lat. 27-18 N., Long 179-59 E. Weather clear. Sea calm.
0900	Received message from Com Task Force Seven. Enemy submarine approaching MIDWAY. Position at 0830, (+12), 345 miles bearing 230 from MIDWAY on course 045, speed 18.

0908	Changed course to 153 T. heading for southern boundary of area.
0930	Received message from Com Task Force Seven changing original orders. Vessels of Task Group 7.1 ordered to maintain submerged patrol during daylight and be ready to surface and pursue enemy units.
1030	Commenced submerged patrol.
1855	Surfaced. Weather clear. Sea calm.

31 May 1942

0439	Submerged.
0900	Intercepted message to Task Forces Sixteen and Seventeen directing them to converge on Lat. 32-00 N., Long. 173-00 W. daily. Task Force Sixteen to operate North and West; Task Force Seventeen North and East of this point.
1905	Surfaced. Weather clear. Sea calm.

1 June 1942

0438	Submerged.
0900	Intercepted message from Cincpac reporting contacts by Midway air patrols at 2200 G.C.T. May 31. One MITSUBISHI two engined heavy bomber bearing 262 T. 450 miles from MIDWAY and one four-motored bomber bearing 213, 480 miles from MIDWAY.
1300	Intercepted message assigning GROUPER designation G7.1.7 and patrol station between 320 T. and 340 T. from MIDWAY, at radius of 150 miles.
1909	Surfaced. Weather clear. Sea calm.
2000	Intercepted Cincpac Bulletin giving location of enemy unit by DF as 26-00 N., 178-00 E.

2 June 1942

0430	Submerged.
0800	Received message from CTF7 to G7.1 directing each submarine this task group to operate within a circle of 20 miles radius from center of patrol line. FLYING FISH and CACHALOT excepted. Own surface forces, including carriers, may operation eastward of 180° Longitude.
1919	Surfaced. Weather clear. Sea calm.

3 June 1942

0425	Submerged.
0430	Received instructions from Com Task Force Seven regarding reports. The success of our forces in the coming battle will depend on timely and accurate contact and damage reports.
0953	Patrol planes contacted two Jap cargo vessels 470 miles, 247 T. from MIDWAY; and eleven Jap ships including warships, 261 T., 700 miles from MIDWAY at 2100 G.C.T.
1000	Intercepted information Bulletin substance as follows. Japanese forces include the following: Special repair units to refit and repair flying facilities, special planes for MIDWAY aboard aircraft tenders and carriers, ground crews, munition supplies, landing force, guns captured at WAKE. Heavy bombers and patrol planes standing by at WAKE. Primary objective is EASTERN ISLAND.
1230	Intercepted message from Cincpac. The force sighted is believed to be the combined occupation and attack forces. Striking force is expected to be separate.
1300	Received further intelligence of forces sighted the A.M. Force consists of eleven ships on course 090 T. speed 19 knots.

1916	Surfaced.
1940	Sighted running lights of two unidentified planes. Submerged for twenty minutes.
2100	Further intelligence gives composition enemy attack and occupation group as 2–3 BB, 2–3 CA and other units to a total of eleven vessels on course 090 T speed 18 knots.
2353	Further information states that occupation and attack force includes 1 CV. Force attacked by B-17 bomber and one battleship and one transport set afire.

4 June 1942

0047	Intelligence reports air patrol sighted a large submarine being serviced by submarine tender seven hundred miles bearing 261 T. from Midway.
0332	Received report of moonlight torpedo attack by aircraft on enemy attack and occupation force. No information on results.
0415	Submerged. Weather clear. Sea calm.
0426	Report of moonlight torpedo attack: One hit on large transport. Enemy force now consists of 10 ships 500 miles bearing 260 T. from MIDWAY.
0525	Sighted Catalina patrol plane headed west.
0615	Enemy planes reported approaching MIDWAY, distant 150 miles, bearing 320 T.
0720	Patrol plane contacted Striking Force, 180 miles from MIDWAY on course 135 T at 25 knots. Heavy bombers despatched to intercept this force.
0750	Received orders to surface and proceed to attack this force.
0750	Surfaced, course 090 T.
0755	Radar contact on plane 18 miles, plane moved in to 9 miles. Submerged. Changed course to 070 T.
0821	Surfaced, speed 18 knots.

0829	First report of initial attack on MIDWAY. A.A. shot down 18 Jap planes. Power house EASTERN ISLAND destroyed. Minor damage to runways.
0853	Changed course to 030 T.
0910	Radar contact on plane distant 12 miles, closing rapidly. Submerged. Plane not sighted.
0913	Changed course to 090 T.
0940	Surfaced. Set course 040 T. at 18 knots.
1000	Heavy bomber reports damaging one heavy cruiser of Striking Force.
1200	Position Lat. 28-02.7 N., Long. 179-37.1 W.
1201	From Cincpac: Our aircraft attacking striking force, sighted two CA and eight to ten other ships. Force screened by fighters to 10 miles from formation. Dive bombers scored two hits on heavy cruiser. Attack and occupation force are now 330 miles from MIDWAY bearing 265 T. Possibly a CV or BB in this force.
1204	Sighted Catalina patrol plane on course 070 T.
1248	Carrier reported last sighted on course 125 T. speed 18, 320 T., 135 miles from MIDWAY at 2130 June 4. Summary of damage: to enemy attack and occupation force torpedo hit on transport, bomb hit on battleship; to striking force, two bomb hits on carrier and carrier burning, two torpedo or bomb hits on battleship.
1505	Enemy forces in Lat 30-38 N., Long. 179-30 W. reported attacked by air groups of task forces 16 and 17. Probably composition of enemy force as follows: 4 CV, 2 BB, 4 CA, and 6 DD. Attack occurred between 0930 and 1130 L.C.T. All four carriers badly damaged. Two other heavy ships hit.
1556	Changed course to 020 T.
1604	Sighed several unidentified planes, bearing 285 T., distant 8 miles, submerged.

1705	Surfaced. Speed 18 knots.
1810	Three burning ships reported 170 miles, 338 T. from MIDWAY.
1814	Changed course to 006 T.
1825	Three enemy ships reported badly damaged and burning 170 miles bearing 320 from MIDWAY. Note: We don't know which bearing, 320 or 338, is correct.
1831	Changed course to 325 T.
1842	Com Task Force Seventeen Flag in ASTORIA. YORKTOWN badly damaged and dead in water. Task Force 17 will cover YORKTOWN and Task Force Sixteen will continue to pursue and engage enemy.
1900	Patrol plane reports three burning ships of striking force are carriers. Two cruisers and four destroyers undamaged bearing 320 T. 170 miles from MIDWAY.
1922	Task unit 7.1.6 (1SS) ordered by CTF7 to investigate burning ships bearing 320 T. 170 miles from MIDWAY
1950	Intelligence indicates one Jap CV possibly still operating. 20 B-17s attacked one CA and left it burning at 0500 GCT 5th. No position.
2000	Position Lat. 29-42 N., Long. 179-54 W.
2018	Slowed to five knots. Assumed that message containing new instructions was missed while submerged. Waiting for 2100 Fox Schedule on Radio.
2027	Intercepted information that NAUTILUS scored three hits on damaged carrier of SORYU class at 1400 L.C.T.
2115	Orders from Com Task Force Seven: 12 submarines of Task Group 7.1 to form on circle at radius of 100 miles from MIDWAY. Each submarine

	assigned a ten degree sector between bearings 230 and 350 True from MIDWAY. All units to arrive on station and dive before dawn. Encounters with friendly surface forces during night possible. TAMBOR assigned 250 T. to 260 T.
2117	Changed course to 185 T., speed 18 knots.
2119	4 CA, 2 AO, 2AK reported 400 miles, 264 T. from MIDWAY on course 085, speed 12 at 0945 L.C.T. and 8 cruisers on course 080 T, 25 knots, 430 miles 265 T. from MIDWAY at 1000 L.C.T.
2207	Intercepted report of attack on striking force by Task Force 16 between 1700 and 1800 L.C.T. 1 CV attacked by bombers, hit and left burning, four bomb hits on battleship. At 1745 enemy force retiring to westward from position L30-40 N., L177-41 W., at 15 knots.
2250	Fortresses from PEARL reports sighting three burning ships, and scored three hits on one of these, bearing 320° 170 miles from MIDWAY. Also sighted two other burning ships 125 miles on same bearing.
2346	Sighted submarine on starboard bow. Assumed to be friendly. Changed course to 160 T.
2349	Changed course to 140 T.
5 June 1942	
0005	Resumed course 185 T. Submarine no longer in sight.
0215–0602	Encounter with Japanese CA's [*sic*] and DD's. At 0215 in position 279 T, 89 miles from MIDWAY, on course 185 T speed 18.5 knots, weather clear, sea calm, sighted the loom of four large ships on the horizon distributed across our bow. Estimated range 3 miles. Estimated angle on the bow 45 port.

Ignorant of the location and exact composition of our own surface forces and forewarned that they might cross the submarine area during the night, we turned to starboard (at 0217) to shadow these ships from the westward (it being just after moonrise) and try to identify them by silhouette. While turning three other ships were sighted to the southwestward with small angle on the bow. We put these astern of us, steadying on course 030 T. We maintained speed 18 knots. They drew slowly to starboard. At 0229, having lost contact, we changed course to the left to 270 T. and at 0234 again to the left to 180 T. Regained contact at 0238, the ships bearing southwestward and heading northward. Changed course to 000 T. to parallel them. At 0251 they altered course to the left and we came left with them to 310 T., and seven minute later to 270 T., trying to get them in the moonstream. At 0306 lost contact and came left to 250 T. Regained contact at 0311, with the ships in south edge of the moonstream, to the eastward, on a northwesterly course. We paralleled them on course 310 T. then but lost contact shortly afterward. At 0319 began altering course to the southward to regain contact and at 0325 steadied on course 200 T. At 0342 regained contact with two ships, apparently maneuvering on southerly courses, bearing still to the eastward. Changed course to 235 T., trying to gain bearing to the southward before daybreak.

We were still uncertain as to whether or not the ships were enemy. We judged that those in sight were destroyers and that those first contacted were larger ships, probably heavy cruisers. We estimated that these latter were beyond the destroyers to the eastward now.

We had transmitted a radio report of the contact with "many unidentified ships", giving their position, and received a receipt from MIDWAY for it at 0306 but if anyone knew from that report that the ships could not be units of our own surface forces he did not give us information.

At 0412, with visibility range increasing as dawn approached, the enemy character of the ships was definitely established when the near one turned to head directly for us, challenging "XJ" by flashing light. We submerged immediately and rigged for depth charge attack. Estimated range at time of diving was 4000 yards.

At 0437 having been unable to detect propeller noises by sound, made a periscope exposure and sighted two MOGAMI cruisers. The near one bore 109 T. distant 9000 yards and the far one 105 T. distant 13,000 yards. The far cruiser was on course about 265 T., the near one on about 235 T. Each ship was doing a great deal of signaling with a brilliant all-directional blinker light at the foremast-head.

This latter fact indicated (a) that the contact at 0342 was not with destroyers but with two of the "large ships" sighted at 0215, (b) that their larger silhouettes had caused us to underestimate their distance when "challenged", (c) that we had not been challenged at all, nor sighted, but that (d) instead the two ships had begun using the all-directional light for maneuvering signals shortly before

APPENDIX I • 149

daybreak, and (e) that they had been maneuvering at considerable distance to the eastward of us while we were awaiting depth charge attack.

Even so, we were in fair initial position for an attack on the far cruiser provided he held his course, as we were less than 6000 yards from his track. He apparently followed the other cruiser on a jog to the southwestward, however, for at 0458, after we had been running at full speed for twenty minutes on course 200 T., the distance to his track had opened to 8000 yards and his angle on the bow increased to 60 starboard. Both cruisers then were on course about 270 T. During the next twenty minutes more signaling and maneuvering ensued and at 0504, just after a periscope observation, we heard the sound of a distant explosion. With renewed hope we again made a long run at full speed but at 0516 there was no improvement in the situation.

It noted before the explosion that the trailing cruiser had about forty feet of her bow missing. Her speed by plot was 17 knots.

At last observation, 0602, both ships were heading west, distant about 20,000 yards. At 0617 obtained receipt from both MIDWAY and HONOLULU for our contact report of "Two MOGAMI Cruisers" giving their course, speed, and position.

0715 Received message directing all units to Task Group 7.1 to surface and proceed in assigned sectors to radius of 5 miles from MIDWAY at best possible speed.

0718	Changed course to 139 T.
0722	Surfaced. Speed 18.5 knots.
0740	Changed course to 128 T. Passed thorough heavy oil slick trending 090–270.
0800	Posit Lat. 28-09.2 N., Long. 179-32.2 W. Weather clear, wind and sea E. force 2.
	Received summary of operations June 4 from CTF 7 as follows. Enemy forces were divided into two parts. The first, approaching MIDWAY on a course approximately 081 T. was 500 miles from MIDWAY at dawn 4 June, composed of 3 BBs, CAs, DDs, possibly a CV, and auxiliaries, total force 20 ships. The second force was bearing 320 T., 200 miles from MIDWAY and contained 4 CV, 2 BB, 4 CA, and DDs. This force was heavily attacked and 4 CV, 1 BB, and 1 CA left burning. At 1740 this force was in position Lat. 30-40 N., Long. 177-40 W. retiring on a westerly course. CTF 7 stated he believed the enemy would still attempt a landing on MIDWAY.
0810	Contacted unidentified plane on radar, range 10 miles. Submerged when range had closed to 5 miles without sighting. Kept down until 1030 by plane hovering over us. Had radar contacts at 0826, 0838, and 0921, range from 2½ to 4 miles. Sighted plane heading for periscope at 0921. Identified as light monoplane, believed to be enemy bent on strafing us when we surfaced. Probably has no bombs.
0925	Changed course to 086 T.
1030	Surfaced. Speed 18.5 knots.
1109	Instructions from CTF 7: Change station from 5 to 17 miles from MIDWAY.
1123	Warned by CTF 7 to be on lookout for own surface forces pursing enemy to westward of MIDWAY.

APPENDIX I • 151

1036	Changed course to 100 T.
1200	Position Lat. 28-05.6 N., Long. 178-58.7 W.
1238	From CTF 7: Task forces 16 and 17's movements west of MIDWAY are not limited. Be careful and do not attack them.
1311	Changed course to 081 T.
1337	Intercepted patrol plane report of contact with 3 CA trailing a group of 6 AP escorted by 2 CL. Two of the CA's were damaged and one was leaving a large oil slick. This force 265 T., 125 miles from MIDWAY at 0600 L.C.T.
1452	Sighted ship. Identified as submarine. Presumably friendly.
1458	Changed course to 270 T. Speed 18.5 knots. This in response to orders just received to proceed to Lat. 27-50 N., Long. 179-00 E. and search for battleship reported bombed and circling with heavy list at Lat. 27-55 N., Long. 179-00 E. TROUT to go to position 5 miles and GRAYLING 10 miles north of TAMBOR's.
	Also intercepted report that our Fortresses and dive bombers had scored one direct hit and close misses astern of a BB 125 miles 264 T. from MIDWAY, causing her to circle and list heavily to starboard.
1515	Changed course to 261 T.
1700	Changed course to 266 T.
1718	From CinCPac: Enemy has probably abandoned landing because of lack of air support and is retiring.
	From CTF 7 to TU7.1.10 (CUTTLEFISH): If no contact by dark proceed PEARL. Assume that CAs will be beyond you by then.
2100	Changed course to 258 T.

2120	Slowed to 9 knots in order to arrive at assigned position after moonrise.
	From CinCPac: Enemy forces retiring, some to westward, other probably to northwestward where visibility is low. At dark there remained within bombing range one group of 1 BB 5 DD which TF 16 was attacking and 2–3 CA 2 DD to the west being attacked by long range bombers. Results of these attacks not yet reported. The retirement may be temporary. All forces must be alert and prepared for further enemy action.
2130	Changed course to 240 T.
2303	Changed course to 265 T.
	Intercepted from CINCPAC: MIDWAY will search sector 220–330 to 600 miles commencing 0430 tomorrow.

6 June 1942

0100	Sighted running lights of unidentified aircraft astern. Changed course to 235 T. Started Radar. Plane approached to port beam then turned off running lights. Radar range on plane dropped from 8 to 3 miles. Clear night with heavy phosphorescence in water. Submerged and changed course to 265 T. at 0113. Plane hovered. We surfaced and submerged again on close radar contacts three times before 0451.
0451	Surfaced. Course 261 T. Speed 16 knots.
	Reported to CTF 7 that we had been kept down and asked if the planes bothering us could have been friendly. Three hours later he replied that they could not be identified. Estimated that the planes were probably Jap cruiser planes engaged

APPENDIX I • 153

	in moonlight search for ships in pursuit, that we were not more than 100 miles from some Jap unit, and that we had been detected and reported.
0514	Arrived at assigned station, changed course to north, searching for damaged Jap BB.
0550	Changed course to 081 T.
0620	Changed course to 000 T.
0636	Changed course to 061 T.
0808	From CTF 7: Continue west at best possible speed in search of enemy if contact not already made. Will give further information after morning plane search. Expect some cripples this morning.
0810	Changed course to 270 T.
0912	From CTF 7: MIDWAY has emergency diesel fuel.
1117	Intercepted message from CinCPac: MIDWAY will attack cruiser group with 12 Fortresses.
1200	Position Lat. 27-51 N., Long. 177-22 E.
1336	Changed course to 250 T in response to orders from CTF 7 (just received) to intercept 2 heavy cruisers and 2 destroyers which at 0650 were at Lat. 28-54 N., Long. 175-11 E. on course 215 T. at 15 knots. These ships are to be attacked this afternoon by Flying Fortresses. CUTTLEFISH, returning from westward, also after them.
1400	Sighted ten Fortresses heading out on westerly course.
1500	Sighted five more Fortresses outbound.
1629	Sighted five Fortresses returning to MIDWAY.
1700	Long Range Radar contacts, assumed to be Fortresses. Overcast. Planes not sighted.
1845	Changed course to 270 T.

Estimated that this course would take us through the scene of the attack on the cruisers by the Fortresses which we had seen go out and return.

2000	Position Lat. 27-25 N., Long. 174-55 E.
2036	Sighted (2) two white lights on the horizon bearing 180 T. Slowed to 15 knots. Changed courts to 210 T. to close.
2100	Increased speed to 18.5 knots.
2108	Changed course to 225 T.
2130	No developments. Resumed course 270 T., at 18.5 knots.
2200	From CinCPac: MIDWAY air search June 7th 230–326 to 350 miles. Fortresses got two 1600 lb. bomb hits on a cruiser who sank in 15 seconds. Note: This is the only report of the Fortress attack transmitted by HONOLULU. It gave no information as to the course, speed, location, and composition of the force attacked, which was quite disappointing. Also disappointing was the short radius of Catalina search. It appeared that henceforth we would have no assistance in finding cripples or any targets.

7 June 1942

0025	TAMBOR, TROUT and GRAYLING ordered by CTF 7 to continue pursuit. Other units stationed on circle radius 25 miles from MIDWAY.
0030	From CTF 7: TU7.5.7 attempt to intercept 2 CA and 2 (?) DD reported L 28-54 N., L 175-11 E. C 215, sp 15 at 1850 GCT June 6th. (Note: other messages intercepted gave time as 1815 GCT June 6th)
0045	Sighted green flare astern.
0050	Slowed to 6 knots.
0056	Stopped, changed course to 225 T.
0140	Went ahead 18.5 knots, course 215 T.
0152	Sighted several green flares resembling "very signals" between 090 T. and 125 T. Stopped.

0200	From CTF 7: TU7.1.10 return and sink apparently damaged BB Lat. 28-55 N. Long. 173-08 E. Cruiser and DDs, some damaged in same action, 2200 GCT June 6th, last sighted on course west. (We are an information addressee).
0210	Went ahead 18.5 knots.
0220	Sighted another flare on starboard quarter. Changed course to 090 T.
0223	Changed course to 270 T. Were at estimated position of cruiser attacked and reported sunk by Fortresses in afternoon. Judged that signals were being made by survivors in boats as nothing could be seen or heard by sound.
0533	Radar contact 15 miles. Sighted flying boat bearing 090 T on northerly course. Probably from WAKE.
0630	Sighted scout plane bearing 230 T. distant 8 miles on southeasterly course.
0720	Radar contact, range 7 miles decreasing. Made quick dive to 140 feet. Plane not sighted.
0722	When at 135 feet we were severely shaken by two depth bombs exploding close aboard. Inspection revealed following damage: Much glass shattered throughout the ship, cork on forward conning tower bulkhead loose, housing of starboard air compressor cracked, casings of all four battery blower motors cracked, #1 battery blower vibrates badly, section of ventilation duct containing moisture trap in forward battery well cracked, upper window and prism of #1 periscope broken and low-power #2 periscope rendered unusable.
0740	Changed course to 180 T.
0800	Position Lat. 27-15 N., Long. 171-59 E.
1042	Rose to periscope depth. Radar contact 3 miles. 200 feet. Changed course to 090.
1200	Position Lat. 27-10 N., Long. 172-08 E.

1515	Surfaced on course 090 T. speed 14 knots. Informed CTF 7 that we had been down since 0720, and that we had suffered non-essential damage by depth bombs, and requested any late information or orders. Also reported the position and course of the planes sighted early in the morning.
1623	Changed course to 110 T.

Estimate: There were probably some Jap ships within 100 miles of us when we sighted the cruiser plane this morning. They were probably bearing about 290°, judging from the course of the scout plane. If so they are apparently making good at least 15 knots to the westward and are now well out of our reach. It is barely possible, however, that the plane was on a return leg to a unit on the reverse bearing which we passed to the southward during the night.

Also there may be a cripple ship still afloat, or a rescue ship, in the vicinity of the green flares sighed last night. Decided to proceed on course 110° during the four hours remaining until dark, and then to proceed to investigate in daylight the area of the green flares the flowing morning.

1630	Commenced zig-zagging to widen our search band.
1700	Increased speed to 17 knots.
2000	Position by DR Lat. 26-42 N., Long. 173-29 E. Slowed to 14 knots. Stopped zig-zagging. Sky overcast, visibility 10 miles. Sea moderate.
2032	Changed course to 000 T.
2359	In response to orders from ComSubPac (just received) changed course to 294 T and proceeded at 17 knots to Lat. 29-30 N., Long. 168 E. TROUT will be 30 miles south and GRAYLING 60 miles south. All of us are to search on course

APPENDIX I • 157

	090 T. Sent message reporting position, as required by the order.
8 June 1942	
0800	Position Lat. 27-52 N., Long. 171-26 E. by D.R. Weather overcast, squally, wind SW force 3. Visibility poor.
0930	Changed course to 315 T. Slowed to 11 knots.
1200	Position by D.R. Lat. 28-20 N., Long. 170-41 W. Weather overcast, squally, wind SW force 3, low visibility.
2000	Position by D.R. Lat. 29-21 N., Long. 169-32 E.
2005	Changed course to 270 T. Slowed to 5 knots. By dead reckoning we are on our assigned track and will be in position to commence the search on reverse course at daybreak tomorrow.
9 June 1942	
0023	Received message directing TUNA and TROUT to search in vicinity of Lat. 28-52 N., Long. 173-18 E. Wreckage reported there.
0505	Changed course to 090 T., increased speed to 14 knots.
0601	Changed course to 000 T. Fix at 0500 showed a drift of 30 miles, 129 T. since last fix at 0500 June 7.
0700	Intercepted message from CTF 7 directing GRAYLING to investigate Japanese unit reported at Lat. 28-31 N., Long. 170-40 E. on course 180 speed 4 knots.
0800	Position Lat. 29-26 N., Long. 169-25 E. Weather still overcast with visibility 2–10 miles.
1200	Position Lat. 29-26.4 N., Long. 170-256 E. Visibility still spotty with frequent squalls.

2000	Position by D.R. Lat. 29-27 N., Long. 172-38 E. Weather overcast, visibility poor. Changed course to 270 T. Slowed to 5 knots.
2342	Received message ordering TAMBOR, TROUT, and GRAYLING to return to PEARL HARBOR.

USS *Trout* (SS-202): Fourth War Patrol[12]

21 May 1942

1400 (VM)	Departed PEARL for assigned station in company with U.S.S. TAMBOR and GRAYLING, under escort of U.S.S. LAMBERTON and WASMUTH.
1748 (X)	Escorting vessels left formation, this vessel set course for assigned station, speed 12.5 knots.

26 May 1942

0140 (Y)	Arrived at northern boundary of assigned patrol sector (260°T to 280°T from MIDWAY ISLAND, median distance 150 miles) and commenced surface patrol on course 180°T and reverse, speed 10 knots.
1105 (Y)	Received Comtaskforce 7 despatch directing conduct of a periscope patrol during daylight, guarding low frequency FOX schedules submerged. Although this vessel had been equipped with a new type antenna coupling unit prior to departure PEARL, these schedules could not be heard on the underwater loop. Failure of reception on the underwater loop made it necessary to constantly maintain a keel depth of 55 feet to expose the vertical antenna sufficiently for solid reception. (Rough weather could have seriously interfered with reception by this method) Submerged patrol was conducted at a speed of 2.8 knots and surface

patrol at 10 knots. During the period of the submerged patrol MIDWAY patrol planes were sighted daily as listed in detail in paragraph 6.

4 June 1942

0755 (Y)   Decoded Comtaskforce 7 041837 directing Task Group 7.1 less CACHALOT, CUTTLEFISH and FLYING FISH to go after enemy force which was on course 135°T, speed 25 knots, bearing 320°T from MIDWAY, distance 180 miles, at 1804 ZED June 4, 1942. Surfaced immediately and set course 060°T, speed 18 knots in an attempt to intercept.

0812 (Y)   Sighted Japanese Zero Fighting Plane maneuvering to attack from astern at an altitude of 500 feet. Dived and shortly after reaching 150 feet heard a series of explosions believed to be light bombs. Throughout the remaining daylight period several attempts were made to proceed on the surface, but in each case this vessel was forced down by the appearance of unidentified planes on attack courses. Plane contacts were made during frequent RADAR and periscope exposures while submerged.

1946 (Y)   Surfaced and set course 135°T, speed 13 knots. At 2030 (Y) June 4, 1942, decoded Comtaskforce 7 050325 assigning patrol stations on 100 miles circle from MIDWAY.

5 June 1942

0140 (Y)   Commenced patrolling the chord of newly assigned sector, modified by Comtaskforce 7 050029, bearing 260°T to 270°T from MIDWAY.

0810 (Y)   Received orders to proceed to MIDWAY 5 mile circle in present sector (Comtaskforce 7 051847). Surfaced, set course 081°T, speed 17 knots.

1410 (Y)	Arrived on station, modified to 12 mile circle from MIDWAY by Comtaskforce 7 052129 and commenced periscope patrol. While proceeding to station this vessel was forced to dive on three occasions for short periods while unidentified planes passed overhead.
1443 (Y)	Decoded Comtaskforce 7 060024. Surfaced and set course 264°T, speed 18 knots, proceeding as directed to a position bearing 264°T, distance 125 miles from MIDWAY to "finish off" damaged enemy battleship.

6 June 1942

1340 (Y)	Decoded Comtaskforce 7 062357 directing interception of two enemy CA and two DD reported at 0650 (Y) June 6, 1942 in position latitude 28°51' N, longitude 175°11' E, course 215°T, speed 15 knots; set course 225°T to intercept.
1450 (Y)	Decoded CINCPAC 070041 reporting six groups of B-17's attacking four unidentified ships, distance 525 miles, bearing 277° from MIDWAY on course 200°T, speed 30 knots. On the basis of this report and earlier observation of B-17's flying westward, changed course to 235°T to intercept possible cripples.
1950 (Y)	Set course for Pearl as directed by Comtaskforce 7 070055, speed 14 knots.

7 June 1942

0321 (Y)	Decoded Comtaskforce 7 070700 directing TAMBOR, TROUT and GRAYLING to continue the chase. Resumed course 235°T and increased speed to 16.5 knots. At 0815 (Y) June 7, 1942 changed course to 270°T.

1440 (Y)	Decoded Comtaskforce 7 080105 directing TROUT to pass through point latitude 29°N, longitude 168°E, at two engine speed and then to search on course 090°T. Set course 309°T to comply, speed 14 knots.

8 June 1942

1515 (Y)	Passed through designated position on course 090°T, speed 14 knots.
2100 (Y)	Decoded Comtaskforce 7 090915 directing a search of area in latitude 28°25' N, longitude 173°18' E and salvage of identifying wreckage.

9 June 1942

1220 to 1606 (Y)	Entered large oil slick and searched for wreckage, recovering: the bow section of a ship's boat, one swab, one charred piece of wood, and a sample of oil. Rescued two Japs from what appeared to be a large wooden hatch cover which was too large for recovery and which bore no identifying markings. Resumed course and speed. At 2350 decoded Comtaskforce 7 100816 directing TROUT to proceed PEARL via designated points. Set course to comply.

APPENDIX 2

Patrol Reports of U.S. Task Group 7.2 Submarines

USS *Plunger* (SS-179): Second War Patrol[1]

Patrol report indicates *Plunger* ended first war patrol on February 4, 1942. Patrol report indicates *Plunger* departed on second war patrol from Midway on June 9, 1942. Patrol report does not contain any information on Midway activities.

USS *Trigger* (SS-237): First War Patrol[2]

Patrol report indicates *Trigger* departed on first war patrol from Pearl Harbor on June 26, 1942. Patrol report does not contain any information on Midway activities.

USS *Narwhal* (SS-167): Third War Patrol[3]

Last entry for second war patrol ends on March 28, 1942. First entry for fourth war patrol begins on July 8, 1942. Between second and fourth patrol reports, document contains the following pertaining to the third war patrol: "The so-called THIRD WAR PATROL for the period 28 May–13 June 1942 is not held by the Operational Archives, Naval Historical Center. This was actually the second patrol conducted by this submarine during World War II."

APPENDIX 3

Patrol Reports of U.S. Task Group 7.3 Submarines

USS *Finback* (SS-230): First War Patrol[1]

Patrol report indicates *Finback* departed from Pearl Harbor on first patrol June 25, 1942. Patrol report does not contain any information on Midway activities.

USS *Growler* (SS-215): First War Patrol[2]

Patrol report indicates *Growler* departed from Pearl Harbor on first patrol June 20, 1942. Patrol report does not contain any information on Midway activities.

USS *Pike* (SS-173): Fifth War Patrol[3]

30 May 1942

1140	Underway in company with TARPON, escorted by LITCHFIELD, standing out of Pearl Harbor, T.H., en route operating area via Kauai Channel. After dark proceeded independently to assigned station at Lat. 26° - 30' N, Long. 157° - 50' W.

31 May 1942

0730	Sighted nothing except two "PBY's" [*sic*].
1251	Sighted one plane believed to be a type "JRS".

1500	Sighted one plane believed to be a "PBY".
1535	On station.
1 June 1942	Conducted a submerged patrol in assigned area.
3 June 1942	
0827	Sighted a land plane bomber believed to be a Flying Fortress.
5 June 1942	
1850	Sound picked up a loud clacking noise on the port bow moving aft. The noise could not be identified until surfacing when a number of whales were seen in the area.
1940	Surfaced and proceeded to new station bearing 330°T, on the 250 mile circle from the center of Oahu in accordance with dispatch orders.
6 June 1942	
0640	Arrived on new station and conducted submerged patrol.
1255	Surfaced and proceeded toward rendezvous with LITCHFIELD, TARPON, FINBACK and GROWLER, but returned to station the same evening upon cancellation of orders.
1638–1720	Sighted three "PBY's" patrolling on south to easterly courses.
7 June 1942	
2040	Remained on station until 2040 June 7, at which time proceeded to new rendezvous at Lat. 21° - 30' N, Long. 157° - 15' W, at 0600, and from there proceeded to Pearl Harbor.

USS *Tarpon* (SS-175): Fourth War Patrol[4]

30 May 1942

1145 (VM)   Underway in company with PIKE, escorted by LITCHFIELD, proceeding north through Kauai Channel. Parted company at dark.

31 May 1942

1630 (VW)   Arrived on station and started submerged patrol in accordance with operation order.

6 June 1942

0545 (VW)   After submerging, deciphered Cincpac 060751, which had been received just before diving. This message was a correction to the routine report of location of our ships and stated that the four submarines which had been located 500 miles north of Oahu had shifted to an area 250 miles, bearing 325 from Oahu. No orders directing this change of area had been received, but assuming that the dispatch so directing had been missed, course was set for new area. Ran submerged this day because we were 100 miles outside of the new bombing restricted zone and in order to prevent confusion that would arise if we were sighted and reported; also it was hoped to receive while submerged and prior to arrival in the new area a possible repetition of the message directing the change.

2100–2215 (VW)   Endeavored to send my 070600 to ComSubPac on 4265 KC series, requesting information as to exact location of new stations of Task Group 7.3. This message was broadcast five times during this period on both frequencies but no receipt could be obtained.

7 June 1942

0400 (VW)   Above mentioned message was sent and receipted for. Arrived on new station, assuming that it bore the same relation to the center of the new area as had the station previously occupied.

APPENDIX 4

Patrol Reports of U.S. Submarines on Patrol

USS *Drum* (SS-228): First War Patrol[1]

31 May	Submerged 5 miles off INUBO SAKI.
1 June	Started to base.
3 June	
1118	Radar contact, 12 miles. Submerged.
1230	Surfaced.
5 June	Received orders from Commander Task Force SEVEN to close MIDWAY and look for burning enemy BB. Continued return route as best course to comply.
6 June	Received orders from Commander Task Force SEVEN to patrol a line to intercept a damaged enemy CV.
1400 (LOVE)	Attained position on prescribed line and commenced search.
7 June	
0724 (Mike)	Sighted unidentified airplane, distant about 3 miles. Submerged.
0746	Surfaced.

0918	Radar contact, 7 miles. Submerged.
0942	Surfaced. Crossed International Date Line. |//
7 June	
1500 (Y)	Received orders from Commander Task Force SEVEN to return to PEARL. |//
12 June	Effected rendezvous with NARWHAL, TRIGGER, and escort, and arrived PEARL.

USS *Greenling* (SS-213): First War Patrol[2]

June 1, 1942

0448 (K)	Began closing TRUK. |//
June 2, 1942	
2000 (K)	Passed 18 miles east of KUOP Island, TRUK. |//
June 4, 1942	
0243 (K)	Received first information of attack on Dutch Harbor.
0800 (K)	Departed from area in accordance with directive of operation order. Lat. 10-00 N, Long 154-50 E. Set course for Pearl via point thirty (30) miles north of Pt. 18. |//
June 5, 1942	Intercepted large number of messages concerning engagement near MIDWAY.
2130 (K)	Received radio directive from CTF 7 to report position, course, speed, fuel and torpedoes.
2215 (K)	Delivered reply to above message to NPM on 8470 Kcs.

June 6, 1942

0505 (K)	Received radio directive from CTF 7 to proceed toward MIDWAY. Proceeded to carry out directive, increased speed to 80–90 on two engines.
1625 (K)	Slowed to one engine speed to increase fuel endurance.

June 7, 1942

0008 (L)	Received radio directive from CTF 7 to attempt to intercept 2 CA's [sic] and 2 DD's [sic] heading for vicinity of WAKE. Heading and key word garbled so message not identified as addressed to us at once. Changed course to north and increased speed in order to intercept enemy force along his reported track before it reaches close vicinity of WAKE.
1600 (L)	Arrived directly ahead of reported enemy force on its track as extended. Dived and commenced submerged patrol to avoid detection by aircraft and to rest personnel who were now showing definite signs of fatigue. Sky nearly 100% cloudy, sea glassy, visibility excellent, radar operative intermittently. Position, 150 miles, bearing 055°T from WAKE.
2145 (L)	Stopped screws and noisy machinery in order increase efficacy of sound watch.
2320 (L)	Most probable time of contacting enemy force passed. Continued patrol in vicinity of reported track of enemy.

June 9, 1942

	Conducted submerged patrol during the day across reported enemy track, the same conditions prevailing as during the previous day.
2123 (L)	Sent message to ComSubPac reporting lack of contacts, position, course, speed and fuel. Receipt obtained from NPM on 8470 Kcs.

2332 (L)   Received message from CTF 7 giving positions of two enemy units and stating they were headed for Mandates. This message had undoubtedly been first transmitted earlier in the day but was not received submerged at this distance from Pearl. Decided, in view of fuel available and present position, to attempt to intercept these forces only if headed for eastern Mandates, especially KWAJALEIN. Plot showed that at 15 kts they were already to the south of us, although we had patrolled across their possible tracks during the day. Commenced patrol along and across possible track of C-in-C 2nd Fleet to KWAJELEIN.

June 10, 1942   Started day patrolling on surface, but later submerged for most of remainder of day in view unfavorable sky and sea conditions, our wake at 6 kts being visible for 10 to 15 minutes on the ripply surface. Considered any enemy force sighted would have an air screen from WAKE, now about 200 miles distant.

2320 (L)   Received radio directive from CTF 7 to proceed to Pearl. Headed toward Pearl.

USS *Pollack* (SS-180): Third War Patrol[3]

June 1

0930 (I)   Sighted Aoga Shima 1 point on port bow.
0956 (I)   Submerged to make passage through Islands.
1948 (IK) Surfaced.

June 4   Sent message to Commander Task Force Seven giving course, speed, position, etc. Sent early because of intercepted messages indicated enemy activity at Midway.

APPENDIX 4 • 173

June 6

1055 (KL)   Received orders from Commander Task Force Seven to get on line from a point, distance 250 miles, bearing 335 from Midway to southern edge of Honshu, in order to intercept a wounded carrier. Changed course to 000°T, increased speed to 12 knots (two engines).

1853 (L)   Arrived on line and changed course to 092°T, speed 9 knots (one engine).

June 7

0902 (L)   Increased speed to 13.5 knots to intercept carrier before dark.

1620 (L)   Slowed to 9 knots.

June 8

1116 (LM)   Number four torpedo starting leaver was tripped as the safety stick was removed while the torpedo was being reloaded after routine inspection. Propeller lock kept engine from turning out before stop valve could be closed considerable damage was done to torpedo. Tube was loaded with a reload.

June 9   Sent routine message to Commander Task Force Seven when 600 miles from Midway.

June 10   Changed course from a point 109 miles south of Midway in accordance with orders received.

June 11

1337 (M)   Crossed date line, changed date to June 10. Intercepted message concerning anti countermining device. Prepared one torpedo forward and one after for possible shot in accordance with dispatch

	[sic]. Received despatch [sic] about possible meeting with U.S.S. TUNA and U.S.S. TAMBOR.
June 11	Sighted two patrol planes, U.S.S. TUNA and cargo vessel escorted by corvette and patrol plane. Exchanged recognition signals.
June 12	Received message about U.S.S. TAMBOR passing us. Sent routine message about rendezvous.

USS *Pompano* (SS-181): Second War Patrol[4]

June 6–7	Patrolling direct route from Tokyo and Yokohama to New Britain, New Zealand, Solomon Island, E. and S.E. Australian ports, etc.
June 7	
0100 (K)	Intercepted information indicating large Jap force near Midway had been defeated and was retiring westward. Proceeded at 13 knots on N.E. course to intercept enemy. Informed ComSubPac of action taken and requested assignment. Directed proceed to 33-00 N., 150-00 E. and thence eastward to point bearing 335 distance 250 miles from Midway; opposite direction to enemy.
0500 (K)	Cleared area.
June 7–13	Scouting for enemy along assigned course en route Midway.
June 13	Arrived Midway.

USS *Porpoise* (SS-172): Third War Patrol[5]

20 May 1942	Transited MANIPA STRAIT for the third time this month.

21 May 1942	Proceeding to PEARL.
6 June 1942	
2230 (L)	Received orders to report position, course and speed to Commander Task Force SEVEN which was given as 17 N., 162 E., speed 140 miles per day.
8 June 1942	
0010 (L)	Received orders to intercept enemy force of two heavy cruisers and two destroyers. Information given shows they are on course for PONAPE and that we can be on their daylight position circle southeast of WAKE by dawn of the ninth.
2300 (L)	On enemy's position circle for dawn. Took up patrol on fifteen miles line normal to enemy's course.
9 June 1942	Not having seen enemy, and plot showed that they should have passed by during day, abandoned patrol at sunset and set course for PEARL.
2300 (L)	Received dispatch which gave positions of two enemy forces and stated that they were headed toward the Mandates. This information was so vague as to be almost useless but analysis showed that if they were headed for the Eastern MARSHALLS by holding course and speed we could be on the dawn position circle of one force and the dusk circle of the other, assuming they were making 15 knots, during the tenth. As we did not have speed or time to intercept on any other assumption we held on and kept a sharp lookout during the day.
10 June 1942	Received orders to proceed direct to PEARL. Set course accordingly.

USS *Silversides* (SS-236): First War Patrol[6]

9 June 1942

0200 (I)   Received Comtaskfor 7's despatch regarding location of units of Japanese fleet retiring from Midway. Decided to start back toward Pearl in hope of intercepting fleet. Decision based on fact that if we didn't leave at once our chances of intercepting would be considerably lessened. Nothing we were likely to get within the remaining four days allowed us in the area would be worth missing a chance at the big show. Since we were already off ASHIZURI SAKI decided to complete investigation of that area during forenoon. Closed to estimated eight miles but sighted no traffic. Our position very doubtful because of four days of constant rain.

1027 (I)   While off the point, sighted trawler patrolling or trolling on north–south line. He remained in our vicinity until about 1500. Similar to patrol sighted off ICHIYE SAKI.

11 June 1942

0030 (I)   Left patrol area after 29 days on station.

0500 (I)   At daybreak while passing between HACHIJO SHIMA and MIKURA SHIMA sighted 2 small coast steamers on northerly course toward TOKYO. Since they were 10000 yards astern and we were abaft their beam, we did not pursue.

12 June 1942

0400 (K)   Resumed surface patrol during day. At 0900 (K) with a definite indication at 15 miles by radar, submerged for 45 minutes to evade detection by plane.

21 June 1942

0958 (VW) Arrived Submarine Base, Pearl Harbor, T.H.

USS *Triton* (SS-201): Third War Patrol[7]

May 17, 1942	Working back toward area; at —
1803 (I)	Latitude 29°-25' N Longitude 134°-09' E Sighted Japanese submarine with rising sun painted on conning tower; bearing 284°T, distance 6200 yards (#16 of paragraph 5).
1817 (I)	ATTACK NO.8. Fired one torpedo—Hit submarine near stern. Part of ship was blown about 100 feet into air. Saw crew abandon ship. Submarine sank by the stern in 2 minutes with bow high in the air and pointed vertically.
1827 (I)	Heard series of 42 explosions through hull and sound gear.
1845 (I)	Sighted about 30 survivors clinging to deck grating. Could not possibly accommodate all; so continued toward area. This ship must have been submerged, and surfaced just before sighted by TRITON.

USS *Tuna* (SS-203): Second War Patrol[8]

2 June

0235 (I)	Passed 18 miles south of Sofu Gan.
2300 (K)	Received message from Comtaskfor 7 altering return route to go via Point H. Changed course to proceed thence via great circle course.

4 June

2030 (K)	Received orders from Comtaskfor 7 to close Midway. Changed course direct for Midway. Fuel on hand is estimated at 10,000 gal., more than minimum requirements to reach Pearl Harbor.

In view of 1500 mile distance from Midway, continued to proceed at 11.5 kts., saving fuel for high speed running to intercept enemy returning from Midway.

5 June

0746 (K)	Sighted plane bearing 020°T., distance 3 miles. Submerged. Lat. 21-00 N., Long. 152-00 E.
0758 (K)	Came to periscope depth and saw plane turning to attack course. Went to 150 ft. and c/c from 093°T. to 180°T.
0930 (K)	c/c to 093°T. and came to periscope depth. No plane in sight, but radar indicated one at 3.5 to 4 mi. Returned to 150 ft.
1150 (K)	Radar and periscope indicated no planes. Surfaced.
1156 (K)	Sighted another plane bearing 090°T, distance 5 mi. Submerged again.
1236 (K)	c/c to 045°T. to increase distance from Marcus I., which was assumed to be the base from which planes were patrolling.
2033 (L)	Surfaced and proceeded to northeastward.
2100 (L)	Received message from Comtaskfor 7 to report position, etc. Delayed reply because the radio contact would be added to plane contacts and we would be within bombing range following day.

6 June

0942 (L)	Radar indicated a plane. Submerged. About two minutes after contact, at 100 ft. depth, from 1 to 3 bombs exploded on port quarter. Attack came from ahead, out of the sun. Experience of previous day indicated that planes would continue to patrol area during the day. Remained submerged. Lat. 29-48 N., Long. 159-40 E.

2030 (L)	Cleared message to Comtaskfor 7 giving position, course, speed, fuel, torpedoes and information of planes. c/c to 120°T. and changed speed to 16.8 kts.
2400 (L)	Received orders from Comtaskfor 7 to intercept enemy carrier on track to northward.

7 June

0018 (L)	c/c to 000°T., speed 16.8 kts.
0600 (L)	Radar indicated 2 planes approaching. Submerged. Lat. 31-15 N., Long. 161-40 E.
0709 (L)	Surfaced and proceeded at 11 kts.
1600 (L)	On line to intercept enemy force. c/c to 092°T., speed 11 kts.

8 June

0950 (L)	Received message from Comtaskfor 7 ordering ship to proceed to Pearl Harbor searching for abandoned enemy BB en route.
1030 (L)	c/c to 133°T. and changed speed to 15 kts to be on probable enemy course at his 11 kt. position circle at morning twilight.
2320 (L)	Sighted flashes to eastward at irregular intervals and finally concluded they were lightning.

9 June

0333 (L)	Reached enemy course line. Changed course to 100°T. to run to position of BB reported.
1040 (L)	Sighted 2 engine bomber, land plane, olive drab camouflage, bearing 020°T., course 200°T., distance 4 miles, headed for us. Submerged.
1125 (L)	Surfaced and changed speed to 16.5 kts.
1845 (M)	Entered oil slick extending about 4 mi. north and south.
1944 (M)	Arrived at reported position of enemy BB.

2025 (M)	Reached end of oil slick which was heaviest near eastern and western parts. Estimated it to be 24 miles long.
2140 (M)	Transmitted results of search to Comtaskfor 7, giving course 107°T., speed 11 kts. for Pearl.

10 June

0100 (M)	Received orders from Comtaskfor 7 to search for wreckage.
0144 (M)	c/c to 283°T. to proceed to position of wreckage.
0808 (M)	Received orders from Comtaskfor 7 to return to Pearl via point 10 miles south of Midway.
0714 (M)	Sighted first of wreckage. Material picked up was examined, photographed and sketched as follows:

TIME	ITEM	POSITION	
0715 (M)	Bow of boat	28-39 N	173-12 E
0914 (M)	Bow of boat (name plate obtained)	28-42 N	173-10 E
1014 (M)	Raft and body of Japanese (clothing removed from body which was then thrown overboard).	28-47 N	173-15 E
1107 (M)	Wooden chest, containing cleaning gear & gas mask.	28-48 N	173-15 E
Various times	3 wooden tubs	various positions	
	3 mattresses, blue & white striped ticking.		
	1 large cylindrical fender covered with woven rope.		
	Oil slicks (sample obtained).		

1044 (M)	c/c for point ten miles south of Midway I.
1049 (M)	sighted PBY type of plane which did not close us. Lat. 28-48 N., Long 173-19 E.
1950 (M)	Sighted 3 red flares bearing about 300°T., estimated distance 12 to 15 miles. The first flare was the brightest. Lat 28-59 N, Long. 175-19 E was our position at the time.
2154 (M)	Sent message to Comtaskfor 7 about the flares. Enemy interference delayed the transmission and KFS interfered on the alternative frequency. Message was cleared by increasing power to get through the interference. c/c to 180°T. to move off the course line about 20 miles.

11 June

0858 (M)	Sighted U.S. PBY plane and exchanged signals in Lat. 28-16 N., Long. 177-45 E.
1455 (M)	Sighted U.S.S. FLYING FISH and exchanged signals in Lat. 28-10 N., Long. 178-50 E.

11 June [*Author's note: Crossed International Date Line*].

0630 (Y)	Sighted U.S.S. POLLACK, Lat. 27-55 N., Long. 177-45 W.
0710 (Y)	17 miles south of Midway I. c/c to 131°T.
1500 (Y)	Changed speed to 12.5 knots average to arrive at Pearl Harbor on 15 June.
2227 (Y)	Sent 1000 mile report of return to Comtaskfor 7.

14 June

1705 (W)	Sighted U.S.S. CUTTLEFISH and exchanged signals.

APPENDIX 5

Extracts From the United States Strategic Bombing Survey: Interrogations of Japanese Officials

Interrogation of Captain Takahisa Amagai, IJN, Air Officer on CV KAGA at Battle of Midway.

When asked, "What was the mission of the Carrier Task Group (containing the four fleet carriers AKAGI, KAGA, SORYU and HIRYU)?" He responded, "To attack MIDWAY, to help the occupation."[1]

Interrogation of Captain Susumu Kawaguchi, IJN, Air Officer on CV HIRYU at Battle of Midway.

When asked, "When you left Japan, what was the mission of the air fleet at Midway?" He responded, "It was to seize Midway."

When asked, "Why didn't the occupation force and Grand Fleet continue on to Midway?" He responded, "Because we could not occupy the island having lost our air attack force."[2]

Interrogation of Captain Y. Watanabe, IJN, Gunnery Officer on BB YAMATO at Battle of Midway.

When asked, "What were the plans leading up to the attack?" He responded, "We intended to capture MIDWAY because on 18 April we were attacked in TOKYO for the first time. We thought the planes came from MIDWAY."[3]

Interrogation of Captain H. Ohara, IJN, Executive Officer on CV SORYU at Battle of Midway.

When asked, "What was the mission of your air fleet?" He responded, "We were to bomb MIDWAY in preparation for a landing operation to be made by transports approaching from the southwest."[4]

Interrogation of Lieut. Comdr. S. Yunoki, IJN, Gunnery Officer on DD escorting transports at Battle of Midway.

When asked, "What was your mission at MIDWAY?" He responded, "I was gunnery officer on a destroyer. We escorted supply and troop transports to occupy MIDWAY. Second Destroyer Squadron, JINTSU flagship. 12 destroyers about 15 transports. About 1000 Marines were to land at SAND Island and about 1000 Army on EASTERN Island. There were also some engineers."[5]

Interrogation of Captain Yasuji Watanabe, IJN, Gunnery Officer on Admiral Yamamoto's staff, Commander in Chief, 2nd Fleet at Midway Battle, June 1942.

When asked, "Did you lack any special equipment for the landing force?" He responded in part, "The failure of the air force to maintain an adequate search for the American carrier fleet at MIDWAY, plus the fact that the JAPANESE submarine line running north and south between 165W and 170W, was too far east to locate the American fleet, are the reasons given for the loss of the Battle of MIDWAY."[6]

APPENDIX 6

Interrogation of Vice Admiral Paul H. Weneker

Former German naval attaché who Left Japan in 1937 to command the pocket battleship Deutschland. *He returned to Japan in February 1940 and remained there until November 1945.*

It was expressed of the German Naval Ministry that every possible effort be made to induce the Japanese to exert their maximum effort in attack against U.S. merchant shipping in the Pacific. Notes were repeatedly exchanged between my office and Berlin on this subject and directive from home instructed me to press the matter further. The Japanese had one invariable answer, namely, that they must conserve their submarines for attack against the U.S. Fleet. They argued that merchant shipping could be easily replaced with the great American production capacity, but that naval vessels represented the real power against what they fought and that these vessels and their trained crews were most difficult to replace and hence were the one logical target. If, therefore, they were to hazard their subs it must be against the U.S. Navy.

The Japanese Navy thought always of the U.S. carriers. They talked about how many were building, and how many were in the Pacific and that these must be sunk; but it was always carriers they talked about. Next after that they would attack battleships and lesser ships but never the merchantmen except under most favorable conditions. On instructions from Berlin I suggested specifically that they concentrate on certain supply lines, with a chance of attacking tankers and transports, but they refused. I suggested the desirability of attacking the route between Honolulu and the West Coast because that would force the use of convoys and would force the withdrawal of many escorts from the Western Pacific. Again the answer was negative; the mission was the American carriers and they could not be changed on this principle.[1]

APPENDIX 7

Navy Cross Citation for Lieutenant Commander William Herman Brockman, Jr.

BROCKMAN, WILLIAM HERMAN, JR.

(First Award)

Citation:

The President of the United States takes pleasure in presenting the Navy Cross to William Herman Brockman, Jr., Lieutenant Commander, U.S. Navy, for extraordinary heroism and distinguished service in the line of his profession as Commanding Officer of the U.S.S. NAUTILUS (SS-168), in the Battle of Midway. On 4 June 1942, Lieutenant Commander Brockman aggressively developed a contact with major enemy forces and doggedly pushed home a torpedo attack on a screened aircraft carrier against determined and repeated enemy counter measures by gunfire barrage, depth charging and bombing from the air. The attack culminated successfully and Lieutenant Commander Brockman is credited with closing and sinking of a 10,000 ton enemy aircraft carrier. His skill, determination, courage and fortitude were in keeping with the highest traditions of the Naval Service.

Commander in Chief, Pacific Fleet: Serial 3277 (August 16, 1942)

Note: Brockman would go on to win two gold stars in lieu of a second and third Navy Cross in subsequent actions during the war.[1]

Endnotes

1. Introduction

1. John A. Adams, *If Mahan Ran the Great Pacific War: An Analysis of World War II Naval Strategy* (Bloomington, IN: Indiana University Press, 2008), 124.
2. Thomas J. Culora, "Japanese Operational Plans in World War II: Shortfalls in Critical Elements," (Newport, RI: Naval War College Joint Military Operations Department; Springfield, VA: June 1994), 15–17.
3. Robert E. Kuenne, *The Attack Submarine: A Study in Strategy* (New Haven, CT: Yale University Press, 1965), 160.
4. Keith Wheeler, *War Under the Pacific* (Richmond, VA: Time Life Inc., 1998), 106.
5. Richard W. Bates, *The Battle of Midway Including the Aleutian Phase, June 3 to June 14, 1942. Strategical and Tactical Analysis* (Newport, CT: U.S. Naval War College, 1948), 26.
6. W. J. Holmes, *Undersea Victory: The Influence of Submarine Operations on the War in the Pacific* (New York: Doubleday & Company, Inc., 1966), 135.
7. William Tuohy, *The Bravest Man: The Story of Richard O'Kane and U.S. Submarines in the Pacific War* (Gloucestershire, Great Britain: Sutton Publishing Limited, 2001), 49.
8. Thomas G. Hunnicutt, "The Operational Failure of U.S. Submarines at the Battle of Midway and Implications for Today," (Newport, RI: Naval War College Joint Military Operations Department; Springfield, VA: May 1996), 8.
9. Emily O. Goldman, *Sunken Treaties: Naval Arms Control Between the Wars* (University Park, PA: The Pennsylvania State University Press, 1994), 106.
10. W. D. Puleston, *The Armed Forces of the Pacific: A Comparison of the Military and Naval Power of the United States and Japan* (New Haven: Yale University Press, 1941), 171–72.
11. Carl Boyd and Akihiko Yoshida, *The Japanese Submarine Force and World War II* (Annapolis, MD: Naval Institute Press, 1995), 77–78.
12. John Keegan, *The Price of Admiralty: The Evolution of Naval Warfare* (New York: Viking Penguin Inc., 1989), 205–08.
13. E. B. Potter and Chester W. Nimitz, *Triumph in the Pacific: The Navy's Struggle Against Japan* (Englewood Cliffs, NJ: Prentice-Hall Inc., 1963), 16.
14. Culora, "Japanese Operational Plans in World War II," 18.

15. Ibid., 17.
16. Potter and Nimitz, *Triumph in the Pacific*, 16.
17. Jonathan Parshall and Anthony Tully, *Shattered Sword: The Untold Story of the Battle of Midway* (Washington, D.C.: Potomac Books, 2007), 98.
18. Even two days late, the submarines of SubRon 5 were still on station before Yamamoto's timeline predicted the U.S. forces would leave Pearl Harbor and head toward Midway. Claiming SubRon 5 was late cannot be used as a factor for Japan's defeat at Midway.
19. Jack Greene, *The Midway Campaign* (Conshohocken, PA: Combined Books, Inc., 1995), 197.
20. Parshall and Tully, *Shattered Sword*, 359.

2. Japanese Naval Doctrine

1. Sadao Asada, *From Mahan to Pearl Harbor: The Imperial Japanese Navy and the United States* (Annapolis, MD: Naval Institute Press, 2006), 283.
2. John T. Kuehn, *Agents of Innovations: The General Board and the Design of the Fleet That Defeated the Japanese Navy* (Annapolis, MD: Naval Institute Press, 2008), 150.
3. Alfred T. Mahan, *Mahan on Naval Warfare: Selections from the Writings of Rear Admiral Alfred T. Mahan*, ed. Allan Westcott (Mineola, NY: Dover Publications, Inc. 1991), xvi; Ronald H. Spector, *Eagle Against the Sun: The American War with Japan* (New York: The Free Press, 1985), 43.
4. Philip A. Crowl, "Alfred Thayer Mahan: The Naval Historian," in *Makers of Modern Strategy from Machiavelli to the Nuclear Age*, ed. Peter Paret (Princeton, NJ: Princeton University Press, 1986), 458.
5. Kuehn, *Agents of Innovation*, 150.
6. James B. Wood, *Japanese Military Strategy in the Pacific War* (New York: Rowman & Littlefield Publishers, Inc., 2007), 72–73.
7. Toshi Yoshihara and James R. Holmes, "Japanese Maritime Thought: If Not Mahan, Who?" *Naval War College Review*, 59 (Summer, 2006): 27.
8. Ibid., 26.
9. Ibid., 27.
10. Mark P. Parillo, "The Imperial Japanese Navy in World War II," in *Reevaluating Major Naval Combatants of World War II*, ed. James J. Sadkovich (New York: Greenwood Press, 1990), 70.
11. Yoshihara and Holmes, "Japanese Maritime Thought," 27.
12. Ibid., 27–28.
13. Atsushi Oi, "The Japanese Navy in 1941," in *The Pacific War Papers: Japanese Documents of World War II*, eds. Donald M. Goldstein and Katherine V. Dillon (Washington, D.C.: Potomac Books, 2006), 9–10.
14. Spector, *Eagle Against the Sun*, 44.
15. Culora, "Japanese Operational Plans in World War II," 5.

16. Asada, *From Mahan to Pearl Harbor*, 41.
17. Yoshihara, "Japanese Maritime Thought," 28; Asada, *From Mahan to Pearl Harbor*, 41.
18. Yoshihara, "Japanese Maritime Thought," 29.
19. Culora, "Japanese Operational Plans in World War II," 3.
20. D. Clayton James, "American and Japanese Strategies in the Pacific War," in *Makers of Modern Strategy from Machiavelli to the Nuclear Age*, ed. Peter Paret (Princeton, NJ: Princeton University Press, 1986), 706.
21. Ibid., 707.
22. Jeffrey G. Barlow, "World War II: U.S. and Japanese Naval Strategies," in *Seapower and Strategy*, eds. Colin S. Gray and Roger W. Barnett, (Annapolis, MD: Naval Institute Press, 1989), 250.
23. Asada, *From Mahan to Pearl Harbor*, 107.
24. Ibid., 179.
25. Yôichi Hirama, "Japanese Naval Preparations for World War II," *Naval War College Review*, 44 (Spring, 1991): 72.
26. Gerhard L. Weinberg, *A World at Arms: A Global History of World War II* (New York: Cambridge University Press, 2005), 257.
27. Mark Stille, *Imperial Japanese Navy Submarines 1941–1945* (New York: Osprey Publishing Ltd., 2007), 5.
28. Haruo Tohmatsu and H. P. Willmott, *A Gathering Darkness: The Coming of War to the Far East and the Pacific, 1921–1942* (Lanham, MD: SR Books, 2004), 41–42.
29. Barlow, "U.S. and Japanese Naval Strategies," 250; John Costello, *The Pacific War 1941–1945* (New York: William Morrow and Company, Inc., 1981), 82.
30. Minoru Genda, "Tactical Planning in the Imperial Japanese Navy," *Naval War College Review*, 22 (October 1969): 46; Asada, *From Mahan to Pearl Harbor*, 107, 50; Masanori Ito, *The End of the Imperial Japanese Navy* (New York: W. W. Norton & Company, Inc., 1962), 23.
31. Barlow, "U.S. and Japanese Naval Strategies," 249.
32. Sadao Asada, *Culture Shock and Japanese–American Relations: Historical Essays* (Columbia, MO: University of Missouri Press, 2007), 144; Genda, "Tactical Planning," 45.
33. Costello, *The Pacific War*, 82.
34. Kuehn, *Agents of Innovation*, 151; Asada, *From Mahan to Pearl Harbor*, 182.
35. Kennosuke Torisu and Masataka Chilhaya, "Japanese Submarine Tactics," United States Naval Institute *Proceedings*, 87 (February 1961), 78.
36. Asada, *From Mahan to Pearl Harbor*, 182.
37. Asada, *Culture Shock*, 144.
38. Carl Boyd, "The Japanese Submarine Force and the Legacy of Strategic and Operational Doctrine Developed Between the World Wars," in *Selected Papers from the Citadel Conference on War and Diplomacy, 1978*, ed. Larry H. Addington et al., (Charleston, S.C.: Citadel Press, 1979), 33.
39. Culora, "Japanese Operational Plans in World War II," 3–4.
40. Kuehn, *Agents of Innovation*, 151.

41. Adams, *If Mahan Ran the Great Pacific War*, 49.
42. Asada, *Culture Shock*, 144.
43. Wood, *Japanese Military Strategy*, 76.
44. Spector, *Eagle Against the Sun*, 48–49.
45. Boyd, "The Japanese Submarine Force and the Legacy of Strategic and Operational Doctrine," 32; Barlow, "World War II: U.S. and Japanese Naval Strategies," 269.
46. Anthony Newpower, *Iron Men and Tin Fish: The Race to Build a Better Torpedo During World War II* (Westport, CT: Praeger Security International, 2006), 113–14.
47. Vincent P. O'Hara, W. David Dickson, and Richard Worth, *On Seas Contested: The Seven Great Navies of the Second World War* (Annapolis, MD: Naval Institute Press, 2010), 202.
48. Barlow, "World War II: U.S. and Japanese Naval Strategies," 269.
49. Wood, *Japanese Military Strategy*, 59.
50. Peter Padfield, *War Beneath the Sea: Submarine Conflict During World War II* (New York: John Wiley & Sons, Inc., 1995), 36.
51. Samuel Eliot Morison, *History of United States Naval Operations in World War II Volume IV: Coral Sea, Midway and Submarine Actions, May 1942–August 1942* (Boston, MA: Little, Brown and Company, 1988), 196–98.
52. O'Hara, *On Seas Contested*, 202–03.
53. Kuenne, *The Attack Submarine*, 169–70.

3. Japanese Submarine Strategy and Tactics

1. Carl von Clausewitz, *On War*. Edited and Translated by Michael Howard and Peter Paret (New York: Alfred A. Knopf, 1993), 209.
2. O'Hara, *On Seas Contested*, 175–76.
3. David C. Evans and Mark R. Peattie, *Kaigun: Strategy, Tactics, and Technology in the Imperial Japanese Navy 1887–1941* (Annapolis, MD: Naval Institute Press, 1997), 433–34.
4. Evans and Peattie, *Kaigun*, 433.
5. Ibid.
6. Stille, *Imperial Japanese Navy Submarines*, 6.
7. Evans and Peattie, *Kaigun*, 433.
8. Stille, *Imperial Japanese Navy Submarines*, 6.
9. Kuenne, *The Attack Submarine*, 169.
10. Kennosuke Torisu and Masataka Chilhaya, "Japanese Submarine Tactics and the Kaiten," in *The Japanese Navy in World War II*, 2nd ed, ed. David C. Evans (Annapolis, MD: Naval Institute Press, 1986), 440; I. J. Galantin, *Submarine Admiral* (Urbana, IL: University of Illinois Press, 1995), 96–97; Morison, *Naval Operations, Volume 4*. 197.
11. Atsushi Oi, "Why Japan's Antisubmarine Warfare Failed," in *The Japanese Navy in World War II*, 2nd ed, ed. David C. Evans (Annapolis, MD: Naval Institute Press, 1986), 414.

12. Boyd and Yoshida, *The Japanese Submarine Force*, 191–192.
13. Spector, *Eagle Against the Sun*, 44; O'Hara, *On Seas Contested*, 176.
14. Carl Boyd, "American Naval Intelligence of Japanese Submarine Operations Early in the Pacific War," *The Journal of Military History* 53 (April 1989): 172.
15. Ibid.
16. Parillo, "The Imperial Japanese Navy in World War II," 63–64; Wood, *Japanese Military Strategy in the Pacific War*, 63.
17. Barlow, "World War II: U.S. and Japanese Naval Strategies," 269.
18. Evans and Peattie, *Kaigun*, 434.
19. Boyd and Yoshida, *The Japanese Submarine Force*, 5; Stille, *Imperial Japanese Navy Submarines*, 6.
20. Morison, *Naval Operations, Volume 4*, 197.
21. Morison, *Naval Operations, Volume 4*, 198.
22. O'Hara, *On Seas Contested*, 176.
23. Ibid., 164.
24. Weinberg, *A World At Arms*, 384.
25. Donald D. Gerry, "Japanese Submarine Operational Errors in World War II: Will America's SSNs Make the Same Mistake?" (Newport, RI: Naval War College Joint Military Operations Department, May 1996), 2.
26. Dorr Carpenter and Norman Polmar, *Submarines of the Imperial Japanese Navy*. (Annapolis, MD: Naval Institute Press, 1986), 9–11. Japan believed large, long-range submarines could attack the U.S. fleet as it moved westward, reducing its strength through attrition while at the same time reporting its movements in preparation for the decisive battle. Thus, was born the strategic concept for the Japanese submarine force. (Carpenter and Polmar, *Submarines of the Imperial Japanese Navy*, 1). The Japanese Navy sought through repeated submarine attacks to reduce the fighting capabilities of the United States fleet by about thirty percent on its trans-Pacific passage; and second, to seek a decisive encounter with U.S. forces after they had advanced to the western Pacific. The Naval Operational Plan of 1936 stipulated, "A portion of the Combined Fleet's submarine force will advance, as soon as hostilities commenced, to Hawaii and the Pacific Coast of the United States." Japanese submarines would scout the moves of the enemy main fleet, attack it on its trans-Pacific passage, and eventually join the Combined Fleet in the main decisive encounter. For this purpose, the Japanese Navy built large, high-speed submarines in great numbers. (Asada, *Culture Shock*, 144).
27. Kennosuke Torisu and Masataka Chilhaya, "Japanese Submarine Tactics," 442. Kaiten were essentially crewed torpedoes used by the Imperial Japanese Navy in the final stages of World War 2. These were "special attack" weapons, whose successful operational use brought an inevitable death of the crew.
28. Stille, *Imperial Japanese Navy Submarines*, 6.
29. Gerry, "Japanese Submarine Operational Errors," 7.
30. Keith Wheeler, *War Under the Pacific*, 207; William B. Hopkins, *The Pacific War: The Strategy, Politics, and Players That Won the War* (Minneapolis, MN: Zenith Press, 2008), 207; Adams, *If Mahan Ran the Great Pacific War*, 365.

31. U.S. Naval Technical Mission to Japan, "Ship and Related Targets: Japanese Submarine Operations." Index No. S-17 (Washington, DC: Operational Archives, U.S. Naval History Division, 1946), 8.
32. Ibid., 21.
33. Gerry, "Japanese Submarine Operational Errors," 7.
34. Gary E. Weir, "Silent Victory 1940–1945," Winter 1999, accessed May 12, 2009, http://www.navy.mil/navydata/cno/n87/usw/issue_6/silent_victory.html.
35. Boyd, "American Naval Intelligence of Japanese Submarine Operations," 170–71.
36. Wheeler, *War Under the Pacific*, 97; George W. Baer, "U.S. Naval Strategy 1890–1945." *Naval War College Review*, 44 (Winter, 1991): 23.
37. Mochitsura Hashimoto, *Sunk: The Story of the Japanese Submarine Fleet 1941–1945* (New York: Henry Holt and Company, 1954), 62; Wheeler, *War Under the Pacific*, 97.
38. Holger H. Herwig, "Innovation Ignored: The Submarine Problem – Germany, Britain and the United States, 1919–1939," in *Military Innovation in the Interwar Period*, ed. Williamson Murray and Allan R. Millett (New York: Cambridge University Press, 1996), 256.
39. Adams, *If Mahan Ran the Great Pacific War*, 364.
40. U.S. Naval Technical Mission to Japan, 11.
41. United States Strategic Bombing Survey (Pacific), Naval Analysis Division. *Interrogations of Japanese Officials, Volume 2* (Washington, D.C.: Government Printing Office, 1946), 293.
42. U.S. Naval Technical Mission to Japan, 11.
43. Ito, *The End of the Imperial Japanese Navy*, 23.
44. U.S. Naval Technical Mission to Japan, 11.
45. Boyd and Yoshida, *The Japanese Submarine Force*, 4.
46. U.S. Naval Technical Mission to Japan, 11.
47. Barlow, "U.S. and Japanese Naval Strategies," 269; Spector, *Eagle Against the Sun*, 48; Oi, "The Japanese Navy in 1941," 12.
48. Carpenter and Polmar, *Submarines of the Imperial Japanese Navy*, 22.
49. Gerry, "Japanese Submarine Operational Errors," 4.
50. USSBS, *Interrogations of Japanese Officials, Volume 2*, 292.
51. Gerry, "Japanese Submarine Operational Errors," 5–6.
52. Ibid., 6.

4. United States Naval Doctrine

1. Colin S. Gray, *Modern Strategy* (New York: Oxford University Press, 1999), vii.
2. Thomas C. Hone and Trent Hone, *Battle Line: The United States Navy 1919–1939* (Annapolis, MD: Naval Institute Press, 2006), 68.
3. Baer, "U.S. Naval Strategy," 18.
4. Trent Hone, "Building a Doctrine: USN Tactics and Battle Plans in the Interwar Period," *International Journal of Naval History* 1, no. 2 (October 2002), accessed

February 19, 2010, http://www.ijnhonline.org/volume1_number2_Oct02/articles/article_hone1_doctrine.doc.htm.
5. Trent Hone, "U.S. Navy Surface Battle Doctrine and Victory in the Pacific," *Naval War College Review*, 62 (Winter, 2009), 70.
6. Hone, "Building a Doctrine," *International Journal of Naval History*.
7. Spector, *Eagle Against the Sun*, 147.
8. Hone, "U.S. Navy Surface Battle," 67.
9. Trent Hone, "The Evolution of Fleet Tactical Doctrine in the U.S. Navy, 1922–1941," *The Journal of Military History* 67 (October 2003): 1108.
10. Hone, "Building a Doctrine," *International Journal of Naval History*.
11. Spector, *Eagle Against the Sun*, 147; Peter Padfield, *The Battleship Era* (New York: David McKay Company, Inc., 1972), 280.
12. Padfield, *The Battleship Era*, 283.
13. Ibid., 290.
14. Spector, *Eagle Against the Sun*, 148.
15. O'Hara, *On Seas Contested*, 228; Galantin, *Submarine Admiral*, 48–49.
16. Craig C. Felker, *Testing American Sea Power: U.S. Navy Strategic Exercises, 1923–1940* (College Station, TX: Texas A&M University Press, 2007), 62.
17. Galantin, *Submarine Admiral*, 47.
18. Galantin, *Submarine Admiral*, 49; Felker, *Testing American Sea Power*, 62.
19. Felker, *Testing American Sea Power*, 62.
20. Ernest Andrade, Jr., "Submarine Policy in the United States Navy, 1919–1941," *Military Affairs*, 35, no. 2 (April 1971): 55.
21. James F. DeRose, *Unrestricted Warfare: How a New Breed of Offers Led the Submarine Force to Victory in World War II* (Edison, NJ: Castle Books, 2000), 4.
22. *Silent Service: Submarine Warfare in WWII, Disc 2: Captains of World War II*. DVD. A&E Television Networks, 2000.
23. Douglas V. Smith, "Preparing for War: Naval Education Between the World Wars," *International Journal of Naval History* 1, no. 1 (April 2002), accessed February 19, 2010, http://www.ijnhonline.org/volume1_number1_Apr02/article_smith_education_war.doc.htm.
24. Galantin, *Submarine Admiral*, 77.
25. Ibid. The cleanliness and material condition of his boat, the smart appearance and discipline of his crew, and timeliness of his reports were critical factors more apparent to his division commander than the less measurable qualities of aggressiveness and leadership under stress.
26. Padfield, *War Beneath the Sea*, 31; Stephen Peter Rosen, *Winning the Next War: Innovation and the Modern Military* (Ithaca, NY: Cornell University Press, 1991), 135; Harris, *The Navy Times Book of Submarines*, 310; DeRose, *Unrestricted Warfare*, 4; Joel Ira Holwitt, *Execute Against Japan: The U.S. Decision to Conduct Unrestricted Submarine Warfare* (College Station, TX: Texas A&M University Press, 2009), 78.
27. DeRose, *Unrestricted Warfare*, 4.
28. William Tuohy, *The Bravest Man*, 49.

29. Herwig, "Innovation Ignored: The Submarine Problem," 259.
30. Barrett Tillman, *Clash of the Carriers* (New York: NAL Caliber, 2005), 45.
31. DeRose, *Unrestricted Warfare*, 4.
32. Daniel E. Benere, "A Critical Examination of the U.S. Navy's Use of Unrestricted Submarine Warfare in the Pacific Theater During World War II." (Newport, RI: Naval War College Joint Military Operations Department, May 1992), 6; DeRose, *Unrestricted Warfare*, 4.
33. Drew Middleton, *Submarine: The Ultimate Naval Weapon: Its Past, Present & Future* (Chicago: Playboy Press. 1976), 96–97.
34. DeRose, *Unrestricted Warfare*, 4.
35. Hone and Hone, *Battle Line*, 68.
36. John B. Hattendorf, *Naval History and Maritime Strategy: Collected Essays* (Malabar, FL: Krieger Publishing Company, 2000), 116.
37. Puleston, *The Armed Forces of the Pacific*, 232.

5. United States Submarine Strategy and Tactics

1. Thomas G. Mahnken, "Strategic Theory," in *Strategy in the Contemporary World*, 2nd ed, eds John Baylis et al (Oxford: Oxford University Press, 2007), 67.
2. Wheeler, *War Under the Pacific*, 26.
3. Hone, "U.S. Navy Surface Battle Doctrine," 72; H. P. Wilmott, *The Last Century of Sea Power, Volume Two: From Washington to Tokyo, 1922–1945* (Bloomington, IN: Indiana University Press, 2010), 486; Galantin, *Submarine Admiral*, 9.
4. Gary E. Weir, "Silent Defense: 1900–1940," Summer 1999, accessed July 27, 2008, http://www.navy.mil/navydata/cno/n87/usw/issue_4/silent_defense.html.
5. Gary E. Weir, "The Search for an American Submarine Strategy and Design, 1916–1936," *Naval War College Review*, 44 (Winter, 1991): 34; Hone, "U.S. Navy Surface Battle Doctrine," 72.
6. Weir, "The Search for an American Submarine Strategy and Design," 34.
7. Weir, "Silent Defense."
8. Weir, "The Search for an American Submarine Strategy and Design," 40.
9. Carl Boyd, *American Command of the Sea Through Carriers, Codes, and the Silent Service* (Newport News, VA: The Mariners' Museum, 1995), 32; Galantin, *Submarine Admiral*, 28; Felker, *Testing American Sea Power*, 66.
10. Weir, "Silent Defense."
11. Puleston, *The Armed Forces of the Pacific*, 220.
12. H. P. Willmott, *The Last Century of Sea Power, Volume Two: From Washington to Tokyo, 1922–1945* (Bloomington, IN: Indiana University Press, 2010), 486.
13. Kuenne, *The Attack Submarine*, 173; Felker, *Testing American Sea Power*, 68.
14. Galantin, *Submarine Admiral*, 81–82.
15. Middleton, *Submarine*, 97; George W. Baer, *One Hundred Years of Sea Power: The U.S. Navy, 1890–1990* (Stanford, CA: Stanford University Press, 1994), 145.

16. Thomas Parrish, *The Submarine: A History* (New York: Viking, 2004), 342.
17. Middleton, *Submarine*, 95.
18. Rosen, *Winning the Next War*, 137.
19. ULTRA was the name given to information gained from the deciphering of messages passed by the enemy in code during the war.
20. Wheeler, *War Under the Pacific*, 25–26; Rosen, *Winning the Next War*, 133; Costello, *The Pacific War*, 453; Jim Christley, *U.S. Submarines 1941–45* (New York: Osprey Publishing Ltd., 2006), 39–40.
21. Richard W. Durham, "Operational Art in the Conduct of Naval Operations," (Fort Leavenworth, KS: School of Advanced Military Studies, United States Army Command and General Staff College, March 1998), 15.
22. Peter C. Smith, *Midway: Dauntless Victory, Fresh Perspectives on America's Seminal Naval Victory of World War II* (Barnsley, South Yorkshire, England: Pen & Sword Books Limited. 2007), 91.
23. Robert Gannon, *Hellions of the Deep: The Development of American Torpedoes in World War II* (University Park, PA: The Pennsylvania State University Press, 1996), 74–75; Frederick J. Milford, "U.S. Navy Torpedoes, Part Two: The Great Torpedo Scandal, 1941–1943." *The Submarine Review*, October 1996, 82–83; Theodore Roscoe, *United States Submarine Operations in World War II* (Annapolis, MD: Naval Institute Press, 1949), 251.
24. Middleton, *Submarine*, 103; Rosen, *Winning the Next War*, 143.
25. Middleton, *Submarine*, 97; Hone and Hone, *Battle Line*, 120.
26. Andrade, "Submarine Policy in the United States Navy," 55. In 1922, all naval powers signed a treaty providing for prohibition of attacks by submarines on merchant shipping. (Weir, "The Search for an American Submarine Strategy and Design," 43). All the participants agreed that unrestricted submarine warfare was illegal, but Japan and the United States argued strongly for retention of submarines, stressing their value as reconnaissance and screening assets for their fleets. (Kuehn, *Agents of Innovation*, 28). Even though many naval strategists recognized the submarine's effectiveness as a commerce weapon and gave some attention to problems of commerce during fleet exercises, the U.S. Navy was hesitant to adopt a policy opposed by both national feeling and treaty.
27. Goldman, *Sunken Treaties*, 77.
28. Padfield, *War Beneath the Sea*, 29–31; Miller, *War Plan Orange*, 319. Most authors assert America made the decision to wage and execute unrestricted submarine warfare in reprisal for Japan's surprise attack on Pearl Harbor. Talbott claims that unrestricted submarine warfare was the probable outcome of decisions made as early as 1919 and pursued throughout the interwar period. (J. E. Talbott, "Weapons Development, War Planning and Policy: The US Navy and the Submarine, 1917–1941," *Naval War College Review* 37 (May–June, 1984): 54–56). Although the submarine force doctrine acknowledged the remote possibility of unrestricted submarine warfare, "at the lower levels, in its operational and tactical preparations,

the service held a consistent view: the U.S. Navy would not allow its submarine captains to attack merchant shipping without warning." (Holwitt, *Execute Against Japan*, 81–82). American interwar naval planners judiciously avoided suggesting that the Navy's submarines should attack merchant vessels. (Weir, "The Search for an American Submarine Strategy and Design," 43).

29. Padfield, *War Beneath the Sea*, 29–31; Edward S. Miller, *War Plan Orange: The U.S. Strategy to Defeat Japan, 1987–1945* (Annapolis, MD: Naval Institute Press, 2007), 319.
30. Miller, *War Plan Orange*, 152.
31. Weir, "The Search for an American Submarine Strategy and Design," 43.
32. Miller, *War Plan Orange*, 152.
33. Galantin, *Submarine Admiral*, 47
34. Tuohy, *The Bravest Man*, 50.
35. Baer, "U.S. Naval Strategy," 23.
36. Baer, *One Hundred Years of Sea Power*, 144.
37. O'Hara, *On Seas Contested*, 228.
38. Boyd, *American Command of the Sea*, 32.
39. Durham, "Operational Art in the Conduct of Naval Operations," 19.

6. Japanese Submarine Actions at Midway

1. Hashimoto, *Sunk*, 87.
2. Zenji Orita and Joseph D. Harrington, *I-Boat Captain* (Canoga Park, CA: Major Books, 1976), 74.
3. Orita, *I-Boat Captain*, 62. To reconnoiter Hawaii prior to the Midway operations, the Combined Fleet ordered the execution of the Second "K" Operation between the latter part of May and before June 3 (Gordon Prange, *Miracle at Midway* (New York: McGraw-Hill Book Company, 1982), 31; Japanese Monograph No. 110. "Submarine Operations in Second Phase Operations, Part I, April–August 1942." (Washington, D.C.: Department of the Army, 1952), 17). I outline the Second "K" Operation in the next section of this chapter.
4. Padfield, *War Beneath the Sea*, 231.
5. Orita, *I-Boat Captain*, 74; Padfield, *War Beneath the Sea*, 231; Carpenter and Polmar, *Submarines of the Imperial Japanese Navy*, 24.
6. Peter C. Smith, *The Battle of Midway: The Battle that Turned the Tide of the Pacific War* (Staplehurst, Great Britain: Spellmount Ltd., 1996), 54; Carpenter and Polmar, *Submarines of the Imperial Japanese Navy*, 24.
7. Prange, *Miracle at Midway*, 31; Bates, *The Battle of Midway*, 109.
8. Orita, *I-Boat Captain*, 63; Bates, *The Battle of Midway*, 25–26.
9. Smith, *Midway*, 18.
10. Bates, *The Battle of Midway*, 109.
11. Japanese Monograph No. 110, 21–22; Smith, *Midway*, 18; Orita, *I-Boat Captain*, 63. *I-171* was to be on station at Latitude 19° N, Longitude 174°20' West. *I-174*

had lifeguard duty 200 miles at 200° from Keahole Point, which is on the west side of the main island of Hawaii.
12. Bates, *The Battle of Midway*, 26; Orita, *I-Boat Captain*, 63; USSBS, *Interrogations of Japanese Officials, Volume 2*, 465; Smith, *The Battle of Midway*, 55.
13. Boyd and Yoshida, *The Japanese Submarine Force*, 81.
14. Mitsuo Fuchida and Masatake Okumiya, "The Battle of Midway," in *The Japanese Navy in World War II*, 2nd ed, ed. David C. Evans (Annapolis, MD: Naval Institute Press, 1986), 124.
15. W. J. Holmes, *Undersea Victory*, 131; Bates, *The Battle of Midway*, 26; USSBS, *Interrogations of Japanese Officials, Volume 2*, 465.
16. Japanese Monograph No. 110, 22–23; Bates, *The Battle of Midway*, 26.
17. Fuchida and Okumiya, "The Battle of Midway," 124; Smith, *The Battle of Midway*, 55.
18. Bates, *The Battle of Midway*, 109.
19. Mitsuo Fuchida and Masatake Okumiya, *Midway: The Battle That Doomed Japan, The Japanese Navy's Story* (Annapolis, MD: Naval Institute Press, 1955), 117.
20. Fuchida and Okumiya, *Midway*, 110–11; Bates, *The Battle of Midway*, 32; Morison, *Naval Operations, Volume 4*. 87–89; Boyd and Yoshida, *The Japanese Submarine Force*, 202.
21. Prange, *Miracle At Midway*, 33; Padfield, *War Beneath the Sea*, 231–32; Morison, *Naval Operations, Volume 4*, 89; Orita, *I-Boat Captain*, 76; Carpenter and Polmar, *Submarines of the Imperial Japanese Navy*, 24; Boyd and Yoshida, *The Japanese Submarine Force*, 34; Parshall and Tully, *Shattered Sword*, 49.
22. Prange, *Miracle at Midway*, 31; Japanese Monograph 110, *Submarine Operations in Second Phase Operations*, 18.
23. Fuchida and Okumiya, *Midway*, 117; Japanese Monograph No. 110, 17, 22–23; Prange, *Miracle at Midway*, 31; Andrieu D'Albas, *Death of a Navy: Japanese Naval Action in World War II* (New York: The Devin-Adair Company, 1957), 118; Hashimoto, *Sunk*, 87.
24. Boyd and Yoshida, The Japanese Submarine Force, 202; Japanese Monograph No. 93. "Midway Operations, May–Jun. 1942." (Washington, D.C.: Department of the Army, 1962), 24; Bates, *The Battle of Midway*, 25; Boyd and Yoshida, 202; Japanese Monograph 93, 24.
25. Dallas Woodbury Isom, *Midway Inquest: Why the Japanese Lost the Battle of Midway* (Bloomington, IN: Indiana University Press, 2007), 98; Carpenter and Polmar, *Submarines of the Imperial Japanese Navy*, 24.
26. Orita, *I-Boat Captain*, 65.
27. Wheeler, *War Under the Pacific*, 106.
28. Orita, *I-Boat Captain*, 67; Carpenter and Polmar, *Submarines of the Imperial Japanese Navy*, 24; Orita, *I-Boat Captain*, 74.
29. Wheeler, *War Under the Pacific*, 106.
30. Holmes, *Undersea Victory*, 133.
31. John B. Lundstrom, *Black Shoe Carrier Admiral: Frank Jack Fletcher at Coral Sea, Midway, and Guadalcanal* (Annapolis, MD: Naval Institute Press, 2007), 221.

32. John Prados, *Combined Fleet Decoded* (New York: Random House, 1995), 322.
33. Fuchida and Okumiya, *Midway*, 153; Parshall and Tully, *Shattered Sword*, 98.
34. Wheeler, *War Under the Pacific*, 106.
35. Smith, *The Battle of Midway*, 56.
36. Parshall and Tully, *Shattered Sword*, 98. Yamamoto's plans called for an air attack on Midway by the carrier task force for June 4 and the landing by the occupation force on June 6. After the completion of the operation and even after the withdrawal of the surface forces, the submarine group operating around Midway and Hawaii was to continue its operations for the time being with Midway as its base. In case the U.S. fleet did not sortie, the Combined Fleet was to prepare itself to draw the enemy fleet out to the vicinity of the invasion point. In this case, SubRon 3 and SubRon 5 would deploy northeast of Midway. If the U.S. fleet advanced westward in force and the whole Japanese fleet was required to fight a decisive battle, the 1st Submarine Group of the Northern Force from the Aleutians would also be put under the command of the commanding officer of the Submarine Force (Japanese Monograph 110, 16–17).
37. Fuchida and Okumiya, *Midway*, 173–74; Prange, *Miracle at Midway*, 170.
38. Japanese Monograph 110, 17; Orita, *I-Boat Captain*, 63–64; Boyd and Yoshida, *The Japanese Submarine Force*, 202; Japanese Monograph 110, 22–23.
39. Yahachi Tanabe and Joseph D. Harrington, "I Sank the *Yorktown* at Midway," in *Submarines in Combat*, ed. Joseph B. Icenhower (New York: Franklin Watts, Inc., 1964), 32.
40. Prange, *Miracle at Midway*, 145.
41. Bates, *The Battle of Midway*, 25.
42. Ibid., 108.
43. Prange, *Miracle at Midway*, 296. Captain Kameto Kuroshima, Combined Fleet's operations officer, suggested removing the submarine cordon from its position between Hawaii and Midway (Cordon A) and concentrating it in the battle area.
44. Boyd and Yoshida, *The Japanese Submarine Force*, 83. Cordon C, about two hundred miles long and 500 miles east of Midway, ran along meridian 168° 40' W.
45. Robert Schultz and James Shell, "Strange Fortune," *World War II*, May/June 2010, 63.
46. Prange, *Miracle at Midway*, 305; United States Navy. *The Japanese Story of the Battle of Midway* (Washington D.C.: Office of Naval Intelligence, 1947); Padfield, *War Beneath the Sea*, 240; E. B. Potter and Chester W. Nimitz, *The Great Sea War: The Dramatic Story of Naval Action in World War II* (Englewood Cliffs, NJ: Prentice-Hall Inc., 1960), 240.
47. Prange, *Miracle at Midway*, 322–23.
48. United States Navy. *The Japanese Story of the Battle of Midway*. Yamamoto determined the cruisers, unable to complete their mission before dawn's light, would be vulnerable to air attack, so he canceled the bombardment and recalled the ships. (Robert Schultz and James Shell, "Strange Fortune," 63).
49. Prange, *Miracle at Midway*, 322–23.

50. H. P. Willmott, *The War with Japan: The Period of Balance May 1942–October 1943* (Wilmington, DE: Scholarly Resources, Inc., 2002), 80.
51. Padfield, *War Beneath the Sea*, 240. *I-168* fired its first round at 0130 on June 5.
52. Willmott, *The War with Japan*, 81.
53. Willmott, *The War With Japan*, 85–86; Padfield, *War Beneath the Sea*, 241; Hashimoto, *Sunk*, 83.
54. Boyd and Yoshida, *The Japanese Submarine Force*, 83. The new geographical location was a north–south line on meridian 180° W for all submarines except for *I-168* which Yamamoto previously ordered to find and sink *Yorktown*.
55. Japanese Monograph 110, 26–27.
56. Willmott, *The War With Japan*, 85–86; Padfield, *War Beneath the Sea*, 241; Hashimoto, *Sunk*, 3.
57. Willmott, *The War with Japan*, 87.
58. Potter and Nimitz, *The Great Sea War*, 245.
59. Bates, *The Battle of Midway*, 184; Japanese Monograph 93, 84. These submarines were to attack the American forces and furnish intelligence in cooperation with search operations from Marshall Island air bases.
60. Japanese Monograph 110, 26–27; Boyd and Yoshida, 83–84.
61. Bates, *The Battle of Midway*, 184. The submarines searched as far eastward as 173° West Longitude.
62. Boyd and Yoshida, *The Japanese Submarine Force*, 84; CINCPAC, "Action Report Battle of Midway, Second Supplementary Report" (Washington, D.C.: Navy Department, 1942); USSBS, *Interrogations of Japanese Officials, Volume 2*, 465; Holmes, *Undersea Victory*, 145.
63. Japanese Monograph 100, 26–27; Japanese Monograph 93, 86.

7. United States Submarine Actions at Midway

1. Admiral Chester Nimitz, quoted in Adams, *If Mahan Ran the Great Pacific War*, 118.
2. Nathan Miller, *War at Sea: A Naval History of World War II* (New York: Scribner, 1995), 246.
3. Costello, *The Pacific War*, 276.
4. Miller, *War at Sea*, 246.
5. John Winton, *ULTRA in the Pacific: How Breaking Japanese Codes & Ciphers Affected Naval Operations Against Japan* (London: Leo Cooper, 1993), 58.
6. Paul J. Jaeger, *Operational Intelligence at the Battle of Midway* (Newport, CT: U.S. Naval War College, 1998), 9.
7. Edwin T. Layton, *And I Was There: Pearl Harbor and Midway: Breaking the Secrets* (New York: William Morrow and Company, Inc., 1985), 411–12. The Japanese would launch their carrier aircraft at a point 175 miles from Midway on a bearing of 325°.
8. Prange, *Miracle at Midway*, 121.

9. Prange, *Miracle at Midway*, 121–22; Potter and Nimitz, *The Great Sea War*, 227; Roscoe, *United States Submarine Operations*, 124; Kenneth Poolman, *The Winning Edge: Naval Technology in Action, 1939–1945* (Annapolis, MD: Naval Institute Press, 1997), 149.
10. Kuenne, *The Attack Submarine*, 159; Padfield, *War Beneath the Sea*, 234; H. P. Willmott, *The Barrier and the Javelin: Japanese and Allied Pacific Strategies, February to June 1942* (Annapolis, MD: Naval Institute Press, 1989), 309; Willmott, *The War with Japan*, 32. This was the first time that Pearl Harbor submarines interrupted their raiding patrols to operate as a task force with the Pacific Fleet (Roscoe, *United States Submarine Operations*, 123).
11. Roscoe, *United States Submarine Operations*, 124.
12. Padfield, *War Beneath the Sea*, 232.
13. Willmott, *The Barrier and the Javelin*, 308.
14. Smith, *The Battle of Midway*, 54; Roscoe, *United States Submarine Operations*, 124; Willmott, *The Barrier and the Javelin*, 308.
15. Padfield, *War Beneath the Sea*, 232; Bates, *The Battle of Midway*, 67; Willmott, *The War With Japan*, 32.
16. Willmott, *The Barrier and the Javelin*, 308; Roscoe, *United States Submarine Operations*, 126; Bates, *The Battle of Midway*, 67; National Archives, *USS Tambor War Patrol Report 3* (College Park, MD: National Archives and Records Administration, 1942), 5.
17. Willmott, *The Barrier and the Javelin*, 308; Bates, *The Battle of Midway*, 67; Willmott, *The Barrier and the Javelin*, 308.
18. Willmott, *The Barrier and the Javelin*, 309; Bates, *The Battle of Midway*, 67.
19. Bates, *The Battle of Midway*, 67; Clay Blair Jr., *Silent Victory: The U.S. Submarine War Against Japan* (Philadelphia: J.B. Lippincott Company, 1975, 213.
20. Holmes, *Undersea Victory*, 133.
21. Japanese Monograph 93, 27; Holmes, *Undersea Victory*, 133.
22. Holmes, *Undersea Victory*, 133; Prange, *Miracle at Midway*, 54; Orita, *I-Boat Captain*, 74.
23. Japanese Monograph 93, 27; Fuchida and Okumiya, *Midway*, 152.
24. Fuchida and Okumiya, "The Battle of Midway," 125–27.
25. Ito, *The End of the Imperial Japanese Navy*, 60.
26. National Archives, *USS Cuttlefish War Patrol Report 2* (College Park, MD: National Archives and Records Administration, 1942), 13; Holmes, *Undersea Victory*, 133.
27. Bates, *The Battle of Midway*, 80; National Archives, *USS Cuttlefish War Patrol Report 2*, 14.
28. Isom, *Midway Inquest*, 95; Keegan, *The Price of Admiralty*, 208.
29. Matome Ugaki, *Fading Victory: The Diary of Admiral Matome Ugaki, 1941–1945*, trans. Masataka Chihaya, Donald M. Goldstein and Katherine V. Dillon, eds. (Annapolis, MD: Naval Institute Press, 1991), 131.

30. Isom, *Midway Inquest*, 95.
31. Ito, *The End of the Imperial Japanese Navy*, 60.
32. Bates, *The Battle of Midway*, 87; Holmes, *Undersea Victory*, 138.
33. Bates, *The Battle of Midway*, 88.
34. Potter and Nimitz, *The Great Sea War*, 234; Roscoe, *United States Submarine Operations*, 126; Walter Karig and Eric Purdon, *Battle Report, Pacific War: Middle Phase* (New York: Rinehart and Company, Inc., 1947), 47.
35. Potter and Nimitz, *The Great Sea War*, 234. The patrol report indicates *Nautilus* fired two torpedoes at a battleship at an estimated range of 4,500 yards.
36. Larry Kimmett and Margaret Regis, *U.S. Submarines in World War II* (Kingston, WA: Navigator Publishing, 1996), 44.
37. Ronald W. Russell, *No Right to Win* (New York: iUniverse, Inc., 2006), 290–91.
38. Potter and Nimitz, *The Great Sea War*, 234; National Archives, *USS Nautilus War Patrol Report 1* (College Park, MD: National Archives and Records Administration, 1942), 2.
39. Morison, *Naval Operations, Volume 4*, 129; Newpower, *Iron Men and Tin Fish*, 163; National Archives, *USS Nautilus War Patrol Report 1*, 3.
40. d'Albas, *Death of a Navy*, 129.
41. Karig and Purdon, *Battle Report, Middle Phase*, 47.
42. Morison, *Naval Operations, Volume 4*, 129.
43. National Archives, *USS Nautilus War Patrol Report 1*, 12; Potter and Nimitz, *The Great Sea War*, 239.
44. Fuchida and Okumiya, *Midway*, 220.
45. Newpower, *Iron Men and Tin Fish*, 163.
46. National Archives, *USS Nautilus War Patrol Report 1*, 3.
47. Bates, *The Battle of Midway*, 146–47; CINCPAC, "Action Report Battle of Midway," 3.
48. Miller, *War at Sea*, 257.
49. Schultz and Shell, "Strange Fortune," 61–62. Admiral English warned his submarines that friendly ships might cross their patrol lines during the night.
50. Potter and Nimitz, *The Great Sea War*, 241.
51. Bates, *The Battle of Midway*, 146, 165; Potter and Nimitz, *The Great Sea War*, 241; CINCPAC, "Action Report Battle of Midway," 3.
52. Willmott, *The War With Japan*, 81; Bates, *The Battle of Midway*, 163–65.
53. Schultz and Shell, "Strange Fortune," 64.
54. Holmes, *Undersea Victory*, 144; Padfield, *War Beneath the Sea*, 240. English sent the order to TG 7.1 at 0929 on June 5, the order to TG 7.2 at 0935, and the order to TG 7.3 at 1247.
55. *Trigger* complied with English's order, but *Narwhal*, because of engine trouble, proceeded directly to the 12-mile circle.
56. Bates, *The Battle of Midway*, 167.

57. National Archives, *USS Cuttlefish War Patrol Report 2*, 14.
58. Bates, *The Battle of Midway*, 162. Apparently English did not communicate to CNAS Midway his conclusions that he and Nimitz still expected a landing attempt on Midway.
59. Bates, *The Battle of Midway*, 166.
60. Holmes, *Undersea Victory*, 147.
61. Bates, *The Battle of Midway*, 181.
62. Ibid. Why English issued this order is obscure, as he issued it about thirty-six hours after a Midway search with excellent coverage reported all contacts made in the searched area were retiring.
63. Bates, *The Battle of Midway*, 181; Holmes, *Undersea Victory*, 147.
64. Bates, *The Battle of Midway*, 187.
65. At 1930, *Cuttlefish* reported being bombed by Japanese planes at 1300, 420 miles from Midway. No damage was sustained, and *Cuttlefish* arrived at Pearl Harbor on June 15.
66. Bates, *The Battle of Midway*, 187–88.
67. CINCPAC, "Interrogation of Japanese Prisoners Taken after Midway Action, 9 June 1942" (Washington, D. C. Navy Department, 1942), 3.
68. Bates, *The Battle of Midway*, 187–88; Holmes, *Undersea Warfare*, 147.

8. Analysis: Undersea Warfare at Midway

1. Mao Tse-tung, quoted in Sun Tzu, *The Art of War*, Translated by Samuel B. Griffith (Oxford: Oxford University Press, 1971), 54.
2. Padfield, *War Beneath the Sea*, 231.
3. Spector, *The Eagle Against the Sun*, 44.
4. Adams, *If Mahan Ran the Great Pacific War*, 12.
5. Culora, "Japanese Operational Plans in World War II," 5.
6. H. P. Willmott, "Isoroku Yamamoto: Alibi of a Navy (1884–1943)." In *The Great Admirals: Command at Sea, 1587–1945*, ed. Jack Sweetman (Annapolis, MD: Naval Institute Press, 1997), 447.
7. Baer, *One Hundred Years of Sea Power*, 217.
8. Sun Tzu, *The Art of War*, 100.
9. Mark McNeilly, *Sun Tzu and the Art of Modern Warfare* (New York: Oxford University Press, 2001), 54–55.
10. Wheeler, *War Under the Pacific*, 96–97; d'Albas, *Death of a Navy*, 114.
11. Japanese Monograph 93, 13.
12. Adams, *If Mahan Ran the Great Pacific War*, 108; Willmott, "Isoroku Yamamoto," 447; d'Albas, *Death of a Navy*, 114.
13. Willmott, *The Barrier and the Javelin*, 367–68. Sun Tzu would warn, "When I have won a victory I do not repeat my tactics but respond to circumstances in an infinite variety of ways. There are in war no constant conditions. Thus, one able to gain

the victory by modifying his tactics in accordance with the enemy situation may be said to be divine." (Sun Tzu, *The Art of War*, 100–01).
14. Fuchida and Okumiya, *Midway*, 104–05.
15. Sun Tzu warns, "When you are ignorant of the enemy but know yourself, your chances of winning or losing are equal." (Sun Tzu, *The Art of War*, 84).
16. Winton, *ULTRA in the Pacific*, 53. If Yamamoto had applied Sun Tzu's teachings, he would have understood that "In war, numbers alone confer no advantage. Do not advance relying on sheer military power. It is sufficient to estimate the enemy situation correctly and to concentrate your strength to capture him." (Sun Tzu, *The Art of War*, 122).
17. Willmott, "Isoroku Yamamoto," 448. Clausewitz wrote that superiority of numbers in a given engagement is only one of the factors that determine victory. Superior numbers, far from contributing everything, or even a substantial part, to victory, may actually contribute very little, depending on the circumstances. (Clausewitz, *On War*, 229).
18. Willmott, "Isoroku Yamamoto," 448. Chen Hao's commentary of Sun Tzu said, "In planning, never a useless move; in strategy, no step taken in vain." (Sun Tzu, *The Art of War*, 87).
19. Adams, *If Mahan Ran the Great Pacific War*, 109; Valerie A. Moulé, *A Comparison of Operational Leadership in the Battle of Midway* (Newport, CT: U.S. Naval War College, 1995), 4–5. Sun Tzu indicated there were five circumstances in which victory may be predicted. The first of these is "He whose ranks are united in purpose will be victorious." (Sun Tzu, *The Art of War*, 82).
20. Layton, *And I Was There*, 408; Prange, *Miracle at Midway*, 379; Ian Speller and Christopher Tuck, *Amphibious Warfare: The Theory and Practice of Amphibious Operations in the 20th Century* (St. Paul, MN: MBI Publishing Company, 2001), 52.
21. Edwin P. Hoyt, *How They Won the War in the Pacific: Nimitz and His Admirals* (Guilford, CT: The Lyons Press, 2002), 95; Speller and Tuck, *Amphibious Warfare*, 52.
22. Fuchida and Okumiya, *Midway*, 165.
23. Prange, *Miracle at Midway*, 379.
24. Willmott, "Isoroku Yamamoto," 447–48; Clausewitz, *On War*, 240.
25. Adams, *If Mahan Ran the Great Pacific War*, 124.
26. Michel T. Poirier, "Results of the American Pacific Submarine Campaign of World War II," accessed July 19, 2008, http://www.navy.mil/navydata/cno/n87/history/pac-campaign.html.
27. Winton, *ULTRA in the Pacific*, 53.
28. Boyd and Yoshida, *The Japanese Submarine Force*, 79; Wheeler, *War Under the Pacific*, 106; Bates, *The Battle of Midway*, 26; Gerry, "Japanese Submarine Operational Errors," 3.
29. Spector, *Eagle Against the Sun*, 167. Yamamoto designed his plans for Midway to engage the U.S. fleet in the time-honored way. Cordons of submarines would be placed across the likely avenues of approach from Pearl Harbor to scout and to

snipe at the enemy. Then the carriers would strike at the U.S. fleet; finally, the Japanese battle line would weigh in to strike the decisive blow.

30. Willmott, "Isoroku Yamamoto," 447; Parshall and Tully, *Shattered Sword*, 50.
31. Fuchida and Okumiya, *Midway*, 272.
32. Prange, *Miracle at Midway*, 358. Watanabe was a Staff Gunnery officer in the Combined Fleet. Kuroshima was one of the planners of the Midway operation.
33. Fuchida and Okumiya, Midway, 272.
34. Orita, *I-Boat Captain*, 87.
35. Ugaki, *Fading Victory*, 139; Parshall and Tully, *Shattered Sword*, 97.
36. Willmott, *The Barrier and the Javelin*, 351; Prange, *Miracle at Midway*, 32; Parshall and Tully, *Shattered Sword*, 97.
37. Bates, *The Battle of Midway*, 33.
38. Boyd and Yoshida, *The Japanese Submarine Force*, 79.
39. Bates, *The Battle of Midway*, 34; Boyd and Yoshida, *The Japanese Submarine Force*, 79; Smith, *The Battle of Midway*, 54.
40. Willmott, *The Barrier and the Javelin*, 351.
41. Orita, *I-Boat Captain*, 87.
42. Bates, *The Battle of Midway*, 25.
43. Boyd and Yoshida, *The Japanese Submarine Force*, 79. Japanese submarines did not spot any ships until after all Japanese carriers sank
44. Willmott, *The Barrier and the Javelin*, 352.
45. John Toland, *The Rising Sun: The Decline and Fall of the Japanese Empire 1936–1945, Volume 1* (New York: Random House, 1970), 409–10. One of the captains of the First Carrier Striking Force discovered after the battle that the submarines had gone to the wrong lines because the Combined Fleet had made errors in transmitting coordinates. This officer alleged the Combined Fleet attempted to cover up its mistake (Willmott, *The Barrier and the Javelin*, 352).
46. Japanese Monograph 110, 22–23.
47. James Boling, "Campaign Planning: A Doctrinal Assessment Through the Study of the Japanese Campaign of 1942," (Fort Leavenworth, KS: School of Advanced Military Studies, April 1997), 28.
48. Isom, *Midway Inquest*, 98.
49. Willmott, "Isoroko Yamamoto," 448.
50. John Ellis, *Brute Force: Allied Strategy and Tactics in the Second World War* (New York: Penguin Group, 1990), 452.
51. Willmott, *The Barrier and the Javelin*, 303. Clausewitz wrote, "What is the object of defense? Preservation. It is easier to hold ground than to take it." (Clausewitz, *On War*, 427).
52. Clark G. Reynolds, "The U.S. Fleet-in-Being Strategy of 1942," *The Journal of Military History* 58 (January 1994): 110–11.

53. Ibid., 109; Julian S. Corbett, *Principles of Maritime Strategy* (Mineola, NY: Dover Publications, Inc., 2004), 213.
54. Mark Stoler, *Allies and Adversaries: The Joint Chiefs of Staff, the Grand Alliance, and U.S. Strategy in World War II* (Chapel Hill, NC: The University of North Carolina Press, 2006), 68; Ellis, *Brute Force*, 452–53.
55. Prange, *Miracle at Midway*, 103.
56. Potter and Nimitz, *The Great Sea War*, 227.
57. Kuenne, *The Attack Submarine*, 161; Benere, "A Critical Examination," 3–4.
58. Roscoe, *Unites States Submarine Operations*, 123.
59. Kuenne, *The Attack Submarine*, 161; Randy Papadopoulos, "Between Fleet Scouts & Commerce Raiders," *Undersea Warfare* 7, no. 4 (Spring 2005), accessed February 14, 2010, http://www.navy.mil/navydata/cno/n87/usw/issue_27/scouts.html.
60. Benere, "A Critical Examination," 3–4. Sun Tzu said, "Just as water adapts itself to the conformation of the ground, so in war one must be flexible; he must often adapt his tactics to the enemy situation." (Sun Tzu, *The Art of War*, 43).
61. Holmes, *Undersea Victory*, 135.
62. Potter and Nimitz, *The Great Sea War*, 227.
63. Willmott, *The Barrier and the Javelin*, 308. There is no record of the origin of the submarine plans of operation, but it is most probable that English had little say about the strategy of submarine employment. (Holmes, *Undersea Victory*, 135).
64. Padfield, *War Beneath the Sea*, 232; Prange, *Miracle at Midway*, 121–22.
65. Willmott, *The Barrier and the Javelin*, 308; Clausewitz, *On War*, 427.
66. Tuohy, *The Bravest Man*, 49; Holmes, *Undersea Victory*, 135; Padfield, *War Beneath the Sea*, 234.
67. Thomas G. Hunnicutt, "The Operational Failure of U.S. Submarines at the Battle of Midway," 8. He states in his abstract that "U.S. submarine operational failure led to tactical insignificance at the Battle of Midway. This was a remarkable outcome since interwar U.S. policy, submarine design, and fleet exercises dictated fleet support by submarines." (Hunnicutt, "The Operational Failure of U.S. Submarines at the Battle of Midway," ii).
68. Reynolds, "The U.S. Fleet-in-Being," 116–18.
69. Costello, *The Pacific War*, 277.
70. Speller and Tuck, *Amphibious Warfare*, 51, 58.
71. Mark Healy, *Midway 1942: Turning-point in the Pacific* (New York: Osprey Publishing Ltd., 1993), 28.
72. Paul S. Dull, *A Battle History of the Imperial Japanese Navy (1941–1945)* (Annapolis, MD: Naval Institute Press, 2007), 138. Midway was not all that was at stake. Admiral King estimated that the enemy's plans included an attempt to trap a large part of the U.S. fleet.
73. Jaeger, *Operational Intelligence*, 11.

74. Adams, *If Mahan Ran the Great Pacific War*, 118; Costello, *The Pacific War*, 278. Clausewitz wrote, "Tactically, every engagement, large or small, is defensive if we leave the initiative to our opponent and await his appearance before our lines. From that moment on we can employ all offensive means without losing the advantages of the defensive." (Clausewitz, *On War*, 248).
75. Keegan, *The Price of Admiralty*, 204; Miller, *War at Sea*, 246.
76. Jaeger, *Operational Intelligence*, 14.
77. Potter and Nimitz, *The Great Sea War*, 227.
78. CINCPAC, "Battle of Midway – Submarines report of," (Washington, D.C.: Navy Department, 1942), 3.
79. CINCPAC, "Action Report Battle of Midway, Second Supplementary Report," 1.
80. CINCPAC, "Battle of Midway," 3–4.
81. CINCPAC, "Action Report Battle of Midway, Second Supplementary Report," 1; CINCPAC, "Battle of Midway," 3–4; Holmes, *Undersea Victory*, 144; Padfield, *War Beneath the Sea*, 240.
82. Speller and Tuck, *Amphibious Warfare*, 52.
83. CINCPAC, "Action Report Battle of Midway, Second Supplementary Report," 2.
84. Roscoe, *U.S. Submarine Operations*, 123.
85. Blair, *Silent Victory*, 211; Holmes, *Undersea Victory*, 138.
86. Bates, *The Battle of Midway*, 71; Hunnicutt, "Operational Failure," 6; Lundstrom, *Black Shoe Admiral*, 227; Roscoe, *U.S. Submarine Operations*, 123.

9. Midway Submerged: Conclusions

1. Sun Tzu, *The Art of War*, 84.
2. Japanese and American strategists envisioned using their submarines as auxiliaries to the battle fleet in scouting roles or lying in wait across the enemy's route of advance or outside his bases, picking off heavy ships as they passed. Then, in fleet action, they would attack the enemy's battle line from below. (Spector, *Eagle Against the Sun*, 480).
3. Miller, *War at Sea*, 10.
4. Padfield, *War Beneath the Sea*, 36; Boyd and Yoshida, *The Japanese Submarine Force*, 34; *Silent Service: Japanese Submarines/Submarines of Russia*. DVD. Timeless Media Group, 2010.
5. Padfield, *War Beneath the Sea*, 32.
6. Wood, *Japanese Military Strategy*, 77.
7. Torisu and Chilhaya, "Japanese Submarine Tactics," 78.
8. Wood, *Japanese Military Strategy*, 76.
9. Parshall and Tully, *Shattered Sword*, 410.
10. Baer, *One Hundred Years of Sea Power*, 219–20.
11. Parillo, "The Imperial Japanese Navy in World War II," 62–63.

12. Baer, *One Hundred Years of Sea Power*, 220. Yamamoto's plan followed a classic line: he sent part of his forces to the Aleutians, the other part to invade Midway. He further divided the Midway force into the Strike Force, the Support Force, and the Occupation Force.
13. Walter Lord, *Incredible Victory: The Battle of Midway* (Short Hills, NJ: Burford Books, Inc., 1967), 285.
14. Potter and Nimitz, *The Great Sea War*, 224; d'Albas, *The Death of a Navy*, 151; Parshall and Tully, *Shattered Sword*, 410; Lord, *Incredible Victory*, 285.
15. Padfield, *War Beneath the Sea*, 32.
16. Nobutake Kondo, "Some Opinions Concerning the War," In *The Pacific War Papers: Japanese Documents of World War II*, eds. Donald M. Goldstein and Katherine V. Dillon (Washington, D.C.: Potomac Books, 2006), 312. Sun Tzu said, "When you are ignorant of the enemy but know yourself, your chances of winning or losing are equal." (Sun Tzu, *The Art of War*, 84).
17. Padfield, *War Beneath the Sea*, 239; Ito, *The End of the Imperial Japanese Navy*, 62–63.
18. Lord, *Incredible Victory*, 285.
19. Ito, *The End of the Imperial Japanese Navy*, 62.
20. Bernard Brodie, *A Guide to Naval Strategy* (Princeton, NJ: Princeton University Press, 1944), 249. Sun Tzu warns, "If I am able to determine the enemy's dispositions while at the same time, I conceal my own then I can concentrate and he must divide. And if I concentrate while he divides, I can use my entire strength to attack a fraction of his. There, I will be numerically superior. Then, if I am able to use many to strike a few at the selected point, those I deal with will be in dire straits." (Sun Tzu, *The Art of War*, 98).
21. Orita, *I-Boat Captain*, 76–77. Japan developed its entire submarine force for action against the enemy's capital units, first to find them far from Japan, and then to attack and destroy them while they steamed toward Imperial waters, finally to join the battle fleet in action against the remnants that entered the perimeter where the decisive battle was to be fought. It was the strategy of attrition adopted by all the weaker battle fleet powers, adapted to the great distances and island groups of the Pacific. (Padfield, *War Beneath the Sea*, 33).
22. Orita, *I-Boat Captain*, 78.
23. Wheeler, *War Under the Pacific*, 106.
24. Orita, *I-Boat Captain*, 73.
25. Padfield, *War Beneath the Sea*, 36–37.
26. Bates, *The Battle of Midway*, 34.
27. Ibid.
28. Japanese Monograph 110, 16.
29. *Silent Service: Submarine Warfare in WWII, Disc 4: Attack Plans of World War II.* DVD. A&E Television Networks, 2000.
30. Janet M. Manson, *Diplomatic Ramifications of Unrestricted Submarine Warfare, 1939–1941* (New York: Greenwood Press, 1990), 159, 179.

31. Miller, *War Plan Orange*, 352; *Silent Service: Submarine Warfare in WWII, Disc 4: Attack Plans*.
32. Edward C. Whitman, "Rising to Victory: The Pacific Submarine Strategy in World War II, Part 1: Retreat and Retrenchment," Spring 2001, accessed July 27, 2008, http://www.navy.mil/navydata/cno/n87/usw/issue_11/rising_victory.html; W. J. Holmes, *Double-Edged Secrets: U.S. Naval Intelligence Operations in the Pacific During World War II* (Annapolis, MD: Naval Institute Press, 1979), 104.
33. Roscoe, *United States Submarine Operations*, 132.
34. Padfield, *War Beneath the Sea*, 238–39; Holmes, *Undersea Victory*, 147.
35. Roscoe, *United States Submarine Operations*, 132.
36. Ibid., 132–33.
37. Roscoe, *United States Submarine Operations*, 132.
38. Keegan, *The Price of Admiralty*, 220.
39. Roscoe, *United States Submarine Operations*, 132.
40. Layton, *I Was There*, 438.
41. CINCPAC, "Action Report Battle of Midway, Second Supplementary Report," 1–2.
42. CINCPAC, "Battle of Midway – Submarines report of," 7.
43. Sun Tzu said, "Thus I say that victory can be created. For even if the enemy is numerous, I can prevent him from engaging. Therefore, determine the enemy's plans and you will know which strategy will be successful and which will not. Thus, one able to gain the victory by modifying his tactics in accordance with the enemy situation may be said to be divine." (Sun Tzu, *The Art of War*, 100–01).

Appendix 1. Patrol Reports of U.S. Task Group 7.1 Submarines

1. National Archives, *USS Cachalot War Patrol Report 2* (College Park, MD: National Archives and Records Administration, 1942), 1.
2. National Archives, *USS Cuttlefish War Patrol Report 2* (College Park, MD: National Archives and Records Administration, 1942), 13–17.
3. National Archives, *USS Dolphin War Patrol Report 2* (College Park, MD: National Archives and Records Administration, 1942), 1–3.
4. National Archives, *USS Flying Fish War Patrol Report 1* (College Park, MD: National Archives and Records Administration, 1942), 1–2.
5. National Archives, *USS Gato War Patrol Report 1* (College Park, MD: National Archives and Records Administration, 1942), 7–8.
6. National Archives, *USS Grayling War Patrol Report 1* (College Park, MD: National Archives and Records Administration, 1942), 1.
7. National Archives, *USS Grenadier War Patrol Report 2* (College Park, MD: National Archives and Records Administration, 1942), 4–6.
8. National Archives, *USS Grouper War Patrol Report 1* (College Park, MD: National Archives and Records Administration, 1942), 1–5.

9. National Archives, *USS Gudgeon War Patrol Report 3* (College Park, MD: National Archives and Records Administration, 1942), 1–5.
10. National Archives, *USS Nautilus War Patrol Report 1* (College Park, MD: National Archives and Records Administration, 1942), 1–4.
11. National Archives, *USS Tambor War Patrol Report 3* (College Park, MD: National Archives and Records Administration, 1942), 1–22.
12. National Archives, *USS Trout War Patrol Report 4* (College Park, MD: National Archives and Records Administration, 1942), 1–3.

Appendix 2. Patrol Reports of U.S. Task Group 7.2 Submarines

1. National Archives, *USS Plunger War Patrol Report 2* (College Park, MD: National Archives and Records Administration, 1942), 1.
2. National Archives, *USS Trigger War Patrol Report 1* (College Park, MD: National Archives and Records Administration, 1942), 1.
3. National Archives, *USS Narwhal War Patrol Report 3* (College Park, MD: National Archives and Records Administration, 1942), 1.

Appendix 3. Patrol Reports of U.S. Task Group 7.3 Submarines

1. National Archives, *USS Finback War Patrol Report 1* (College Park, MD: National Archives and Records Administration, 1942), 1.
2. National Archives, *USS Growler War Patrol Report 1* (College Park, MD: National Archives and Records Administration, 1942), 1.
3. National Archives, *USS Pike War Patrol Report 5* (College Park, MD: National Archives and Records Administration, 1942), 1–2.
4. National Archives, *USS Tarpon War Patrol Report 4* (College Park, MD: National Archives and Records Administration, 1942), 1.

Appendix 4. Patrol Reports of U.S. Submarines on Patrol

1. National Archives, *USS Drum War Patrol Report 1* (College Park, MD: National Archives and Records Administration, 1942), 4–5.
2. National Archives, *USS Greenling War Patrol Report 1* (College Park, MD: National Archives and Records Administration, 1942), 9–12.
3. National Archives, *USS Pollack War Patrol Report 3* (College Park, MD: National Archives and Records Administration, 1942), 7–8.

4. National Archives, *USS Pompano War Patrol Report 2* (College Park, MD: National Archives and Records Administration, 1942), 2–3.
5. National Archives, *USS Porpoise War Patrol Report 3* (College Park, MD: National Archives and Records Administration, 1942), 6.
6. National Archives, *USS Silversides War Patrol Report 1* (College Park, MD: National Archives and Records Administration, 1942), 5.
7. National Archives, *USS Triton War Patrol Report 3* (College Park, MD: National Archives and Records Administration, 1942), 17.
8. National Archives, *USS Tuna War Patrol Report 2* (College Park, MD: National Archives and Records Administration, 1942), 8–13.

Appendix 5. Extracts From the United States Strategic Bombing Survey: Interrogations of Japanese Officials

1. United States Strategic Bombing Survey (Pacific), Naval Analysis Division. *Interrogations of Japanese Officials, Volume 1* (Washington D.C.: Government Printing Office, 1946), 5.
2. Ibid., 6.
3. Ibid., 66.
4. Ibid., 167.
5. Ibid., 191.
6. Ibid. 67.

Appendix 6. Interrogation of Vice Admiral Paul H. Weneker

1. United States Strategic Bombing Survey (Pacific), Naval Analysis Division. *Interrogations of Japanese Officials, Volume 1* (Washington D.C.: Government Printing Office, 1946), 284.

Appendix 7. Navy Cross Citation for Lieutenant Commander William Herman Brockman, Jr.

1. "Full Text Citations for Award of the Navy Cross," Home of Heroes, accessed May 1, 2011, http://www.homeofheroes.com/members/02_NX/citations/03_wwii-nc/nc_06wwii_navyB.html.

Bibliography

Adams, John A. *If Mahan Ran the Great Pacific War: An Analysis of World War II Naval Strategy.* Bloomington, IN: Indiana University Press, 2008.
Andrade, Jr., Ernest. "Submarine Policy in the United States Navy, 1919–1941." *Military Affairs* 35, no. 2 (April 1971): 50–56.
Asada, Sadao. *From Mahan to Pearl Harbor: The Imperial Japanese Navy and the United States.* Annapolis, MD: Naval Institute Press, 2006.
———. *Culture Shock and Japanese–American Relations: Historical Essays.* Columbia, MO: University of Missouri Press, 2007.
Baer, George W. "U.S. Naval Strategy 1890–1945." *Naval War College Review* 44 (Winter, 1991): 6–33.
———. *One Hundred Years of Sea Power: The U.S. Navy, 1890–1990.* Stanford, CA: Stanford University Press, 1994.
Barlow, Jeffrey G. "World War II: U.S. and Japanese Naval Strategies." In *Seapower and Strategy*, edited by Colin S. Gray and Roger W. Barnett, 245–272. Annapolis, MD: Naval Institute Press, 1989.
Bates, Richard W. *The Battle of Midway Including the Aleutian Phase, June 3 to June 14, 1942. Strategical and Tactical Analysis.* Newport, CT: U.S. Naval War College, 1948.
Benere, Daniel E. "A Critical Examination of the U.S. Navy's Use of Unrestricted Submarine Warfare in the Pacific Theater During World War II." Newport, RI: Naval War College Joint Military Operations Department, May 1992.
Blair Jr., Clay. *Silent Victory: The U.S. Submarine War Against Japan.* Philadelphia: J. B. Lippincott Company, 1975.
Boling, James. "Campaign Planning: A Doctrinal Assessment Through the Study of the Japanese Campaign of 1942." Fort Leavenworth, KS: School of Advanced Military Studies, April 1997.
Boyd, Carl. "The Japanese Submarine Force and the Legacy of Strategic and Operational Doctrine Developed Between the World Wars." In *Selected Papers from the Citadel Conference on War and Diplomacy, 1978*, edited by Larry H. Addington et al., 27–40. Charleston, S.C.: Citadel Press, 1979.
———. "American Naval Intelligence of Japanese Submarine Operations Early in the Pacific War." *The Journal of Military History* 53 (April 1989): 169–189.

Boyd, Carl. *American Command of the Sea Through Carriers, Codes, and the Silent Service.* Newport News, VA: The Mariners' Museum, 1995.

Boyd, Carl, and Akihiko Yoshida. *The Japanese Submarine Force and World War II.* Annapolis, MD: Naval Institute Press, 1995.

Brodie, Bernard. *A Guide to Naval Strategy.* Princeton, NJ: Princeton University Press, 1944.

Carpenter, Dorr, and Norman Polmar. *Submarines of the Imperial Japanese Navy.* Annapolis, MD: Naval Institute Press, 1986.

Christley, Jim. *U.S. Submarines 1941–45.* New York: Osprey Publishing Ltd., 2006.

CINCPAC. "Action Report Battle of Midway, Second Supplementary Report." Washington, D.C., Navy Department, 1942.

———. "Battle of Midway – Submarines report of." Washington, D.C., Navy Department, 1942.

———. "Interrogation of Japanese Prisoners Taken after Midway Action, 9 June 1942." Washington, D.C., Navy Department, 1942.

Corbett, Julian S. *Principles of Maritime Strategy.* Mineola, NY: Dover Publications, Inc., 2004.

Costello, John. *The Pacific War 1941–1945.* New York: William Morrow and Company, Inc., 1981.

Crowl, Philip A. "Alfred Thayer Mahan: The Naval Historian." In *Makers of Modern Strategy from Machiavelli to the Nuclear Age*, edited by Peter Paret, 444–477. Princeton, NJ: Princeton University Press, 1986.

Culora, Thomas J. "Japanese Operational Plans in World War II: Shortfalls in Critical Elements." Newport, RI: Naval War College Joint Military Operations Department; Springfield, VA: June 1994, 32.

D'Albas, Andrieu. *Death of a Navy: Japanese Naval Action in World War II.* New York: The Devin-Adair Company, 1957.

DeRose, James F. *Unrestricted Warfare: How a New Breed of Officers Led the Submarine Force to Victory in World War II.* Edison, NJ: Castle Books, 2000.

Dull, Paul S. *A Battle History of the Imperial Japanese Navy (1941–1945).* Annapolis, MD: Naval Institute Press, 2007.

Durham, Richard W. "Operational Art in the Conduct of Naval Operations." Fort Leavenworth, KS: School of Advanced Military Studies, United States Army Command and General Staff College, March 1998, 55.

Ellis, John. *Brute Force: Allied Strategy and Tactics in the Second World War.* New York: Penguin Group, 1990.

Evans, David C., and Mark R. Peattie. *Kaigun: Strategy, Tactics, and Technology in the Imperial Japanese Navy 1887–1941.* Annapolis, MD: Naval Institute Press, 1997.

Felker, Craig C. *Testing American Sea Power: U.S. Navy Strategic Exercises, 1923–1940.* College Station, TX: Texas A&M University Press, 2007.

Fuchida, Mitsuo, and Masatake Okumiya. *Midway: The Battle That Doomed Japan, The Japanese Navy's Story.* Annapolis, MD: Naval Institute Press, 1955.

Fuchida, Mitsuo, and Masatake Okumiya. "The Battle of Midway." In *The Japanese Navy in World War II, 2nd ed,* edited by David C. Evans, 119–155. Annapolis, MD: Naval Institute Press, 1986.

Galantin, I. J. *Submarine Admiral.* Urbana, IL: University of Illinois Press, 1995.

Gannon, Robert. *Hellions of the Deep: The Development of American Torpedoes in World War II.* University Park, PA: The Pennsylvania State University Press, 1996.

Genda, Minoru. "Tactical Planning in the Imperial Japanese Navy." *Naval War College Review* 22 (October 1969): 45–50.

Gerry, Donald D. "Japanese Submarine Operational Errors in World War II: Will America's SSNs Make the Same Mistake?" Newport, RI: Naval War College Joint Military Operations Department; Springfield, VA:, May 1996, 21.

Goldman, Emily O. *Sunken Treaties: Naval Arms Control Between the Wars.* University Park, PA: The Pennsylvania State University Press, 1994.

Gray, Colin S. *Modern Strategy.* New York: Oxford University Press, 1999.

Greene, Jack. *The Midway Campaign.* Conshohocken, PA: Combined Books, Inc., 1995.

Hashimoto, Mochitsura. *Sunk: The Story of the Japanese Submarine Fleet 1941–1945.* New York: Henry Holt and Company, 1954.

Hattendorf, John B. *Naval History and Maritime Strategy: Collected Essays.* Malabar, FL: Krieger Publishing Company, 2000.

Healy, Mark. *Midway 1942: Turning-point in the Pacific.* New York: Osprey Publishing Ltd., 1993.

Herwig, Holger H. "Innovation Ignored: The Submarine Problem – Germany, Britain and the United States, 1919–1939." In *Military Innovation in the Interwar Period,* edited by Williamson Murray and Allan R. Millett, 227–264. New York: Cambridge University Press, 1996.

Hirama, Yôichi. "Japanese Naval Preparations for World War II." *Naval War College Review* 44 (Spring, 1991): 63–81.

Holmes, W. J. *Undersea Victory: The Influence of Submarine Operations on the War in the Pacific.* New York: Doubleday & Company, Inc., 1966.

———. *Double-Edged Secrets: U.S. Naval Intelligence Operations in the Pacific During World War II.* Annapolis, MD: Naval Institute Press, 1979.

Holwitt, Joel Ira. *Execute Against Japan: The U.S. Decision to Conduct Unrestricted Submarine Warfare.* College Station, TX: Texas A&M University Press, 2009.

Home of Heroes. "Full Text Citations for Award of the Navy Cross." Accessed May 1, 2011. http://www.homeofheroes.com/members/02_NX/citations/03_wwii-nc/nc_06wwii_navyB.html.

Hone, Thomas C., and Trent Hone. *Battle Line: The United States Navy 1919–1939.* Annapolis, MD: Naval Institute Press, 2006.

Hone, Trent. "Building a Doctrine: USN Tactics and Battle Plans in the Interwar Period." *International Journal of Naval History* 1, no. 2 (October 2002). Accessed February 19, 2010. http://www.ijnhonline.org/volume1_number2_Oct02/articles/article_hone1_doctrine.doc.htm.

Hone, Trent. "The Evolution of Fleet Tactical Doctrine in the U.S. Navy, 1922–1941." *The Journal of Military History* 67 (October 2003): 1107–1148.

———. "U.S. Navy Surface Battle Doctrine and Victory in the Pacific." *Naval War College Review* 62 (Winter, 2009): 67–105.

Hopkins, William B. *The Pacific War: The Strategy, Politics, and Players That Won the War.* Minneapolis, MN: Zenith Press, 2008.

Hoyt, Edwin P. *How They Won the War in the Pacific: Nimitz and His Admirals.* Guilford, CT: The Lyons Press, 2002.

Hunnicutt, Thomas G. "The Operational Failure of U.S. Submarines at the Battle of Midway – and Implications for Today." Newport, RI: Naval War College Joint Military Operations Department; Springfield, VA: May 1996, 31.

Isom, Dallas Woodbury. *Midway Inquest: Why the Japanese Lost the Battle of Midway.* Bloomington, IN: Indiana University Press, 2007.

Ito, Masanori. *The End of the Imperial Japanese Navy.* New York: W. W. Norton & Company, Inc., 1962.

Jaeger, Paul J. *Operational Intelligence at the Battle of Midway.* Newport, CT: U.S. Naval War College, 1998.

James, D. Clayton. "American and Japanese Strategies in the Pacific War." In *Makers of Modern Strategy from Machiavelli to the Nuclear Age*, edited by Peter Paret, 703–732. Princeton, NJ: Princeton University Press, 1986.

Japanese Monograph No. 93. "Midway Operations, May–Jun. 1942." Washington, D.C.: Department of the Army, 1962.

Japanese Monograph No. 110. "Submarine Operations in Second Phase Operations, Part I, April–August 1942." Washington, D.C.: Department of the Army, 1952.

Karig, Walter and Eric Purdon. *Battle Report, Pacific War: Middle Phase.* New York: Rinehart and Company, Inc., 1947.

Keegan, John. *The Price of Admiralty: The Evolution of Naval Warfare.* New York: Viking Penguin Inc., 1989.

Kimmett, Larry, and Margaret Regis. *U.S. Submarines in World War II.* Kingston, WA: Navigator Publishing, 1996.

Kondo, Nobutake, "Some Opinions Concerning the War." In *The Pacific War Papers: Japanese Documents of World War II*, edited by Donald M. Goldstein and Katherine V. Dillon, 304–317. Washington, D.C.: Potomac Books, 2006.

Kuehn, John T. *Agents of Innovations: The General Board and the Design of the Fleet That Defeated the Japanese Navy.* Annapolis, MD: Naval Institute Press, 2008.

Kuenne, Robert E. *The Attack Submarine: A Study in Strategy.* New Haven, CT: Yale University Press, 1965.

Layton, Edwin T. *And I Was There: Pearl Harbor and Midway—Breaking the Secrets.* New York: William Morrow and Company, Inc., 1985.

Lord, Walter. *Incredible Victory: The Battle of Midway.* Short Hills, NJ: Burford Books, Inc., 1967.

Lundstrom, John B. *Black Shoe Carrier Admiral: Frank Jack Fletcher at Coral Sea, Midway, and Guadalcanal.* Annapolis, MD: Naval Institute Press, 2007.

Mahan, Alfred T. *Mahan on Naval Warfare: Selections from the Writings of Rear Admiral Alfred T. Mahan*. Edited by Allan Westcott. Mineola, NY: Dover Publications, Inc. 1991.
Mahnken, Thomas G. "Strategic Theory." In *Strategy in the Contemporary World*, 2nd ed, edited by John Baylis et al, 66–81. Oxford: Oxford University Press, 2007.
Manson, Janet M. *Diplomatic Ramifications of Unrestricted Submarine Warfare, 1939–1941*. New York: Greenwood Press, 1990.
McNeilly, Mark. *Sun Tzu and the Art of Modern Warfare*. New York: Oxford University Press, 2001.
Middleton, Drew. *Submarine: The Ultimate Naval Weapon—Its Past, Present & Future*. Chicago: Playboy Press. 1976.
Milford, Frederick J. "U.S. Navy Torpedoes, Part Two: The Great Torpedo Scandal, 1941–1943." *The Submarine Review*, October 1996, 81–93.
Miller, Edward S. *War Plan Orange: The U.S. Strategy to Defeat Japan, 1897–1945*. Annapolis, MD: Naval Institute Press, 2007.
Miller, Nathan. *War at Sea: A Naval History of World War II*. New York: Scribner, 1995.
Morison, Samuel Eliot. *History of United States Naval Operations in World War II Volume IV: Coral Sea, Midway and Submarine Actions, May 1942–August 1942*. Boston, MA: Little, Brown and Company, 1988.
Moulé, Valerie A. *A Comparison of Operational Leadership in the Battle of Midway*. Newport, CT: U.S. Naval War College, 1995.
National Archives, *USS Cachalot War Patrol Report 2*. College Park, MD: National Archives and Records Administration, 1942.
———. *USS Cuttlefish War Patrol Report 2*. College Park, MD: National Archives and Records Administration, 1942.
———. *USS Dolphin War Patrol Report 2*. College Park, MD: National Archives and Records Administration, 1942.
———. *USS Drum War Patrol Report 1*. College Park, MD: National Archives and Records Administration, 1942.
———. *USS Finback War Patrol Report 1*. College Park, MD: National Archives and Records Administration, 1942.
———. *USS Flying Fish War Patrol Report 1*. College Park, MD: National Archives and Records Administration, 1942.
———. *USS Gato War Patrol Report 1*. College Park, MD: National Archives and Records Administration, 1942.
———. *USS Grayling War Patrol Report 1*. College Park, MD: National Archives and Records Administration, 1942.
———. *USS Greenling War Patrol Report 1*. College Park, MD: National Archives and Records Administration, 1942.
———. *USS Grenadier War Patrol Report 2*. College Park, MD: National Archives and Records Administration, 1942.
———. *USS Grouper War Patrol Report 1*. College Park, MD: National Archives and Records Administration, 1942.

National Archives, *USS Growler War Patrol Report 1*. College Park, MD: National Archives and Records Administration, 1942.

———. *USS Gudgeon War Patrol Report 3*. College Park, MD: National Archives and Records Administration, 1942.

———. *USS Narwhal War Patrol Report 3*. College Park, MD: National Archives and Records Administration, 1942.

———. *USS Nautilus War Patrol Report 1*. College Park, MD: National Archives and Records Administration, 1942.

———. *USS Pike War Patrol Report 5*. College Park, MD: National Archives and Records Administration, 1942.

———. *USS Plunger War Patrol Report 2*. College Park, MD: National Archives and Records Administration, 1942.

———. *USS Pollack War Patrol Report 3*. College Park, MD: National Archives and Records Administration, 1942.

———. *USS Pompano War Patrol Report 2*. College Park, MD: National Archives and Records Administration, 1942.

———. *USS Porpoise War Patrol Report 3*. College Park, MD: National Archives and Records Administration, 1942.

———. *USS Silversides War Patrol Report 1*. College Park, MD: National Archives and Records Administration, 1942.

———. *USS Tambor War Patrol Report 3*. College Park, MD: National Archives and Records Administration, 1942.

———. *USS Tarpon War Patrol Report 4*. College Park, MD: National Archives and Records Administration, 1942.

———. *USS Trigger War Patrol Report 1*. College Park, MD: National Archives and Records Administration, 1942.

———. *USS Triton War Patrol Report 3*. College Park, MD: National Archives and Records Administration, 1942.

———. *USS Trout War Patrol Report 4*. College Park, MD: National Archives and Records Administration, 1942.

———. *USS Tuna War Patrol Report 2*. College Park, MD: National Archives and Records Administration, 1942.

Newpower, Anthony. *Iron Men and Tin Fish: The Race to Build a Better Torpedo During World War II*. Westport, CT: Praeger Security International, 2006.

O'Hara, Vincent P., W. David Dickson, and Richard Worth. *On Seas Contested: The Seven Great Navies of the Second World War*. Annapolis, MD: Naval Institute Press, 2010.

Oi, Atsushi. "The Japanese Navy in 1941." In *The Pacific War Papers: Japanese Documents of World War II*, edited by Donald M. Goldstein and Katherine V. Dillon, 4–31. Washington, D.C.: Potomac Books, 2006.

———. "Why Japan's Antisubmarine Warfare Failed." In *The Japanese Navy in World War II*, 2nd ed, edited by David C. Evans, 385–414. Annapolis, MD: Naval Institute Press, 1986.

Orita, Zenji, and Joseph D. Harrington. *I-Boat Captain*. Canoga Park, CA: Major Books, 1976.
Padfield, Peter. *The Battleship Era*. New York: David McKay Company, Inc., 1972.
———. *War Beneath the Sea: Submarine Conflict During World War II*. New York: John Wiley & Sons, Inc., 1995.
Papadopoulos, Randy. "Between Fleet Scouts & Commerce Raiders." *Undersea Warfare* 7, no. 4 (Spring 2005). Accessed February 14, 2010. http://www.navy.mil/navydata/cno/n87/usw/issue_27/scouts.html.
Parillo, Mark P. "The Imperial Japanese Navy in World War II." In *Reevaluating Major Naval Combatants of World War II*, edited by James J. Sadkovich, 61–77. New York: Greenwood Press, 1990.
Parrish, Thomas. *The Submarine: A History*. New York: Viking, 2004.
Parshall, Jonathan, and Anthony Tully. *Shattered Sword: The Untold Story of the Battle of Midway*. Washington, D.C.: Potomac Books, 2007.
Poirier, Michel T. "Results of the American Pacific Submarine Campaign of World War II." 30 December 1999. Accessed July 19, 2008. http://www.navy.mil/navydata/cno/n87/history/pac-campaign.html.
Poolman, Kenneth. *The Winning Edge: Naval Technology in Action, 1939–1945*. Annapolis, MD: Naval Institute Press, 1997.
Potter, E. B., and Chester W. Nimitz. *The Great Sea War: The Dramatic Story of Naval Action in World War II*. Englewood Cliffs, NJ: Prentice-Hall Inc., 1960.
———. *Triumph in the Pacific: The Navy's Struggle Against Japan*. Englewood Cliffs, NJ: Prentice-Hall Inc., 1963.
Prados, John. *Combined Fleet Decoded*. New York: Random House, 1995.
Prange, Gordon. *Miracle at Midway*. New York: McGraw-Hill Book Company, 1982.
Puleston, W. D. *The Armed Forces of the Pacific: A Comparison of the Military and Naval Power of the United States and Japan*. New Haven: Yale University Press, 1941.
Reynolds, Clark G. "The U.S. Fleet-in-Being Strategy of 1942." *The Journal of Military History* 58 (January 1994): 103–118.
Roscoe, Theodore. *United States Submarine Operations in World War II*. Annapolis, MD: Naval Institute Press, 1949.
Rosen, Stephen Peter. *Winning the Next War: Innovation and the Modern Military*. Ithaca, NY: Cornell University Press, 1991.
Russell, Ronald W. *No Right to Win*. New York: iUniverse, Inc., 2006.
Schultz, Robert, and James Shell. "Strange Fortune." *World War II* 58 (May/June 2010): 58–65.
Silent Service: Japanese Submarines/Submarines of Russia. DVD. Timeless Media Group, 2010.
Silent Service: Submarine Warfare in WWII, Disc 2: Captains of World War II. DVD. A&E Television Networks, 2000.
———. *Disc 4: Attack Plans of World War II*. DVD. A&E Television Networks, 2000.
Smith, Douglas V. "Preparing for War: Naval Education Between the World Wars." *International Journal of Naval History* 1, no. 1 (April 2002). Accessed February 19,

2010. http://www.ijnhonline.org/volume1_number1_Apr02/article_smith_education_war.doc.htm.

Smith, Peter C. *The Battle of Midway: The Battle that Turned the Tide of the Pacific War.* Staplehurst, Great Britain: Spellmount Ltd., 1996.

———. *Midway: Dauntless Victory, Fresh Perspectives on America's Seminal Naval Victory of World War II.* Barnsley, South Yorkshire, England: Pen & Sword Books Limited. 2007.

Spector, Ronald H. *Eagle Against the Sun: The American War with Japan.* New York: The Free Press, 1985.

Speller, Ian, and Christopher Tuck. *Amphibious Warfare: The Theory and Practice of Amphibious Operations in the 20th Century.* St. Paul, MN: MBI Publishing Company, 2001.

Stille, Mark. *Imperial Japanese Navy Submarines 1941–1945.* New York: Osprey Publishing Ltd., 2007.

Stoler, Mark A. *Allies and Adversaries: The Joint Chiefs of Staff, the Grand Alliance, and U.S. Strategy in World War II.* Chapel Hill, NC: The University of North Carolina Press, 2006.

Talbott, J. E. "Weapons Development, War Planning and Policy: The US Navy and the Submarine, 1917–1941." *Naval War College Review* 37 (May–June, 1984): 53–71.

Tanabe, Yahachi, and Joseph D. Harrington, "I Sank the *Yorktown* at Midway." In *Submarines in Combat*, edited by Joseph B. Icenhower, 30–41. New York: Franklin Watts, Inc., 1964.

Tillman, Barrett. *Clash of the Carriers.* New York: NAL Caliber, 2005.

Tohmatsu, Haruo, and H. P. Willmott. *A Gathering Darkness: The Coming of War to the Far East and the Pacific, 1921–1942.* Lanham, MD: SR Books, 2004.

Toland, John. *The Rising Sun: The Decline and Fall of the Japanese Empire 1936–1945, Volume 1.* New York: Random House, 1970.

Torisu, Kennosuke, and Masataka Chilhaya. "Japanese Submarine Tactics." United States Naval Institute *Proceedings* 87 (February 1961): 78–83.

———. "Japanese Submarine Tactics and the Kaiten." In *The Japanese Navy in World War II*, 2nd ed, edited by David C. Evans, 440–452. Annapolis, MD: Naval Institute Press, 1986.

Tuohy, William. *The Bravest Man: The Story of Richard O'Kane and U.S. Submarines in the Pacific War.* Gloucestershire, Great Britain: Sutton Publishing Limited, 2001.

Tzu, Sun. *The Art of War.* Translated by Samuel B. Griffith. Oxford: Oxford University Press, 1971.

Ugaki, Matome. *Fading Victory: The Diary of Admiral Matome Ugaki, 1941–1945.* Translated by Masataka Chihaya. Donald M. Goldstein and Katherine V. Dillon, eds. Annapolis, MD: Naval Institute Press, 1991.

United States Navy. *The Japanese Story of the Battle of Midway.* Washington, D.C.: Office of Naval Intelligence, 1947.

United States Strategic Bombing Survey (Pacific), Naval Analysis Division. *Interrogations of Japanese Officials, Volume 1.* Washington, D.C.: Government Printing Office, 1946.

United States Strategic Bombing Survey (Pacific), Naval Analysis Division. *Interrogations of Japanese Officials, Volume 2.* Washington, D.C.: Government Printing Office, 1946.

U.S. Naval Technical Mission to Japan. "Ship and Related Targets: Japanese Submarine Operations." Index No. S-17. Washington, D.C.: Operational Archives, U.S. Naval History Division, 1946.

von Clausewitz, Carl. *On War.* Edited and Translated by Michael Howard and Peter Paret. New York: Alfred A. Knopf, 1993.

Weinberg, Gerhard L. *A World at Arms: A Global History of World War II.* New York: Cambridge University Press, 2005.

Weir, Gary E. "The Search for an American Submarine Strategy and Design, 1916–1936." *Naval War College Review* 44 (Winter, 1991): 34–48.

———. "Silent Defense: 1900–1940." Summer 1999. Accessed July 27, 2008. http://www.navy.mil/navydata/cno/n87/usw/issue_4/silent_defense.html.

———. "Silent Victory 1940–1945." Winter 1999. Accessed May 12, 2009. http://www.navy.mil/navydata/cno/n87/usw/issue_6/silent_victory.html.

Wheeler, Keith. *War Under the Pacific.* Richmond, VA: Time Life Inc., 1998.

Winton, John. *ULTRA in the Pacific: How Breaking Japanese Codes & Ciphers Affected Naval Operations Against Japan.* London: Leo Cooper, 1993.

Whitman, Edward C. "Rising to Victory: The Pacific Submarine Strategy in World War II, Part 1: Retreat and Retrenchment." Spring 2001. Accessed July 27, 2008. http://www.navy.mil/navydata/cno/n87/usw/issue_11/rising_victory.html.

Willmott, H. P. *The Barrier and the Javelin: Japanese and Allied Pacific Strategies, February to June 1942.* Annapolis, MD: Naval Institute Press, 1989.

———. "Isoroku Yamamoto: Alibi of a Navy (1884–1943)." In *The Great Admirals: Command at Sea, 1587–1945,* edited by Jack Sweetman, 442–457. Annapolis, MD: Naval Institute Press, 1997.

———. *The War with Japan: The Period of Balance May 1942–October 1943.* Wilmington, DE: Scholarly Resources, Inc., 2002.

———. *The Last Century of Sea Power, Volume Two: From Washington to Tokyo, 1922–1945.* Bloomington, IN: Indiana University Press, 2010.

Wood, James B. *Japanese Military Strategy in the Pacific War.* New York: Rowman & Littlefield Publishers, Inc., 2007.

Yoshihara, Toshi, and James R. Holmes. "Japanese Maritime Thought: If Not Mahan, Who?" *Naval War College Review* 59 (Summer, 2006): 23–51.

Index

Akagi (carrier), 49, 180
Aleutian Islands, viii, 1, 46, 57–58, 79
Amagai, Captain Takahisa, 67
Analysis: Undersea Warfare at Midway, 75–90
    American Fleet Situation, 83–84
    American Submarines at Midway, 85–87
    Battle Preliminaries, 75–79
    Battleship Division 1, 77
    commerce raiding, 85
    complexity and luck, 78
    Fleet opposed invasion–Midway, 87
    fleet-in-being concept, 84
    Intelligence, 87–88
    Invasion, 88–90
    Japanese Submarines, 83
    psychological impact/emotions, 76
    quantitative superiority, 10, 75
    Yamamoto intent/battle plan flaws, 76–77
    Yamamoto's Operational Plan, 79–82
Arashio (destroyer), 51

Battle of Coral Sea, 58, 62, 77
Brockman, Lieutenant Commander William H., 66–68

Chikuma (cruiser), 52, 68
CINCPAC, 3, 86
von Clausewitz, Carl, 79, 85
ComSubPac, 3, 86

Conclusions, 91–101
    American Submarines, 97–101
    commerce raiding, 95, 98
    failure of Japanese intelligence, 93
    failure of surprise, 91–92
    final assessment, 101
    flawed Japanese submarine battle orders, 95
    Japanese invasion of Midway as lure, 96–97
    Japanese Occupation Force as bait, 96
    Japanese Submarines, 92–97
    Japanese victory disease, 92
    Mahanian strategy, 92
    over-specialized units, 91–92
    submarine as offensive weapon, 99–100
    submarines as defensive screen, 100
cordons, xi, 4, 45–49, 51, 54, 78, 80–82, 94
Cordon A, 43, 45–47, 49, 81–83
Cordon B, 46–48, 61, 79, 81–83
Cordon C, 51–52, 82
Cordons R, S and T, 52, 54
Cordons U and V, 54

Daigo, Rear Admiral Tadashige, 48
Doolittle raid, 41, 76

English, Admiral Robert H., xii, 3, 7, 58–65, 68–69, 71–74, 85, 87–90, 98–101

Five-Power Naval Treaty (1922), 11
Fletcher, Admiral Frank Jack, 84, 99
Fremantle, Australia, 35, 58–59

Gotō, Vice Admiral Eiji, 44–45, 96
Great Torpedo Scandal, 37

Hiryu (carrier), ix, 53

I-boats, 15, 18, 19, 41, 43–47, 49–55, 58, 62, 69, 71, 79, 81, 93, 95, 99
Imperial Japanese Navy (IJN), 1, 13
Iura, Commander Shojira, 48

Japanese 13th Submarine Division, 42–43, 47
Japanese Advanced Expeditionary Force, 16, 19, 45–47
Japanese Carrier Striking Force, xi, xii, 3, 5, 6, 44, 51, 58, 60, 62, 65–66, 77–78, 83, 86–90, 99–100
Japanese Combined Fleet, 1, 11, 14–16, 18, 20, 24, 42, 45, 48–49, 54, 64, 77, 82–83, 94, 97
Japanese Naval Command (JNC), 95
Japanese Naval Doctrine, 9–16
   Advance Expeditionary Force, 16
   decisive-battle strategy, 13–14
   Naval Affairs Bureau of the Navy Ministry, 14
   Naval General Staff, 11, 15, 48
   IJN Submarine Doctrine, 15, 18, 20–21
   Yōgeki Sakusen (interceptive operations), 13
Japanese Naval War College, 10
Japanese Occupation Force, xii, 1, 4, 42, 44, 49, 51, 58, 62–64, 68–69, 71, 83, 88, 93, 95–97, 99–100
Japanese Sixth Fleet, 15, 24–25, 41–42
Japanese Submarine Actions at Midway, 41–56

24th Air Flotilla, 42, 44
Cruiser Division Seven, 72
DesOpOrd No. 155, 51
DesOpOrd No. 158, 51
Emily flying boats, 43
French Frigate Shoals (FFS), 41, 43
Japan's N Day, 50
Kwajalein, 42, 44
La Perouse Pinnacle (LPP), 43
Midway Island Reconnaissance, 49
mine-laying submarines, 41
picket-line deployment, 41
Operation "MI", 52
Submarine Division 13, 54
Japanese Submarine Strategy and Tactics, 17–25
   ambush, 24
   close-in-sure-shot, 18
   Commerce Raiding, 18–21, 23
   Primary Tasks- Submarines, 23
   reconnaissance, 24
   screening, 24
   Secondary Tasks—Submarines, 23–25
   stealth over boldness, 18
   Strategy and Tactics, 21–23
   tactical scouting, 23
Japanese Task Force, viii, 9, 33, 93
JN25, 36

Kaga (carrier), 66–68, 99
Kido Butai (Mobile Force), viii, 86
Kimmel, Admiral Husband, 83
King, Admiral Ernest, 6, 100
Kirkpatrick, Lieutenant Commander Charles C., 62
Knox, William, 84
Komatsu, Vice Admiral Teruhisa, 42, 45, 51–52, 54–55, 80, 82–83, 96
Komura, Captain Keizo, 68, 82
Kondō, Admiral Nobutake, 51, 78, 93
Kumano (heavy cruiser), 51
Kurita, Vice Admiral Takeo, 51, 68

Kuroshima, Admiral Kameto, 80–81

Laysan Island, 43, 45
Layton, Edwin T., 58
Lisianski Island, 45, 55

Mahan, Alfred Thayer, 3, 9–11, 13, 15, 27, 29, 34–35, 75, 79, 91–92
McClusky, Lieutenant Commander Wade, 66, 99
midget submarines, 12, 17, 46
Midway Island, viii, 5, 49, 93
Mikuma (heavy cruiser), 51, 69–70, 73, 98–99
Miwa, Vice Admiral Shigeyosh, 24
Mogami (heavy cruiser), 51, 69–70, 98
Murphy, Lieutenant Commander John W. Jr., 68, 70–71

Nagumo, Admiral Chuichi, 5, 49, 64, 78, 80, 87, 95, 98
Navy General Board, 29, 34
Nimitz, Admiral Chester W., iv, viii, xi–xii, 2–3, 6–7, 44, 57, 68–69, 71, 78, 84–90, 94, 99–101
Nisshin (carrier), 46

Office of Naval Intelligence, 3
Operation "MI", 95

Pearl Harbor, vii, ix, 5, 9, 14, 18–19, 21–23, 27–29, 32, 35, 39, 41, 44–45, 47, 49, 54, 58–61, 63, 66, 70–73, 75, 77, 80–81, 83, 91, 94, 96–97
Puleston, Captain W.D., 3–4

Rochefort, Commander Joseph J., 57–58, 87–89, 94, 98–99

Sand Island, 50
Second "K" Operations, 41–42, 44–49, 77–78, 96

Shigeyoshi, Vice Admiral Inoue, 14
Shōkaku (carrier), 58, 62
Sōryū-class carrier, 66–68
Spruance, Admiral Raymond, 69, 71, 84, 94, 98–99
SubRon 3, 3, 41, 43, 45–47, 49, 54–55, 83
SubRon 5, 3, 5, 7, 41, 46–49, 54–55, 58, 62, 79, 80, 83, 94–95, 99
Sun Tzu, 10–11, 75–76
Suzuya (heavy cruiser), 51

Takayasu, Commander Arima, 81
Task Force 7, 59, 61
Task Force 16, 61, 71, 88
Task Force 17, 61, 88
Task Group (TG) 7.1, 44, 59, 61, 64, 68–69, 71–72, 85, 88–90
Task Group (TG) 7.2, 59, 61, 68, 71, 88
Task Group (TG) 7.3, 59, 61, 68, 71–73
Tōgō, Admiral Heihachirō, 13
Tone (Japanese cruiser), 64

U.S. Naval Academy, 30
U.S. Naval Doctrine, 27–32
  Battle Force, 27
  commerce raiding, 31
  cruising, approach and battle formations, 27–28
  Fighting Force, 27
  Interwar Tactics, 32
  night search and attack procedure, 27
  Submarine Doctrine, 29
  Submarine Skipper Problem, 30–31
U.S. Naval War College, 29, 33–34
U.S. Pacific Fleet, vii, 1, 2, 6, 15, 27, 32, 35, 59, 77–78, 85, 92
U.S. Submarine Actions at Midway, 57–74
  CNAS Midway, 70–71
  intelligence, 57–58
  submarine deployment, 59–62, 68

USS *Cuttlefish*, 62–64
USS *Nautilus*, 66–68
USS *Tambor*, 68–70, 72
U.S. Submarine Strategy and Tactics, 33–40
   commerce raiding, 35
   Post World War I, 33–35
   submarines as commerce raiders, 38–39
   submarines as warships and fleet support, 36
   unreliability of torpedoes, 37–38
   unrestricted warfare, 39
U.S. (American) Task Force, 4, 9, 19, 22, 28, 41, 49, 93, 99
Ugaki, Chief of Staff Matome, 64
ULTRA intelligence, 36
USS *Argonaut*, 58
USS *Balch*, 52
USS *Benham*, 53
USS *Cachalot*, 37, 59–61, 65, 72–73, 89
USS *Cuttlefish*, 37, 59–65, 68, 71–73, 88–89, 99
USS *Dolphin*, 37, 55, 59–61, 72–73
USS *Drum*, 59, 62
USS *Enterprise*, viii, 54, 66, 72–73, 89
USS *Finback*, 59–61, 72
USS *Flying Fish*, 59–61, 65, 72–73, 89
USS *Gato*, 59–61, 72–73
USS *Grayling*, 59–61, 72–73
USS *Greenling*, 59
USS *Grenadier*, 59–61, 72–73
USS *Grouper*, 59–61, 64–65, 72–73, 89
USS *Growler*, 59, 61

USS *Gudgeon*, 59–61, 72–73
USS *Hammann*, 53–54, 95
USS *Hornet*, 42, 54, 70–71, 88, 94
USS *Indianapolis*, 17
USS *Narwhal*, 59, 61, 72–73
USS *Nautilus*, 59–61, 64–68, 72–73, 89, 98–99
USS *Pike*, 59–61, 72
USS *Plunger*, 59–61, 73
USS *Pollack*, 59, 62
USS *Pompano*, 59
USS *Porpoise*, 59
USS *Silversides*, 58, 62
USS *Tambor*, 51, 59–61, 68–70, 72–73, 88, 99
USS *Tarpon*, 59–61, 72
USS *Thresher*, 58
USS *Trigger*, 59–61, 72–73
USS *Triton*, 46, 58, 62, 99
USS *Trout*, 59–61, 72–73, 99
USS *Tuna*, 59, 73
USS *Yorktown*, viii–ix, 17, 50, 52–54, 77, 88, 94–95

War Plan Orange, 13, 27
Watanabe, Captain Yasuji, 80, 82
Withers, Commander Thomas, 34

Yahachi, Lieutenant Commander Tanabe, 52
Yamamoto, Admiral Isoruku, viii, ix, xii, 1, 3–5, 7, 14, 25, 41, 45–52, 57, 64, 68, 71, 75–83, 92–93, 95–98, 101
Yamato (battleship), 15, 45, 49, 71